The Years of my Day

An eighty-year-long travelogue

Floyd Schmoe

© 1979, Floyd Schmoe; Azzurri Publishing edition, © 2023 Azzurri Publishing by permission of University of Washington Libraries, Special Collections, Floyd Wilfred Schmoe papers, Accession #0496-008, Box 5, Folder 7, The Years of My Day.

Introduction and Thanks

Peter Wick – Editor/Publisher - Azzurri Publishing

    I first met Floyd Schmoe in 1985. I had begun hanging out with the family as the new boyfriend of his then 19-year-old granddaughter, Liz. I remember Floyd being a fascinating man. He had written books, which was always going to pique my curiosity. He was an artist – he would often talk about his latest efforts at sculpture – and, well, he had been nominated for the Nobel Peace Prize. A year later he would turn 90, and in the process, he became something of a personal hero of mine. It was not just that he had lived so long, or so well (it is not your average 90-year-old who can get out on a pair of skies and self-deprecatingly joke about not having the same balance he had 65 years ago). It was the quality of life he lived. After you read this book, I have no doubt you will agree. I knew him until he passed in 2001 at the age of 105. His entire 90s had been an inspiration to me. He was flying around the world receiving honors and accolades. He was once again nominated for the Nobel Peace Prize. My memory would place that nomination in 1994. We all assumed he would lose to Jimmy Carter, but instead they both lost to Yasser Arafat.

    I remember, back in those days, seeing a xeroxed, hand-bound volume on a family bookshelf, with the handwritten title down the spine, **The Years of My Day**. I had flipped through it a bit. I realize now that that was actually the follow-up to this book, later chapters of his life written in 1989. This volume, though, I consider the main course.

Written in 1979, while Floyd was in his 80s, it is in these pages that he set down the bulk of his...well...his DAY.

In 2018 it was brought to my attention that Japan's NHK Television had produced a documentary about Floyd, titled **Houses For Peace**. As I watched the documentary, I caught a passing reference to Floyd's "memoir," and some sort of lightbulb turned on in my mind. I contacted my now ex-wife Liz (who lives in Seattle), from Los Angeles (where I run Azzurri Publishing with our adult son Morgan, who is of course Floyd's great grandson) and mentioned that I remembered seeing books by Floyd, including a memoir, on family shelves back in the day.

I did not know how many copies of this book Floyd had passed around to the world, but I knew it could not have been more than ten or so.

"I run a small publishing company," I reasoned. "My second in charge is Floyd's great grandson. What if we were to pursue publishing this book?"

To my mild surprise, the idea began to take off. Family members offered their best wishes and support.

In his later years Floyd had donated his "Archives" to the good people at the University of Washington Libraries, Special Collections.

In December, 2019, Myself, my ex-wife Liz, and our son Morgan visited Suzzallo Library, on the UW campus, and spent an afternoon pouring through a fascinating trove of original documents. We made some notes and left with plans to visit again before too much time passed.

Then, a few months into 2020, the COVID-19 pandemic nearly shut down the world. The UW, along with nearly all educational institutions, switched to an all-online education format. Libraries closed. We waited.

    Two years later, in early January, 2022, I was able to visit Suzzallo again, alone, due to COVID restrictions, and finally settled on what we wanted to do, what we wanted to include, and what personal notations, sometimes about people still living, we would leave out. Yes, with the blessing of the family we have made only tiny alterations. The vast majority of everything we have left as is, out of respect to Floyd.

    It has been my absolute pleasure to prepare this unique volume, for what I have come to think of as The Historical Record.

    I want to thank Liz. It might be uncommon for someone, all these years later, to thank an Ex for helping out on a project, but her communication with the rest of the Schmoe family, her help with a few tech issues in creating a modern document with so many very old images, and even her editorial opinions, have been welcome and helpful.

    As for those very old images...you'll see them soon enough. Floyd drew all the little sketches you are about to see, sprinkled throughout the book. Sometimes he even typed his original text on top of a given sketch. We made decisions sketch by sketch. Sometimes you'll notice the obvious truth, we captured the image with words typed across it, and just put it there for you to see. Other times we did our best to clean a given image up and minimize the affect that age had played on the original paper. We hope you will be both forgiving and appreciative of the original artwork, and how we chose to present it. I believe the sketches are an endearing addition to Floyd's legacy.

I want to thank Allee Monheim, Anne Jenner, and Ruba Sadi, at Suzzallo Library Special Collections, on the University of Washington Campus.

Everyone has been a pleasure to work with.

As requested by the Schmoe family, monetary proceeds from this book will be donated to American Friends Service Committee, the Quaker charity that Floyd supported and volunteered for throughout his life.

If you are discovering Floyd for the first time, with this book, I envy you. What fun it would be to discover him anew once again.

If, like me, you have previous knowledge, understanding, or memories of Floyd, I hope this volume will solidify his legacy for you.

For me, this process has been nothing but fun. I write books myself, but publishing this has been my proudest moment as a publisher.

Enjoy!

-Peter Wick

ONE DAY IS WITH THE LORD

AS A THOUSAND YEARS,

AND A THOUSAND YEARS

AS ONE DAY

(II Peter 3,8.)

The Years of my Day
An eighty-year-long travelogue
Floyd Schmoe

This tale of my wanderings and my ruminations is written "for the record" – the family record. It is not intended to amuse or instruct, and it will add little to the history of the times, but, for those to follow, it will perhaps illuminate the past that the future may be more clearly seen.

Otherwise it is the tale of the ambitions, the struggles – which only incidentally involved considerable going to and fro with attendant adventures – and the fruits of a long life, which covered much of the twentieth century.

It should be dedicated – if in fact it should be dedicated – to all the ancestors who went before, and all the friends and family who went along; for no man – as John Don said – is and island, entire of itself; every man is a piece of the continent, a part of the main...

So this is written, published, and
dedicated to the family...the family
Schmoe, who was, and is, and
may yet to be...
In the year nineteen seventy-nine

The Years of My Day

In my 80's and still in excellent health I find retirement pleasant and profitable. With a good wife and companion, with wonderful children and grandchildren, and with a host of good friends and neighbors, I am comfortable and content.

With time to study and books to write I feel my time is well spent. Since retirement in 1958 I have written eight books, not all of which have yet been published. At the moment I have two more in progress and a third planned.

Recently also I have added oil painting to my long time hobbies of gardening, sculpture and ceramics. When I tire of the typewriter and pen I take up the brush or the chisel or - if it Spring and the sun is shining – the shovel and the hoe.

Life is wonderful. It is good. I am thankful for it.

Floyd Schmoe

This picture is of Ruth and I, newly married and newly arrived at Longmire Springs for my first job as a Ranger on Mt. Rainier National Park. It was taken beside the Nisqually River in the Summer of 1922.

The Years of My Day

The picture below is of Ruth and I with Masa Kobori, a friend from Tokyo, at our home in Seattle, about 1956.

Tomiko and I in 1970, newly married and living at our home on Finn Hill.

Floyd Schmoe

The Years of my (comparative)
Innocence
1895-1912
Kansas

The Years of My Day
1900-1910

As I was growing up on the Kansas farm during the first decade of this twentieth century, there were no electric lights, no automobiles, and of course no airplanes or moon rockets.

We did have trains, though most of our neighbors had never ridden on one, and some had never seen one. We had steam engines and hand-crank telephones, and the more prosperous farmers had buggies with folding tops and yellow wheels.

Mom had a bicycle though she seldom rode it because the roads were usually deep in dust when not deeper in mud. We had a lawn swing and a croquet set.

Mom, like most of the other fashionable women, wore "rats" in her hair, high lace collars, corsets, and undergarments padded in the right places both in front and behind. Her "shirtwaists" were tight and her skirts full and long. They brushed the ground when she walked and you saw her high heeled, sharp-toed button shoes only when she gathered up her skirts to mount a horse or climb a stairs. She rode sidesaddle, and only on "Old Charlie," the most docile of our farm horses. When she rode her bicycle or Charlie she wore a little flat sailor hat with a ribbon.

Dad wore denim overalls, even to meeting on Sunday but he did have a proper blue serge suit which he wore only when he went, about once a year, to Kansas City. Or to a funeral.

About once a year we also went to the County Seat at Olathe for a Fourth of July celebration or to Lawrence to see the circus. We got free tickets to the circus almost every Summer because we had an ice house with a blank wall facing on the highway which was a choice place for the big gaudy circus posters.

Ringling Brothers and Barnum and Bailey had combined then and it was truly, as the billboards said, "The greatest show on Earth."

Floyd Schmoe

There have been changes since then, even on the farm, but I think the circus has changed least of all. There were the same elephants, and tigers, and huge dappled horses. The same brass bands, and pretty girls, and funny clowns. The same acts mostly also...the high wire, the flying trapezes, the human cannon ball, the death defying "Loop the loop" – though with a bicycle rather than a motorcycle.

Just as exciting and more familiar was Cousin Bert Moon's steam tractor which pulled his J.I. Case thrashing machine from farm to farm during wheat harvest and pulled the road grader during the rest of the year. Dad was "Road Boss" for several years and Bert would let me ride on the tractor. Sometimes he would allow me to pull the whistle cord at quitting time.

Bert was the indispensable man in the community. He never married and for many years he lived with us, amply repaying his keep by helping Dad on the farm. He helped at butchering time and ice cutting, and if he was around he even helped mom – "Cousin Min" to him – with the week's washing, which in good weather was done on the back porch. Water was heated in the big black soap kettle over an open fire. Bert would tend the fire and pump the water.

Later he lived with "Cousin Clara," mom's older sister, who was Uncle Bill Rice's wife. There he helped in the blacksmith shop, operated Uncle Bill's cider mill in season, and helped him move houses and build bridges. He owned the saw mill. When a dairy cooperative was formed and built a creamery, Bert became its manager and entire staff. He was also custodian of the Prairie Center Cemetery.

Bert was a quiet, unassuming man. He seldom spoke unless spoken to, but, although I doubt if he ever went to school, he was likely the best informed man in the township. At least on technical matters.

The Years of My Day

About the time we left Kansas Cousin Bert built a small cottage beside the creamery and lived there alone for many years. I saw him only once after that, perhaps forty years later. Ruth and I were visiting her cousins John and Hattie Garrison in Hutchinson, Kansas, one time when we happened to pass that way, and there we found Cousin Bert living in a church retirement home. He must have been 90 years old but he seemed like the same quiet person I so well remembered. He showed little interest in what happened to me and I asked few questions. Bert liked to keep it that way.

* * *

One of the annual events of those years on the farm, along with butchering and harvesting, was cutting ice.

Ours was the only ice house in the area. Ice was one of Dad's sidelines but Bert always engineered the ice harvest. During some winters the ice would freeze to a thickness of six inches on the creek which ran across our farm.

When it was judged thick enough Geary and I would skip school and go with Dad and Bert to the creek. Bert would mark off a checkerboard of squares about 3 x 3 feet, and then with a heavy ice saw cut them free. It would be my job to float them, with a large pike pole, to the foot of a chute which Dad had built up the bank and into the wagon. Geary helped haul them up the chute and went with Dad to the ice house to help unload and store the ice.

For insulation the ice was buried in sawdust, and thus kept with very little loss from melting, through the following summer. Although it was a cold, and sometimes wet, job (someone usually slipped and fell during the process), we always looked forward to it almost as we looked forward to Christmas and the Fourth of July.

The first and last days of school were red letter days, and two events which I associate with the opening of school in September are sorghum molasses making and cider making.

Most farmers grew a patch of sorghum cane and a few farmers had apple orchards. Bill Andrews, whose farmhouse was

Floyd Schmoe

across the road from the school house, and who often 'kept' the school teacher, unless he, or she, lived in the area, had a sorghum mill where we usually stopped by after school if the sap was flowing.

Neighbors would bring a wagon load of cane, hitch their team to the long sweep which turned the mill, and remain, often most of the following night, as the juice was boiled down into the thick, amber, syrup which served most of us in place of commercial sugar. If it was our "turn" at the mill I would be allowed to stay out of school to ride the sweep and drive the team around and around, while Dad fed the cane between the heavy iron rollers which pressed out the juice. When it was not our "turn" I would at least stop by for a time, along with the other children, to sample the syrup. Bill Andrews nor the neighbor whose cane was being milled, objected to us dipping our little paddles into the hot bubbling syrup and eating all we could hold. It spoiled our supper and did our teeth no good, but it was fun.

A little later in the month Bert and Uncle Bill Rice would ready the cider mill back of the blacksmith shop and then, some autumn day there would be smoke coming from the chimney and a long line of wagons loaded with apples.

Coming down the road from school we could climb onto the wagons and sample the juicy red Winesaps and Gravensteins, then enter the mill and help ourselves to the fresh sweet juice as it ran from the tall hydraulic press into the waiting kegs and barrels (Bert saw that a large tin cup was always available for cider tasters). Most families wanted at least ten gallons of cider each year to be used fresh as a beverage and to be boiled down into apple butter. What may have been left over was fermented into vinegar unless (though not in our family) it was more desirable as apple brandy.

Mom was an active and enthusiastic member of the W.C.T.U. (Women's Christian Temperance Union). She even named me Floyd Willard after Francis E. Willard, the beloved founder and

The Years of My Day

lifelong President of the militant organization. (The 'Floyd' was of course from my Uncle Floyd, her scalawag, though loveable, young brother.) I later changed the Willard to Wilfred out of sheer macho bias. I didn't want to be named for a woman. Bill we named Wilfred Pickering, though he usually signs "W.P.Schmoe."

Floyd Schmoe

HEARSAY
These things happened before
My day, but my account is based
Upon such good authority as:
My mother told me....
The family bible.....

The Years of My Day
Our Roots

My ancestors (and yours if you are of the Schmoe family) were pioneers, as was, and is, anyone who tears up their roots from the native soil and undertakes a new life in a strange and unfamiliar land, for a pioneer is one who breaks new ground, prepares the way, and opens the doors for those who are to follow. It is a difficult task, made doubly so by the fact that most pioneers are untrained and ill equipped for the work they undertake.

Grandfather Schmoe, whose full Germanic name was Ernest Heinrich Wilhelm, was born in Bremmerhaven, Germany on February 19, 1822, though more likely of Frisian than of German descent. The family name is our best evidence of this since we have found no family history of earlier date. ("sch" is a distinctive Germanic syllable while "moe" is equally typically Scandanavian, and the ancient Frisian language is ancestor to both German and Scandanavian, as well as to the English and Dutch.)*

At around age 20, which would be in the early 1840s, Ernest and his older brother Friedrich came to America and settled in the predominantly German-speaking community of Shelbyville in central Indiana.

On what ship they sailed and at what port they landed, and by what means they traveled inland, I have never learned. That was a period of heavy European migration and the brothers Schmoe most likely joined a party of central European immigrants who traveled from Bremmerhaven or Hamburg by sailing ship, landed

---

* There is, interestingly, a linguistic intermarriage with Yiddish as well. The word schmoe as an adjective rather than as a noun, is common in spoken Yiddish; and Yiddish, which in its formation drew from every language spoken by Jews in Europe, including many Frisian words, as does also modern English, German, Dutch, Danish, and Polish.

Floyd Schmoe

in New York by way Ellis Island, then came overland by train to Indianapolis and Shelbyville.

Some years later the family moved to Juliette, a suburb of Indianapolis. Perhaps it was because grandfather Schmoe had become a carpenter, and work opportunities may have been more promising in the larger city.

In the mean time Ernest had met and married a girl of the community (either Shelbyville or Juliette) named Karlena Ostemeir, and their fourth son, Ernest Antoni Fredrick, was born in Juliette on November 14, 1865. Ernest Fredrick, who later signed his name as "E.C. Schmoe," for some unknown reason, was my father. About 1880, when father would have been only 15 or 16, the family moved again, probably by "immigrant car" some 800 miles westward, this time to the cross-roads village of Prairie Center, Kansas. There, a mile south of the village, Ernest and Karlena bought a farm, built a house, dug a well, and raised their family of four sons and two daughters. And there, some years later, son Ernest Antoni met and married the daughter of a near neighbor, Minta Victoria Moon. That was on August 27th, 1889, at Lawrence, Kansas.

Grandmother Moon, whose maiden name was Barbara Rich, had been born June 10th, 1840, in Indiana, but her ancestors had migrated from England late in the 17th century, to Cape Cod, and being Quakers, had followed what had become almost a fixed migration route for American Quakers; by way of Pennsylvania, to North Carolina, and from there across Tennessee to Indiana. From Indiana they moved to Iowa, and from Iowa to Kansas.* There, in a

---

* From Kansas and Iowa in later years there have been two migratory streams, one to the northwest resulting in the Quaker community of Newburg, Oregon, and the other to the southwest, centering in Whittier, California. Monuments marking this westward path are Quaker colleges; Moses Brown in Providence, Rhode Island, Swarthmore, Bryn Mawr, and Haverford, in Pennsylvania, Guilford in North Carolina, Earlham in

The Years of My Day

Quaker community called Cottonwood, a few miles west of Emporia, Barbara Rich, now 18, met and married a neighbor, Jesse Moon.

The Moons were also of English Quaker descent and had first settled in Virginia some time before 1750.

From Cottonwood Jesse and Barbara reversed the westward flow and moved back east 100 miles to the newer community of Prairie Center.

I have no record of the English Moons but the Riches have a long history dating back to the 14th century. At some point they crossed blood with the Churchill family. Members of the family still like to refer to Winston Churchill as "Cousin Winnie."

Indiana, Penn in Iowa, Friends in Kansas, George Fox in Oregon, and Whittier in California.

Floyd Schmoe

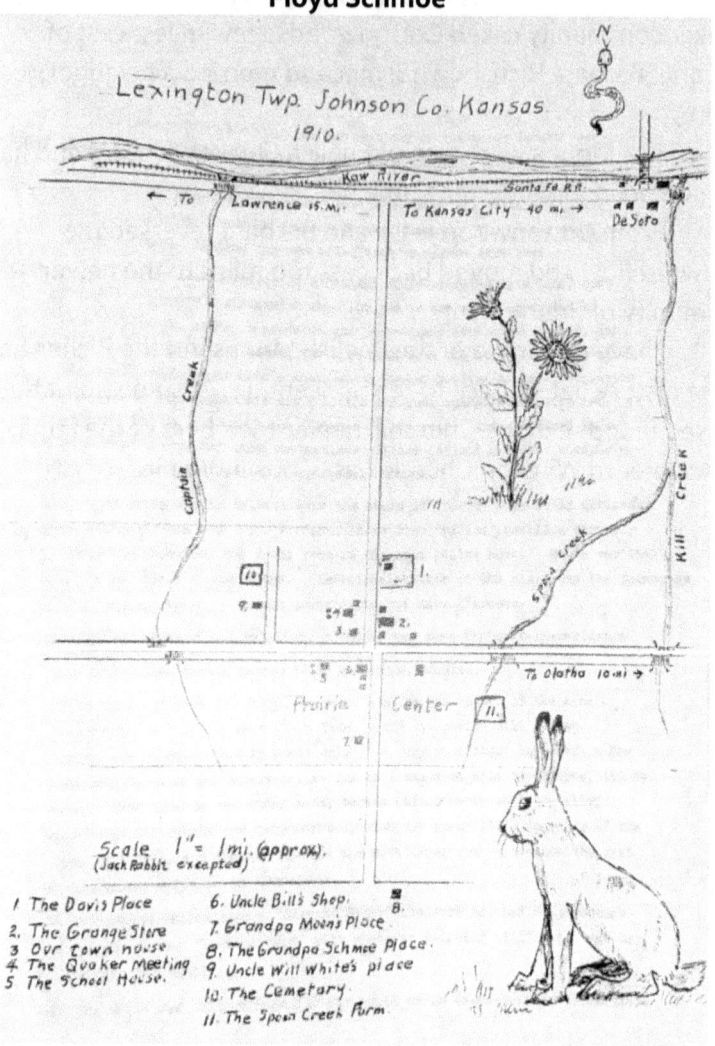

I first appeared center stage on the 21st day of September in the year 1895, second child, second son of Ernest Schmoe and wife Minta Moon Schmoe. The place, a weatherbeaten pioneer shack on a 40 acre farm known as the "Davis Place," and located ¾ of a mile north of the village Prairie Center, Lexington township, Johnson

The Years of My Day

County, Kansas. The county seat, and center of trade, Olathe, lay ten miles east by narrow dirt road.

Prairie Center then consisted of a general store operated by a local coop named "The Grange," a blacksmith shop 100 yards to the south operated by Uncle Bill Rice, master blacksmith and jack of all mechanical trades, and Mom's brother-in-law. Across the dirt road from the store was a one-acre tree-shaded churchyard with a small white Quaker Meeting House. A quarter mile west of the crossroads was a little one-room schoolhouse with two outhouses set at a respectable distance to the rear, and a hundred yards to the east a somewhat more pretentious edifice (it had a modest steeple with bell) the M.E. (Methodist-Episcopal) church.

Scattered about and in between were the homes of four or five solid citizens, most solid of whom was Doc Woodard, whose tiny "office," smelling strongly of laudanum, occupied the front room of his neat little home. Doc's was the first house north of the store. Immediately south of the store was the parsonage of the Meeting House – though Quakers did not have "Parsons."

"Aunt Racher Woodard" (no relation of Doc's) was then minister-in-residence. She lived alone, having never, to my knowledge, married.

Uncle John and Aunt Ida White occupied a house just south of the ornate home of Uncle Bill and Aunt Clara Rice, which sat beside Bill's shop. Uncle John White, who was my "Uncle" only in a very roundabout way, kept a few pigs and chickens but otherwise, so far as I was ever able to observe, did no work. Aunt Ida, on the other hand, became (after Uncle Bill installed telephones throughout the neighborhood, which was about 1900) operator of the local "Central," and thereby perhaps the most important – because the most knowledgeable – woman in the community.

The Methodists relied upon a "Circuit Rider" ministry and had no parsonage. The schoolteacher "boardedround" with whatever neighbor willing to take her, or him, into the family.

Floyd Schmoe

Aunt Ida White was paid perhaps $110 per month by an assessment on subscribers (meaning all persons who owned telephones) and the teacher received a somewhat larger stipend by the local school board who received funds from the county.

At the moment, or say by the turn of the century when I started school, I had an elder brother Geary; John and Ida White had two sons, Ray and Ralph, and a daughter Pearl. Doc and Mrs. Woodard had an older daughter, Gertrude, already past school age, a son Lloyd a bit older than me, and a second daughter, Inez, who was about my age.

My Uncle Will White (John's older brother) and Aunt Molly (Mom's older sister) lived on a farm one mile west of us and had a son, my favorite cousin, Earl, perhaps five years older than me. Uncle Bill and Aunt Clara Rice had two children, Vada and Edwin. Edwin was my age. These children, all of whom walked to school, along with three or four who "commuted" on horseback from farms further away, made up the Prairie Center Public School, District 21.

A widow – a Mrs. Hale – lived just south of us and had a small orchard. Also an old gray horse and a tall gangly daughter Elva. Elva was my first "date." She "took" me, one cold winter night, to a skating party on Captain Creek, west of the schoolhouse, behind her saddle on her gray mare.

I liked Uncle Wills best of all my relatives and liked to visit Earl. Together we hunted Indian arrowheads in the corn fields, fished for sunfish in Captain Creek which crossed their land, played in their apple orchard and barnyard, and explored the graveyard adjacent to their farm.

Cousin Earl came for me one evening and took me behind his saddle to spend the night with him. Next day I returned home to discover I had a baby sister Karlena, named for my dad's mother Karlena whom I had never seen.

The Years of My Day

Year 1900. Memory. My two vivid memories, which came a bit earlier, were of the tearing down of the old shack on our farm and the building of a neat, square, four room house in which my sister was born. Dad also built a substantial barn about the same time. The second memory was of driving our team of horses, Sam and Arch, to a covered wagon, a hundred miles southwest to Cottonwood, Kansas – another Quaker community where lived various uncles, aunts and cousins of Grandfather Moon's family.

We rested at the farm home of Uncle Asa and Aunt Mary Moon for a day, then went on another hundred miles to Wichita where we were to attend the session of Kansas yearly meeting of Friends at the newly established four year college, called by the pretentious name of Friends University. On the second morning after our arrival at Uncle Asa (Mother's uncle) the wagons, now augmented by two or three others from the university, left early for the long drive to Wichita, but Aunt Mary, with me, her four-year-old great-nephew, stayed behind to take the train, since Aunt Mary did not feel well enough to take the trip by wagon.

I, being "under six" could travel free, so she took me with her for my first train ride.

The Santa Fe railroad closely parallels the old Santa Fe trail which was still the wagon road.

On the train next day Aunt Mary allowed me to sit next the window on the righthand side of the coach so that I could watch the road. Sure enough a few minutes out of the Cottonwood station we spotted the small caravan of covered wagons and waved to our slow moving family.

This incident and the tearing down of the old house at home was, I believe, my earliest, my only, nineteenth century clear memory.

In September of 1900 (when I was five and sister Karlena was an infant) my brother Geary was past six and ready for school. But since Geary, being shy and bashful, refused to go to school

Floyd Schmoe

alone, I was sent along to bolster his morale. I remember only one incident of that my first day in school. Much to my embarrassment the young teacher took me to her desk and held me in her lap while she conducted classes.

Sixty-some years later we met in Whittier, California and remembered the occasion, though I cannot today remember her name.

I remember also walking the mile to school that winter when the snow lay a foot or more deep on the road and the temperature dropped below zero. We had no woolen socks or waterproof overshoes and I cried from the cold both going and coming. My feet were freezing.

Another memory of that year is of being allowed to sit in the back of the room with an older student and look at the pictures in his textbooks. The illustrated maps in the geography book fascinated me. It was my first knowledge of Africa, Asia, and South America, of people of other races and of strange animals...huge snakes, crocodiles, elephants, and giraffes.

In the late Spring of that year a most frightening incident occurred. Lightning struck the schoolhouse while classes were in session. It struck the chimney which stood between the two entrance doors. The tall "Round Oak" stove which stood in the middle of the room, was vented to the brick chimney by an overhead stove pipe. There was no fire in the stove but the metal stove pipe was clogged with soot. When the bolt of lightning struck the chimney it not only scattered the bricks but exploded the stove pipe, filling the room with noise and a dense cloud of soot. We thought the house was on fire and students dived out the open windows. In less than a minute the stunned teacher and I were the only remaining inside. The schoolhouse did not burn and when we went outside children were still running in both directions down the road. Some of them did not stop until they reached home.

They did not return that day.

The Years of My Day

There were a few exciting memorable events during the following years. In 1904 my brother Othel was born, and in 1906 my youngest sister Inez arrived. Earlier Dad had sold the old Davis place to Len Weller and we had moved to a larger house owned by Louie Schultz on the corner across from Uncle Bill's blacksmith shop. I believe we at first rented the place and later purchased it. For the next few years the big two-story house with its acre of land was all the property we owned but Dad rented 40 acres on Spoon Creek, a half-mile east. (See map page 6). *[change pg. # as needed]

Now we had land with a creek and a bit of woods and my adventures with wild plants and animals began. In the summer we had picnics by the stream and fished the deep holes. I learned to swim that summer. In the autumn we found ripe paw paws and persimmons and gathered hazel nuts and black walnuts.

Dad built pig sties by the creek and raised wheat and corn in the cleared fields beyond. There was a low limestone bluff, actually a ledge, on the far side and the fields lay above that. Later, against my mother's wishes, Dad allowed me to buy some traps and a single-shot 22 rifle, and I hunted rabbits and squirrels in the fields and woods and trapped skunk, muskrat, and opossum along the stream. There were many racoon and a few mink. I often saw their tracks but I was not skillful enough to catch one. I am grateful for that now, and ashamed that I ever enjoyed the cruel "sport" of hunting and trapping.

Around 1905 someone shipped a car-load of wild horses from Wyoming into Eudora, our nearest railroad station, and sold them at auction. Dad took Geary and me and we bought two beautiful horses for $20.00 each. They had never had a halter on them and fought the restraint all the way home. Geary chose a roan mare with the build of a quarter horse and left me a rangy bay gelding which I named Bill. Geary named his mare Pearl.

As soon as we had arrived home that evening Dad said, "Well, now's the time to ride 'em when they are tired...who's first?"

Floyd Schmoe

We saddled Pearl without much trouble and Geary climbed abord. She wouldn't move. With a lot of coaxing he finally got her to walk around the barn lot.

He unsaddled, rubbed her down, and put her in a box stall. Then it was my turn. Bill was skittish. When we crowded him against the side of the barn and threw the saddle on he shivered all over and rolled his eyes. Dad led him to the middle of the lot and held his head while I mounted. Bill went wild. He ran into the side of the barn and skinned his shoulder. When I turned him toward a low Osage orange hedge he ran straight through it, scratching us both on the thorns. Finally Dad opened the gate and we dashed out. I let him run all the way up the hill to the schoolhouse. When he was covered with lather and nearly exhausted, I was able to turn him and ride back.

I became very fond of "Old Bill" and rode him for several years but I never did "break" him. Whenever he felt like bucking, or didn't feel like working, or whenever something spooked him, or another horse tried to pass him, he took off, and there were many times I did not go along. Pearl became a docile work horse. If pushed too far she would balk and nothing could move her, but mostly she worked. Mom even drove her single to our buggy. I said "nothing" would move her, but three times Dad did outsmart her. Once he hitched her with Charlie to a load of wheat he was taking to the mill in DeSoto. When Dad was ready to go Pearl wouldn't budge. He whipped her until Mom came out and yelled for him to stop. Just then a neighbor came by, I think it was Sam Walker, a farmer-carpenter who lived across from the M.E. Church. He watched for a time and then said, "Pete (no one called Dad "Earnest") let me try something."

Sam took a switch from a nearby tree and squatting beside Pearl began to tap her on one leg until she lifted that foot. Then he tapped her one after another leg until he had her dancing. He then motioned to Dad. Dad said "Gedap" and off they went. Another

The Years of My Day

time Dad took a rope and tied her by the tail to the wagon box. She lunged forward and pulled her half of that load for four miles by her tail.

The third time did not work out so well. Late on a Saturday evening she refused to pull a wagon load of corn out of the field. After Dad had tried all the tricks he knew he took some dry corn husks and built a fire under her. She moved but only far enough so that the fire was under the wagon. He then tied the team to the nearby fence and walked home.

Early Sunday morning Dad went before daylight (so that the neighbors would not see him working on the sabbath), untied the team, got on the wagon and said "Gedap." Both horses started with a lurch and dragged Dad off the wagon. He had not checked in the dark and the horses had milled about so much during the night that they had managed to unhitch themselves completely from the wagon.

In 1909 Dad sold a load of fat hogs and bought train tickets to Seattle and California. The Alaska-Yukon-Pacific Exposition was on in Seattle, and Mom had relatives in southern California. It was their one big travel adventure, and the only train trip they ever took together.

Also it was the first time I ever heard of Seattle and the Pacific Northwest which, as things turned out, was to become my home for most of my life.

While the folks were gone Geary and I plowed some 30 acres of land and planted it to wheat. We had five horses then and two plows, one riding sulky with a three-horse hitch and one walking plow with two horses. Geary was 15 and "boss." The boss got the riding plow. On the whole I enjoyed walking behind a plow, though by the end of a ten hour day, often in temperatures around 100°, I was exhausted.

I enjoyed it because I liked the smell of new-turned earth, and the monotonous turning of the sod had a mesmerizing effect

Floyd Schmoe

on my mind. I felt like I was walking in a trance. This spell was broken frequently as the plow unearthed field mice or snakes and I stopped to rescue them. I had not yet read Robert Burns but I had the same feeling of compassion for these "wee timorous beasties" expressed by the Scottish Bard.

With snakes and their problems I had only an academic concern. I knew all the common species from water snakes, which we thought were poisonous, to the rattlers, copperheads and cottonmouths which we knew were lethal. I once had picked up (with leather gloves) a baby rattlesnake and brought it home. I had it in an empty tin can but it managed to slip through the crack around the lid and disappear. I looked all over for it and mother took the bedding apart. Her greatest fear was that she might happen to get in bed with it. We never saw it again. I think it found a crack under the screen door.

One day when Geary and I were plowing as close to the fence as possible and came upon the platform of an old binder which had been cannibalized for spare parts and left to rust away at the edge of the field. Geary suggested that we turn it up against the fence and thereby gain a few feet of ground.

It was heavy and weed-grown but together we managed to lift it by the cutting bar. When we had it chest high and ready for the final heave we heard a loud, unmistakable "whirrrr." I yelled "Rattler," and jumped back. Geary was slower to react and so was left with a load he could not hold. As it fell the sharp steel finger of the cutter bar raked him from chest to toe, removing most of his clothing and considerable skin. We were not always on the best of terms that summer and from that moment the relationship deteriorated markedly.

The Years of My Day
The Oklahoma-Arkansas Interlude

1912-1915

Mom and Dad brought home a sheaf of picture post cards showing the wonders of the World's Fair in Seattle, the tall trees and the splendid beaches of California. They had gone over to Catalina Island and taken a trip on a "glass-bottomed boat." From this adventure Mom secured an abalone shell. They also told terrible stories of the San Francisco earthquake and fire. Evidence of the destruction was still to be seen all over the Bay Area.

It was that story – not the earthquake but the tall trees and sandy beaches – which caused me to decide that I too would go west sometimes.

Another event of the summer of 1909 was the visit of a young man several years older than me from South China, Maine. Earnest Jones had just graduated from the Yale College of Forestry and had, on his way to Wyoming for a job with the U.S. Forest Service, stopped off to visit with an uncle who, at the moment, was Minister of the Friends Meeting.

Earnest had in his baggage a tennis racket and a couple of balls and, as we batted balls back and forth on our lawn, he introduced me to the profession of forestry. I decided then and there to study forestry and become a forest ranger.

Some years were to intervene. In 1912 we sold out in Kansas and with one team of horses and a few household goods, headed south by covered wagon, looking for more and better land.

Mom had met, perhaps at Yearly Meeting, a famous Quaker missionary called Uncle Jerry Hubbard. "Uncle Jerry," who with his flowing white hair and colorful manner of dress reminded me of a somewhat smaller-than-life Buffalo Bill Cody, was in fact a medicine man, a dispenser of elixirs and remedies guaranteed to ease both spiritual and physical pain. He made a living by the

Floyd Schmoe

manufacture of a blood-red, authentic-smelling ointment which sold locally under the label, "Uncle Jerry's Salve." The label stated that, "His was a secret formula given to him by a famous Indian Medicine Man." Uncle Jerry was also Minister to the small Miami Friends Meeting when not on one of his frequent sojourns among the local Indians.

The Hubbards had a beautiful daughter named Ruby who became a classmate of mine at Miami high School and an occasional date. Ruby helped process and package the salve and, on close contact, smelled like the salve. On Ruby it was not an unpleasant odor.

Having more recently become familiar with the famous "Tiger Balm" King of Hong Kong, and his product, I could believe that Uncle Jerry's Salve bore a blood relationship, in some mysterious manner, to Tiger Balm. We used it for years in our home.

It was because of mom's casual relationship to "Uncle Jerry" that we stopped over in Miami, then a booming mining town, and became acquainted with the small Quaker community there.

Later we settled in Miami, as must have already become evident, but first Dad must explore every possibility for farming land, and all the farms around Miami were on Indian reservations and not available. This search took Dad as far south as the Red River Valley on the border of Texas. The family went along as far as the Arkansas River at Fort Smith Arkansas, but there we camped and Dad went on by train. Mom and the horses were both tired of life on the road.

It was at Muskogee, after Dad had returned disappointed, and we were on our way back to Miami, that I went to jail.

I had refused to sell the bicycle which I bought from Bay White with a few dollars I had earned at trapping, and carried lashed to the side of the wagon when roads were too rough or too muddy to ride it.

The Years of My Day

At Muskogee mom gave me five cents and asked me to take the bike and find the Post Office for the purchase of five-penny post cards. She said they would drive and if I did not overtake them before they reached the bridge over the river about four miles north of town they would wait for me there.

I found the Post Office quickly and purchased the cards, but then I set out to see the town. Perhaps it was because it was the first time I had ever enjoyed the fun of riding on paved streets that I extended my tour for a considerable time. Finally I took off in hot pursuit of my family and reached the bridge at dusk. No family! And the bridge tender (it was a toll bridge) told me that no such outfit had passed that way that day. Thinking I must have missed them on the way I rode back toward town looking for any possible campsite along the way. It was late when I returned to the bridge badly frightened.

The bridge tender gave me a small can of pork and beans and allowed me to sleep on the floor of his toll house. Next morning, without breakfast, I rode back into Muskogee, reasoning that since I had not shown up, Mom would insist that they turn back to search for me. I had no money for food.

I rode back and forth all day searching and asking but no one could help. Hunger and desperation finally drove me to the police. A friendly Irish cop told me to wait: all the day shift will be in soon and somebody will have seen your folks. No one had.

They fed me and I slept in an empty cell in the woman's jail.

I didn't get much sleep. The bed was a grid of iron slats and the mattress was very thin. Then before I could get to sleep the night patrol brought in a dozen drunken prostitutes and dumped them in the cell next to mine. Those girls were not only drunk but they were mad. This I surmised by the fact that for hours they screamed curses at the guards, then fought with each other and tried to break up the joint. The partition was a thin metal plate

Floyd Schmoe

which did not reach the ceiling so I missed very little. I did increase my store of profanity materially.

I was there almost a week. Finally a letter came from the Miami police with a ten dollar bill in it, and I, and my bicycle, took a train north.

Trouble was, there were two roads and two bridges. We had taken different routes. They had turned back to look for me but somehow we had failed to find each other. Dad said, "He's ridden ahead of us. We'll find him in Miami." Mom was worried, and when they didn't find me in Miami she was scared. Then they went to the Police.

Another exciting thing happened while I was a guest of the Muskogee police.

Muskogee is a cotton town. Not only are there large cotton gins there but other gins all over the area ship cotton seed to Muskogee for the production of cotton seed oil. The "cake" left after the oil is expired makes fine cattle feed and at that time thousands of range cattle were shipped to feed lots in Muskogee where they were fattened on cotton seed cake before being shipped on to the Kansas City, Omaha, and Chicago slaughter houses.

One night several hundred of these wild steers broke out of their pens and overtook the town. When the cowboys from the feedlots could not handle the situation the police and the firemen were called out. I rode with the police.

When chased or cornered range cattle can be dangerous. Horses were gored, pedestrians treed, and steers went through plate glass windows. Next morning stray cattle were found in cisterns and in the basements of private homes.

I ate outside the cell block with a few trusties who were assigned to clean-up duty in the jail kitchen. I was not asked to work but I helped out.

The Years of My Day

One afternoon another "trusty" and I were sweeping the corridors of the prison. We came to the front door, went outside and swept down the steps. I returned but my partner kept right on sweeping the sidewalk until he disappeared around the corner.

A couple of hours later (escorted by a patrolman) he returned neatly dressed in a suit of new clothes. He had, it seems, swept himself right into a men's clothing store, tried on a new suit, and walked out without bothering to pay. The police returned the suit and the haberdasher returned the broom.

We bought a house in Miami on the bank of the Neosha River, and Dad got a job hauling for the lead mine nearby, and I entered Miami High School. (I had graduated from the eighth grade at Prairie Center and been voted valedictorian for all the eighth grade classes in Lexington township, so I made my first speech at the commencement exercises which were held on a very hot and humid June evening at the First Baptist Church in DeSoto. It was a very short speech which was a good thing, for I was sick with fright and very nervous. Dad had taken me to a restaurant for supper before the exercises – Mom was having dinner with a friend who lived in town – and I was so nervous that I had to go out back of the church and throw up before the services began.)

I enjoyed my year at high school so much that when the folks moved to Arkansas, I rented a room (for $2.00 per month), got a job as janitor's helper for the high school, and stayed on for a second year.

At Miami High School about half the students were Indians, the town being surrounded by reservations without high schools, and some of the girls became my lifelong friends.

I was most fortunate also in having some very fine teachers and, for the first time in my life, access to good books.

My landlady was a widowed Indian by the name of Gobin. Her husband had been a French hunter and trapper along the Neosha, but whether he had died or absconded I never learned.

Floyd Schmoe

There were two Gobin children, Musa, my age and a classmate, who was dark like her mother and, like her mother also, was beautiful, kind, and considerate. Both she and Mrs. Gobin "mothered" me, did my laundry without pay, and often invited me in for Sunday dinner. It was largely because of their friendly concern, and that of good friends in the community, that I was able to live and pay all my expenses on the $8.00 per month I was paid for sweeping the high school rooms every day and washing blackboard and windows on Saturdays. It also helped that we lived near the railroad yards where I was able to pick up coal that fell (sometimes with a little help) from the local cars to stoke the little stove that kept me warm and on which I warmed the canned beans and boiled the hot dogs which was my usual diet.

This was my dinner diet. For breakfast I usually ate hotcakes with an occasional slice of bacon or sausage pattie, and for lunch I usually went "downtown" to a chili parlor housed in an ancient railway coach, where for ten cents I could have a large
continued page...38

Dad and Geary hated Miami. They were farmers, not city men. Dad did keep a few pigs in a pen down by the river but there was no space on our lot for even a kitchen garden. He had to work for the mines or for the railroad or for the lumberyard. With our team, Sam and Arch, who had brought us from Kansas, he hauled lumber, ore, cement, dirt, whatever needed hauling. He hated working for someone else. He liked being his own boss.
The hardest work of my whole life (to date) was helping Dad and Geary unload carloads of 600 one-hundred-pound bags of cement. Portland cement came in cloth bags in those days and they were stacked six high. I weighed about 130 pounds and that last bag from off the floor was a back breaker.

Because of Friends Meeting and a few good friends, Mom was content. The children were in good schools. There was a

The Years of My Day

Our home by the Neosho.
Miami, Oklahoma.
1912 - 1914

Missionary Society, a chapter of the W.C.T.U. She quilted quilts and hooked rugs.

I loved it. There was the river nearby and woods beyond. We had a rowboat. I enjoyed school, liked my teachers, and was dating girls. And there was Spider Jones, the best school chum I ever had.

Across the street from us lived "Old man Sweasey" and his wife. We almost never saw the wife. She stayed in her own back yard. Sweasey had a wooden leg. He made it himself. I never heard how he lost his real leg. It didn't bother him much. He was dark-skinned, black-bearded and he drooled tobacco juice. He looked, and he talked, like a pirate. He was a pirate of sorts for he fished with illegal nets. I often went with him to tend his nets. We caught catfish, carp and suckers mostly. The Sweaseys ate the carp, sold the catfish, and threw away the suckers. But they did not throw them far enough away. The place smelled to high heaven. When the wind was up river we could smell the fish inside our house even. Mom wouldn't go near the place and that suited the Sweasey's just right. I never saw anyone go near the place. Sweasey peddled his fish door to door.

Floyd Schmoe

Continued from page...36

bowl of steaming chili along with all the crackers I could eat, and a piece of pie.

On Sundays I sometimes went to church but more often, if the weather was good "Spider" Jones and I went arrowhead hunting along the river.

Spider, whose real name I never knew, or at least cannot remember, was my closest male friend. He lived on a farm some miles up river. In bad weather he rode horseback to school, but usually he walked. He also worked as a janitor so we spent a great deal of our time together. Spider's mother was French and a wonderful cook. I had Thanksgiving and Christmas dinners with them and I have liked rice pudding with butter, cinnamon and nutmeg topping ever since.

Then school was out that spring of 1913 I took I took a train from Joplin, Missouri, down the James and White rivers to Calico, Arkansas. Dad met me there riding a mule and leading a small gray gelding named Gilmore. We rode together for fifteen miles along a rugged wagon track through the woods and hills to a tiny mountain hamlet of Wild Cherry where Dad and mom had settled in an ancient log house heated only by huge stone fireplaces. They raised hogs, sheep and cattle, and a bale or two of cotton on the few acres of cleared land behind the house.

I spent a few days that summer "Chopping" (thinning) cotton, but mostly I spent the summer riding through the hills on Gilmore, hunting arrowheads and, under the guidance of some experienced local boys, exploring the several caves in the area.

I had never seen mountains before, such natural phenomenon being unknown in Kansas and Oklahoma (and the Ozarks of southern Missouri and northern Arkansas, though not as magnificent as the Rockies or Sierras, are real mountains by definition) and I found them fascinating and beautiful. There were forests of great oak, maple, red gum, pecan and other hardwood

The Years of My Day

trees, and occasional stands of yellow pine. The only pine trees I had ever seen were pair of tall white pines someone had planted beside the house where I was born in Kansas.

Mom had an older brother who lived in Wichita, Kansas where he owned a small grocery store. Uncle Roy offered to provide room and board if I would deliver groceries evenings and Saturdays. I decided to go to the big city for the remainder of my high school.

There were several children in Uncle Roy's and Aunt Meg's family. The older three were in college at Friends University. A girl, Clara, would be a classmate of mine, and the youngest was still in grade school. The house attached to the store was quite small, and already overcrowded. I had to sleep with one of the older boys.

I enjoyed my cousins and the exciting city life but I soon tired of being "the grocer's boy." This was mainly because I had to feed and care for the ancient horse which pulled the grocer's cart. I have always liked horses but, unlike my brother Geary, I never enjoyed working them. Old Bill had been more of a pal than a workhorse.

One of the older boys, Charles, had an "Eagle route." This got him out of bed at 4:00 a.m. every morning to deliver the morning *Wichita Daily Eagle*.

He was also a fullback on the Friends University football team, and practice took most of his evenings. The other older cousin, Maurice, played in the college band which, with his girl friends and many other extra-curricular activities, occupied all his spare time. Neither had time to deliver groceries.

The following summer I went to Western Kansas to work in the wheat harvest. This was the summer job for many Kansas students because it was always available and paid well. This was before the day of the huge motor driven combines. If you drove a binder you drove six horses. If you stacked wheat or worked a threshing crew you pitched bundles. It was hot, dirty and tiring

Floyd Schmoe

work, and I, at less than 150 pounds, was not built for it. But for a twelve hour day you earned $3.00 and your food. We slept in the straw.

Returning to Wichita in the fall I got a job similar to the one I had in Miami, as an assistant janitor at the high school. I also moved into a room that available in the college dormitory. My roommate was Fred Fellow, a freshman at F.U. We became lifelong friends.

At University Friends Church we had become acquainted with two girls who were also close friends. Double-dating was the order of the day. At all church or school affairs, Fred and Helen, Ruth and I were usually to be found together.

This happy relationship continued, with marriage, for each of us for more than fifty years.

I graduated from high school (in 1916) a year ahead of Ruth, but entered Friends University that autumn largely in order to remain near her. The only academic work I remember favorably was a splendid course in biology with Dr. Fred Emerson.

In the summer of 1917 I returned again to the harvest field and although I now earned $3.50 per day I did not save enough to take me to Seattle where I had decided to study forestry at the University of Washington. This was because I spent most of what I earned on a diamond engagement ring. Even so, it was a very small diamond. it was in September, 1917, with $100.00 borrowed from the bank (with the endorsement of my good friend and dentist Dr. Claude Holmes) I took the train for Seattle.

The outstanding event of that journey was a two-day stopover at Glacier National Park. I hiked into Medicine Lake over the Mount Henry trail, found a small cabin and spent the night. During that night almost two feet of snow fell, blocking all trails and roads. I was rescued by a Blackfoot Indian boy who rode into the park from the reservation adjacent to the park. He was

The Years of My Day

rounding up stray horses and we met by good chance. I rode one of his horses out.

In Seattle I went immediately to the State Museum on campus and presented a letter of introduction from Professor Henry C. Fellow of F.U. (Fred's uncle and my geology professor). F.S. Hall, Director of the museum immediately offered me work as a laboratory assistant in the museum and a room in his home. For walking his huge white mastiff "Prince," I received bed and breakfast. Prince, who had sworn and oath to destroy every other dog in the area, saw that I earned my pay.

I got a job at the campus cafeteria, "The Commons," as busboy and earned my noon lunch. The only time I remember ever having dinner was when good friends of the Friends Memorial Church invited me out.

Within two days of my arrival on campus I was enrolled in the College of Forestry and had my room and board provided for. I eventually repaid my loan but I cannot remember when or how. It was some years later I think for in March of 1918 my draft number came up and, claiming conscientious objection, I went to France with the American Friends Service Committee's Belief and Reconstruction Unit.

Highlights of the following fourteen months were a stint of working ambulance trains during the battle of Chateau-Thierry late in May 1918, of meeting and working with many wonderful people; French, English, Swiss and Germans – including a French girl, Anne Loone (later Dardant) who became like a sister to both Ruth and me – some German prisoners who were assigned to work for us, Henry Scattergood of the American Friends unit, Sir Edmund Harvey and Ruth Frye of the British Friends unit, Jane Addams of Hull House, The Swiss painter Eugene Burnard, his kindly wife and their lovely twin daughters, Mireille and Rita, the American sculptor Lorado Taft, and even Isadora Duncan and her brother who lived

Floyd Schmoe

nearby our Paris hostel and walked by daily in their white roman togas walking Isadora's poodle dog.

Stationed in Paris during the winter of 1918 I was able to take classes in sculpture at the Academe' Juliana, see all the operas of the season at the Paris Opera house (for 'un franc' – 14 cents each), and in the late spring of 1918 convoy a train load of the Hoover commission's food and medical supplies from Paris to Warsaw, where a typhus epidemic was raging.

In late June of 1919 I terminated service and was sent to Brest to await transport of the troop ship George Washington. However, President Wilson returning from Versailles to Washington to "sell" his peace treaty to Congress, commandeered the Washington, leaving me, along with several thousand others, to wait for whatever ship might show up later.

I went to a rest center at La Coquette, at the northwest tip of France, and lived on lobster and good French bread for a week.

On the last day of June 1919 we were called back to Brest to board the confiscated German superliner Vaterland, now converted to a troop ship and renamed the Leviathan. There were 17,000 troops on board and a crew of a thousand more. Bunks were six deep and mine was under the fantail and directly over one of the four huge propellers. The vibration stopped only once (for an hour while nine nets were taken in) until we docked at Hoboken on the evening of July 4th.

After a night at the McAlpin in Manhattan I took a train to Arkansas where Ruth would meet me. Happy meeting. We spent a week of pre-marriage honeymoon hiking and camping in the Ozarks, then returned to Wichita where on August 17th, 1919, we were married in the Quaker manner during a meeting for worship at University Church. We left the next day for Seattle via the Grand Canyon and California.

On the Santa Fe train, where fortunately we had Pullman berths, I developed a high fever. In hundred-degree heat and a 103

The Years of My Day

degree fever we saw the Grand Canyon, then went on to Pasadena where Truman Johnson's good mother nursed and prayed me back to a semblance of health. The problem was a malaria germ donated to me no doubt by an Arkansas mosquito. It stayed with me for two years though, fortunately intermittently.

In Seattle we rented a housekeeping room near the campus and both enrolled for classes. For lunch we both worked at the Commons, she behind the counter and I at my old job as a busboy. We each earned .25 cents per hour, but for .25 cents in 1919 you could buy a satisfactory lunch.

Nevertheless, we were soon dead broke and forced to drop out of school at the end of the first semester.

One of my classmates had told me that he was earning very good money each summer as a guide on Mount Rainier. I took the S.S. Virginia II to Tacoma and went to office of the Mount Rainier National Park Company who operated the hotels and other concessions on the park.

Mr. T. J. Martin, the General Manager of the company, listened to my story and said that there might be an opening on the Guide Force but there would be no such work until July.

There was no way we could live and pay rent until July unless one of us found work. I asked if there was any job open on the park at the moment and was told I could go the Longmire Inn, the lower of two hotels in the park, and shovel snow off the roof. I left by train from Seattle the next morning and was met by the inn's caretaker at Ashford with a two-horse bobsled.

It was dark by the time we reached Longmire Springs 13 miles up the river.

I had only worked a day or so when Mr. Martin called to say that the winter keepers at Paradise Inn had walked out, or otherwise disappeared, and would I take over at Paradise, seven miles and 4,000 feet higher on the side of the mountain?

Floyd Schmoe

There was 30 feet of snow on the ground at the inn, and plenty of shoveling to be done there.

I was given a pair of bear-paw webs and told to follow the telephone line. It was my first experience with snowshoes and long before I reached the inn I hoped fervently that it would be my last.

Mrs. Green, the caretaker's wife, packed a good lunch for me and told me to telephone back as soon as I arrived. That lunch may have saved my life for I was on that trail all day, and for the last several miles, without any guide except up, far above the Narada Falls the telephone line disappeared beneath the snow and there was no other trail marker through the woods. I was very near total exhaustion when I finally came out of the forest and, topping another ridge saw the chimneys of Paradise Inn sticking through the snow. No welcoming smoke rose through the chimneys. I entered through a broken dormer window in the steep roof.

The last light of day entering the dormer windows of the cathedral-like hotel lobby illuminated the huge beams and rafters dimly, but all below was black as midnight. I lowered myself to the floor and began feeling my way around. Occasionally I stopped and called out, then listened carefully for the slightest sound. I may as well have been in the depths of an underground cavern.

I came to a huge stone fireplace at the north end of the lobby and beside it discovered an open door. This led to the spacious dining room. Tables and chairs were stacked in rows and covered with canvas. Following an open aisle, I came to double doors leading into the kitchen. As I moved cautiously about trying to identify the numerous objects with my hands, I inadvertently touched a pile of metal mixing bowls stacked on the drainboard of a sink. These toppled into the sink with a clatter that startled me.

Exploring further in total darkness I reached a door leading into a smaller room which by the presence of ovens and bread pans identified it as the bake shop. At one side an open stairway led to an upper floor. Entering the room above the bakery I

The Years of My Day

immediately became aware of a difference in the atmosphere. There was odor of tobacco sacks and when I found the large wood-burning stove in the middle of the room it was warm and there were still live coals among the ashes. I had an eerie feeling that I was not alone, though by now I hoped fervently that I was. No one answered my calls.

Groping about the walls I discovered the telephone beside a door and, taking the receiver, listened. A low hum indicated that it was "alive." I cranked out two long rings. It was answered promptly by Mrs. Green at Longmire. Immediately the entire atmosphere changed, though miles removed from the closest human being (I hoped) I was not alone. The Green's asked urgently if I had arrived and if I was safe. They had expected a call hours earlier and had already considered the possibility that I was lost.

Mr. Green asked about Gus and Alf, the two winter keepers who had "disappeared" a few days earlier. When I reported that only the hot stove indicated their existence, we were all very puzzled. George (Mr. Green) suggested that one or both of them had left only that morning and that somehow we had missed meeting on the trail. Perhaps they had taken a shortcut down. But why had they not at least reported in at Longmire?

There were a number of question yet to be answered but they could wait until daylight. In the meantime I was cold and exhausted. With a bit of paper I was able to get a light from the coals in the stove and with it find a candle and a Coleman lantern. The candle would serve for the moment. There was firewood in a box behind the stove and I soon had a warming flame roaring up the chimney. There were blankets so I undressed, hung my outer garments behind the stove to dry, and went to bed in what appeared to be the cleaner of the two cots which stood against the wall.

Floyd Schmoe

Aside from the groaning and creaking of the building under the tremendous burden of snow on its roof, there was no sound and I soon fell asleep.

I was awakened late next morning by the ringing of the telephone. George had been calling for an hour or more but the muffled jangle that got through was not loud enough to waken me. I was still groggy and my legs, unused to the terrible strain that is put upon them by the prolonged lifting of snow-weighted webs, were painfully stiff and sore.

There was no word of our missing men and George suggested that I search the place carefully for any clues of their disappearance.

After rebuilding the fire in the stove I melted a pan of snow for water and made breakfast. A cookstove had been set up in the bakeshop below and there was an abundance of food.

Apparently the upper room was, during the summer season, a common room for the hotel kitchen staff, and the bakeshop had been converted for the winter-keeper's kitchen. A pantry between the bakeshop and the large hotel kitchen was stocked with enough supplies to last two people for months.

It was known that Gus and Alf, both Norwegians and ski enthusiasts, had been good friends when they took the job as caretakers in the Fall, and all had gone well with them until Christmas when, apparently, they had managed to brew some potent prune brandy by way of celebrating the happy occasion.

George reported that there had followed long periods of silence when the telephone was unanswered and suspicious mutterings and excuses when it was.

George surmised that the happy relationship had broken down and the two were not speaking to each other as well as to the Greens. He did not say that he feared there might even have been physical violence but I got the impression it was a possibility.

The Years of My Day

I managed to light the Coleman lantern and spent most of the morning searching the 50-room inn, with all its service and storage space, even breaking into the locked area in the basement, which turned out to be a carpenter's shop.

Then, painfully, I went outside, strapped on my despised snowshoes, and walked completely around the huge hotel complex. It had snowed during the night. There were marten tracks where the furry little animals had dashed from one snow-laden tree to another, and the straight-line trail of a bobcat out early on his daily hunt. Gray Jays, blue and black Stellar Jays, and big bold Clarkes nutcrackers, the size of Crows, followed me in short hops from tree to tree, but there was no sign of a man-made trails leading out. This left the possibility that both had departed earlier on the day before and their tracks had been completely obliterated by falling or drifting snow, or that – and the thought disturbed me greatly – in some place and in some condition one or both must still be around.

I knew that there were other buildings in the valley; a ranger station, guide house, stables, a laundry and other service facilities, but as near as I could see these were all buried beneath the snow which lay 30 feet deep on the level, and there were drifts in places twice as deep.

But I was still tired and sore from yesterday's long climb so I returned to my room for lunch and another nap in a warm bed.

Floyd Schmoe

So far as I have ever been able to learn, though I have never pursued the matter, the story of the disappearing caretakers was never solved. For some unknown reason they simply walked out, avoiding the Greens at Longmire and the rangers at the Park entrance. They did not appear even to collect a month's back-pay at the Company offices in Tacoma.

Mr. Martin sent word that if we chose Ruth might join me in Paradise (Valley) and we would have employment until the season opened in July, at which time I would become a mountain guide. The pay would be $100.00 per month and all expenses. It was a good chance to save some money since there was no way of spending any.

The work would consist of shoveling snow off the roof and taking a daily temperature and precipitation reading for the U.S. Weather Bureau, which would be phoned in each evening.

As it turned out about the only snow shoveling it was possible to do was to keep open a tunnel down to the second floor door of our apartment over the bakeshop, and a similar tunnel to

The Years of My Day

let light into a dormer window. The snow drifted so deep over Paradise Inn that winter that snow from the roof would have to be shoveled straight up ten feet and that was impossible. Later in the spring as the snow melted and settled down we were able to clear other dormers though in spite of all we could do several were pushed right off the roof. This happens almost every winter at Paradise Inn even today.

I met Ruth at Longmire a week later. Although she was a strong and healthy girl I knew that the climb back to the inn would be a grueling one as she had never used snowshoes before either. However, she was eager to make the attempt.

Mrs. Green bundled her in woolen sweaters and high boots, and George planned to take two horses to go as far up the trail as the horses could wallow through the three to four feet of snow in the lower valley. He would then return with the horses and we would be on our own. However, on this trip we would have plenty of food, travel very slowly, and spend two days on the climb.

We would spend a night at a ranger station at Narada Falls two miles and a thousand feet below Paradise Inn. We started early in the day. George and I took turns riding the lead horse and Ruth rode all the way.

At the crossing below the Nisqually Glacier George and the horses had to give up. The snow was too deep and the horses were floundering hopelessly. We had gained three miles but it was another two miles to Narada and a much steeper trail. It was dark by the time we arrived.

Even so the two miles yet to go on the morrow would be far more difficult.

Pack rats, who occupy most mountain cabins during the winter months, kept us awake for a time, but we rested and again started out early in the morning.

Floyd Schmoe

Fortunately it had not snowed so the trail that I had made on my way down two days ago was still open and of great help. It was a beautiful day and the Alpine trees of the upper meadow were all mantled in snow and ice. In the low afternoon sun they cast long dark shadows across the glistening snow. Birds followed us; the saucy Gray Jays and Clarks crows were always in sight. A pair of ravens gave us a raucous farewell from the ranger station, and chickadees, nuthatches, and crossbills appeared here and there. We stopped frequently to rest at which times the gray Jays would take food from our hand and, much to Ruth's delight, perch on her head or shoulder. We stopped frequently also to examine animal tracks. The long leaping, neatly paired tracks of the martin were the most numerous but there were snowshoe rabbit, coyote, and bobcat tracks as well. We arrived happy but exhausted in mid-afternoon, and surprisingly Ruth was recovered enough by evening to enjoy another brief stroll outside to enjoy the view of the mountain in moonlight.

There was a piano in our living room, a phonograph and many records, and a few books and magazines. There was more food than we could eat, and since Ruth enjoyed baking and cooking we lived very well.

About once a week I would ski down to Longmire, packing my webs on my back. I made the seven-mile descent once in 45 minutes and the round trip in a single day. The return required four or five hours even with a broken trail. Since there was a stock of rental skis in the guide house I did not pack them back up but used a different pair each trip.

At Longmire I would pick up our mail, some fresh meat and vegetables, and a recent newspaper. Actually we had few needs. We were never sick, our duties were light, it was a second honeymoon.

The Years of My Day

Time passed quickly though Ruth did not see bare ground until the road was opened by snowplows late in June and we did not get out for a visit to Seattle until the 4th of July.

On July 2nd a skeleton crew hiked in from Narada Falls, the road being open only that far, and Ruth prepared dinner for 25 people. Harry Poppi John, the chef, said her lemon meringue pie was the best he had ever tasted.

With the hotel crew came two tall rawboned Swiss guides, Hans and his brother Heinnie Furber, both of whom were to become famous in mountaineering circles both in America and in Canada.

Ruth and I went down on the first bus which came through but I returned in a couple days to help Hans and Heinnie open up the guide house and get climbing gear in shape for the season. Ruth did not return for a week or more by which time there was a bit of bare ground on the sunny slope of Alta Vista where we could build a floor and pitch a tent.

She had informed earlier that spring of 1920 that we were to become parents of a child and that, along with the exciting new job and the magnificent mountain environment, made us both very happy.

There were other guides, some of them like me, inexperienced; so Hans set out immediately to put us through a rigorous training period, first on the glaciers, then some rock work on Pinnacle peak, and finally a warmup climb to the summit of Rainier.

For most of that season I worked as an apprentice guide bringing up the rear of parties led by either Hans or Heinnie. Never in the two seasons I served with the Mount Rainier Guides did I lead a summit party, though I went as second or third guide on some 14 ascents. Most of my trips were traverses of the Nisqually or Paradise glaciers, with an occasional ascent of Pinnacle Peak.

Floyd Schmoe

On my one free day each week, Ruth and I (or with other off duty guides) did a great deal of climbing and exploration.

The season closed on Labor Day and Ruth and I found a two room apartment near the university where I continued my studies on forestry and ecology.

On September 28, 1920, our first child, Kenneth, was born. Life was good to us.

With what we had saved from the summer's work and a small income from an assistanceship in Dendrology we were able to live.

Again in the summer of 1921 I worked as a mountain guide and Ruth kept Kenneth at a small log cabin we had built during the winter overlooking Lake Washington. They came to visit for a few days only once during the season and that summer passed slowly. However I earned enough so that in September we were able to visit friends and family in Wichita, and, with help from a friend I had met on Mount Rainier, go on for a year of study at New York State College of Forestry at Syracuse University.

Kenneth was growing rapidly, my work, turning more into biology and ecology, was fascinating, new and friendly people in anew setting, all this combined to give us a most satisfying year. I graduated in June, 1922, with a Bachelor of Science degree.

Earlier I had been appointed a ranger with the National Park Service, so on the strength of this job, we borrowed money and purchased a second-hand Model T Ford. We would drive cross-country.

I had driven an automobile only once before in my life but that was a trip across Paris in an ambulance. Perhaps that hazardous journey of only a few miles had given me more experience than weeks of driving under highway conditions.

We set out as soon as classes were over, not waiting for commencement exercises, and had six flat tires the first day. I had put too much pressure in old tires and the day was extremely hot.

The Years of My Day

West of Chicago where there was no more hard surface road and the air was cooler we had more trouble with mud but less with tires. It took us 18 days to Seattle.

As a Park Ranger we were provided with a tent at Longmire Springs. It was a very good tent with board floor and walls and a fly. There was a small wood burning stove for heat and electricity for cooking and lighting, but when in December temperatures dropped below zero and snow piled up four feet deep on the ground, it was a very poor shelter. Ruth suffered most trying to keep a fire day and night, bathing and doing laundry every day for Ken with water which had to be carried in and heated on the stove. With only the Greens at the Inn and the Wilsons (a warehouse man and his wife) for neighbors, no church or other social life, it was a long and dreary winter. Only the company and needs of our child, and each other, kept us content.

Fortunately we were able to drive to Seattle about once a month where we still had the cabin and many friends.

After winter set in I had very little work to do. Occasionally after a storm there would be trees fallen across trails to remove, and telephone lines to repair. There was a daily weather report to make, frozen water pipes to thaw, and firewood to be cut and hauled in. Mostly it was only a matter of supplying our own needs. The nearest Post Office and grocery store was 14 miles down river at Ashford.

In early spring a trail crew was hired and I became crew boss. All the trails need repairs after a winter and spring thaw. Not only do trees fall but avalanches occur, trails wash and slide out, bridges are washed out or damaged, beavers raise their dams and flood roads or trails, patrol cabins need opening, and campgrounds put in shape. There is plenty to do. The work often kept me away from home for several days at a time, camping out on the job.

We opened the Paradise trail first, since it is most used. The cabin at Narada Falls became a base camp for work on the upper

Floyd Schmoe

trail. Supplies and materials often had to be packed in on horses. I learned to tie the Diamond Hitch but I never learned to pack shovels, axes, peavies, and six-foot cross-cut saws on a horse so that they would stay on uphill and down. Often the horses had to be repacked several times before arriving with all they started out with.

The second trail we worked was the Indian Henry Trail. It was seven miles long and the upper third, like the Paradise Trail, is very steep. There was a bridge to build and switchbacks on talus slopes always slide out. We camped by the creek for a week, fell cedar logs for stringers, and split cedar puncheon for decking.

In June, 1923 I was transferred to the Paradise District and a new man put on the Longmire District. At Paradise Alley there was an old log cabin which was built even before the National Park was established. Perched high on the side of Alta Vista, it commanded a magnificent view of the valley, the Tatoosh Range, and Mount Adams beyond, but with the hill between us we could see Rainier. Ruth spent happy days gathering huckleberries and making jam. My work that second summer was largely patrol, police and rescue work. With thousands of visitors there was plenty to do. In spite of signs posted along all the trails there were always people who could not resist picking flowers or cutting trees. We seldom arrested anyone; I made only two arrests all summer, one a girl caught picking flowers after being warned once, and the other a drunken driver. Rescue work was more difficult. Seldom has a season gone by without one or more fatal accidents. That summer was bad. A man prodding at loose ice in the Ice Caves under the Paradise Glacier was crushed by falling ice, a young girl waitress at Paradise Inn drowned while swimming in Reflection Lake and Paul Mosher, a young Swiss guide, fell to his death while trying to scale Unicorn Peak. In each case bodies had to be found and carried out to a trail where they could be lashed to a horse to be packed out. Sometimes it was an all night job and never an easy one.

The Years of My Day

Rainier Houses

Our first home on Rainier was a tent at Longmire Springs. 1922-1923.

Our second was the old Log Cabin on Alta Vista. 1924.

The third the Paradise Ranger Station. 1925-1926.

Our last home on Rainier, half a new duplex at Longmire. 1927-1928

Ruth was pregnant again that summer but she felt well and happy. We did quite a lot of climbing and hiking, and she and Ken gathered more blueberries. When we returned to Longmire in the autumn we stored all the office furniture into one room and settled

Floyd Schmoe

ourselves into the remainder of the Administration Building. It was warm and far more comfortable than the tent in which we had spent the previous winter.

On January 11th, 1923, in the midst of a snowstorm, Helen Elizabeth was born. Snow was already three to four feet deep and although the doctor from Ashford tried to get in he was unable to make it. Mrs. Green from the inn provided experienced help and all appeared to go well. Little Elizabeth appeared well and we were happy. However something was wrong, or went wrong, for on the third day I found her crying in a strange way and called Mrs. Green. She was aware that the child was seriously ill and so we called the doctor and sent Mr. Green down the road with the sleigh to meet him. It was several hours before they returned and in the meantime the baby had ceased to cry and appeared to be sleeping. Mrs. Green feared the worst but did not tell us.

When the doctor finally arrived, our Beth was gone. I am sure that was Ruth's saddest hour. While I went to the shop to make a tiny coffin she held her daughter close. When I returned with the little cradle she wrapped our child in a soft blanket and tucked her in. She was the picture of peaceful sleep.

Next day I sealed the small casket, put on my snowshoes, and carried it to the foot of a small cliff above our house where I buried her beneath the snow.

I weep now as after more than fifty years I write Beth's brief history for the first time.

Ken, only two and a half years old was a healthy and happy child and a great comfort to us. Although Ruth wore her grief outwardly well I knew she was deeply hurt and as soon as we felt she was physically able to travel we left the park for a long visit with her family in Wichita.

When we returned in early spring flowers were beginning to bloom, a new house had been built for us at Longmire, and we had purchased a grand piano, but Ruth was not truly happy again

The Years of My Day

until after Christmas when she knew that next Summer she would bear another child.

When in June of 1924 the child was due we decided to be safe and go to Seattle where better medical care would be assured. It was a fortunate coincidence that at just the right time a big cougar wandered into the park looking for deer and was shot by one of the rangers. I did not find it difficult to persuade the Superintendent that such a fine specimen should be mounted for display in the park museum we hoped to build.

While a student at the university in 1917 I had worked as an assistant in the taxidermy laboratory of the State Museum and I was sure that A.J. Albrecht, the taxidermist, would cooperate. So it happened that Ruth with child, and I with cougar, traveled together to Seattle where we rented a small house near the campus and settled in.

I found Albrecht away on a collecting expedition for the American Museum in New York, but the laboratory and the necessary equipment was available. I skinned out my cat and sent the hide to the tannery.

Esther was born without incident on June 3rd and did well from the first day. We were all very happy.

I managed to use up more than a month at my job of mounting the cougar and Esther was a strong and happy little girl when we went back to Paradise Valley in July. Today Esther is a grandmother and "Old Glasseyes," as the rangers have called our cougar, still stands, bug as life, in a new museum at Longmire.

Floyd Schmoe

Old Glass eyes

In June of 1927 out fourth child was due and we went to Seattle again for the happy occasion. Ruth's mother would come again to help and comfort, and this one would be delivered in a hospital. Whether we were growing "modern," or more cautious, or the grateful children of the divine guidance, I am not sure, but I lean toward the latter, for there were complications requiring skilled assistance. Bill had managed to entangle himself in the umbilical cord and was almost strangled to death before he could be delivered.

It was the first time Ruth had experienced a difficult labor, and we were happy to have a competent physician and the loving care of Grandmother Pickering.

Bill was a strong baby and he recovered rapidly. Within hours the blue skin had become pink and healthy and there were no problems, not yet anyway.

It was seven years before our fifth and last child would be born. Ruthanna was not an "afterthought," nor an "accident." We loved children and enjoyed a big family, though we were never able financially to do as much for them as we would have liked. We did manage to feed and clothe them and we gave them all our love. Ruth, especially, was born to love.

The Years of My Day

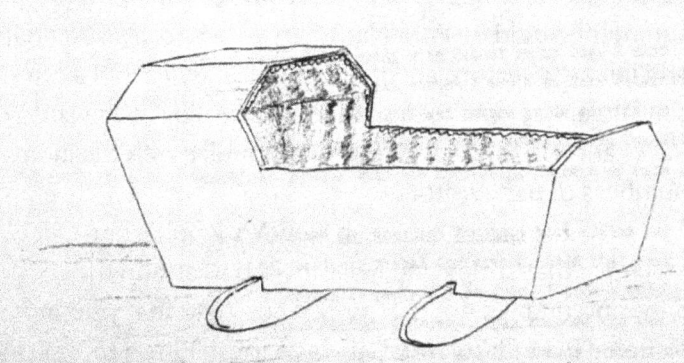

The cradle I made for Ken that first spring at Paradise Inn has also served to cradle his children, and now his grandchildren.

* * *

  Ruth's mother, Elizabeth Pickering, came out from Wichita again that summer to be with us, and as it happened there was an unusually heavy crop of wild blueberries on the hillside just below our cabin. Mrs. Pickering, Ruth, and Kenneth could not bear to see the bears and the birds take all of them so they picked gallons of the luscious fruit. Harry Poppijohn saved mayonnaise jars from the hotel kitchen for Ruth, and together they canned so many that seven years later at our home in Seattle we threw out the last jar. It was still good but we were tired of blueberry jam.
  No rangers wintered in Paradise valley in those days as the road was not kept open and there were few skiers or snowshoers who got that high on the mountain.
  Several new homes were built at Longmire during the summer so we were able to move into a comfortable home for the winter of 1923-24. Esther was beginning to walk and Ken was old enough to enjoy her to and help care for her. This was good because Ruth became ill with anemia and tuberculosis and had to spend much time resting.

Floyd Schmoe

I wrote my first book that winter, often typing with Esther on my lap. I also began to prepare myself for a new job. The next summer I would be Park Naturalist with two assistant naturalists, and initiate a lecture and nature guide service in the park. Earlier a similar service had been pioneered at Yellowstone and Yosemite Parks and was proving useful and popular with the increasing numbers of park visitors.

G.P. Putnam's Sons in New York published *Our Greatest Mountain* that spring and I was invited to attend the Superintendent's Annual Conference, held that year in Mesa Verde National Park in Colorado. It was early in June. I took a Union Pacific train from Seattle to Grand Junction, Colorado, then boarded the one-coach, one-box-car, one caboose, narrow gage, Denver and Rio Grande south through the Colorado Rockies to Mancos, which is the station nearest Mesa Verde Park. The trip took three days.

On the Rio Grande we stopped the evening of the second day at the silver mining town of Telluride and the three man crew left the train along with all the half-dozen passengers. No one told me that we were to spend the night there.

After waiting for an hour for the crew to return from what I supposed was a supper break, I went to the station and found it closed. On a blackboard was chalked; "D & R.G. train #1. Lv. Silverton, Durango and Mancos; 7am." I walked up the one-street town looking for a hotel.

The first several houses were brothels. Girls in doors or windows invited me in. Most of the other establishments were saloons. The SILVER DOLLAR advertised ROOMS. I went in. A Buxom blonde barmaid allowed me to sign the register, took my $2.00, and gave me a key. I soon learned that "room service" was available. (In Japan it's called "pillow service".)

The saloon just below me did not close until 2am; the "room service" did not close at all. I did not sleep well.

The Years of My Day

Returning from Mesa Verde I was invited to ride with Superintendent Thompson and his wife, of Yosemite National Park. We visited Bryce Canyon and Zion National Parks along the way.

Crossing dry lakes in California where for ten miles in every direction the earth is as flat and as smooth as a billiard table Thompson had an urge to test he speed of his new Lincoln Continental. It was the only time I have ever traveled 100 miles per hour in an automobile. At Fresno we stopped overnight and had the car brakes adjusted. The next day, driving down the long, winding, Wawona grade into Yosemite Valley, with Mrs. Thompson driving, we suddenly discovered that we had no brakes. At about 30 miles per hour she tried to shift into low gear but failed. At the next curve we went off the road. About 100 feet down a steep rocky slope we were stopped by heavy mesquite. The car did not overturn and no one said a word. Thompson walked back up the road and found the pin from the brake rod. The mechanic at Fresno had neglected to replace the kotter key.

Next day I took the train to San Francisco, then, to add one more adventure, boarded the S.S. Ruth Alexander for Seattle. The three-day voyage, with splendid food, was relaxing.

When we moved to Paradise Valley that Summer we occupied two small rooms over the Paradise Ranger Station. The District Ranger and his family moved to the cabin on Alta Vista and I turned the lower room into a small natural history museum and Naturalists office.

This became our pattern of life for the next four years; winters at Longmire Springs and Summers at Paradise. We moved up and down, back and forth 13 times during the six years I served with the National Park. It began to get tiresome.

Also Kenneth and Esther needed schooling and we all missed the wider and more stimulating social contacts. And on June 18, 1927, our son Bill was born.

Floyd Schmoe

In 1928 I was offered and accepted the Directorship of the newly founded Puget Sound Academy of Sciences at the University of Washington.

I found the work of organizing a program of popular science lectures, motion pictures, and field trips on the campus not greatly different from the work I had been doing at the park, but the environment and the people far more stimulating; and Ruth and the children were happy to be in a home of our own with gardens, neighbors, schools and church, and with no necessity to move twice a year.

The Academy, though we soon built up a dues paying membership of more than 600, was operating on a very slender budget, and I found the salary of the Director inadequate. Dean Hugo Winkenwerder of the College of Forestry helped out by offering me an assistanceship in dendrology, and I began writing more extensively.

While Park Naturalist I had published a monthly news sheet called Nature Notes, and "moonlighted" a bit by selling a 'Nature' column to a couple of newspapers. The Stockton Record published it weekly and *The Seattle Times* ran it daily in a shorter form.

Now I collected the best of this material and the University Bookstore published it as an attractive book titled "Wilderness Tales." Soon I culled out a series of stories and sketches about interesting plant life and we published it under the title, "Cattails and Pussywillows."

I also enrolled as a part time student in the Graduate School and in 1935 earned a Master of Science degree. Ruthanna came along in 1934.

In 1935, also, Dean Winkenwerder offered me an Instructorship in Forest Ecology. I could carry on my work for the Academy on the side.

With a growing family the old three-room log cabin was becoming somewhat cramped so we purchased an acre of land

The Years of My Day

with an even better view of the lake and the mountains a mile south of our pioneer cabin and began construction of what has ever since been termed "the Big House."

The whole family worked at construction. Ruth and I did most of the carpentry, employing a professional only for help with the heavy framing. Ken and Esther collected used paving bricks which were being discarded by Seattle's Department of streets, carried them home in Ken's old Dodge truck and cleaned them of mortar. Ken and I did the plumbing and wiring. We employed a retired mason to direct the brick work and to build the fireplace and chimney. He was an old Yorkshire man who fell in love with Ruthanna and hired her as his helper. She carried brick. For this he paid her five cents a day and brought her lunch with his. She was now a "big girl," three years old.

The spring after we moved to Seattle Ruth and I decided to build a house of our own. On a bright Sunday afternoon we walked out along the lake shore until we found a lot for sale for 400 dollars, which was all we thought we could borrow from Ruth's mother. It had a view of Mount Rainier and enough second growth fir to build a log cabin.

We cut the trees and built the cabin during the spring and summer. The only lumber we bought was for a floor and window frames. You could see daylight through the shake roof but it didn't leak. We lived there off and on until I came back to the University and we built the "Big House" down the lake.
Ruthanna was born while we lived there. That was on November 19, 1934.

"Chalet Grünwold" The log cabin we built on a bluff above Lake Washington, near Seattle 1920s

Floyd Schmoe

"Moon Gate"--The "Big House," Seattle 1930–195

The "Little House" Seattle, 195 –1968

We lived in the "big house" until the 1950s.

By then Ken, Esther, and Bill were all married and gone. Ruthanna was still in college, and later working as a stewardess. The big house was too big for just Ruth and I.

So we sold it and built the "little house" nearby.

* * *

The war was on. I quit teaching and helped organize a Northwest branch office of the American Friends Service Committee. The immediate job was to protest the threatened internment of all West Coast people of Japanese ancestry, and after that took place, to try to help them get jobs and acceptance outside the restricted zone, and eventually to return to their homes.

This work kept me away from home much of the time. I made frequent trips to the relocation centers in Idaho, Wyoming,

The Years of My Day

and California. I was in Minidoka, Idaho, or Heart Mountain, Wyoming, each of the Christmases of 1942, '43, and '44. We were also helping with European refugees, mostly Jewish people, some of whom came directly to Seattle after having fled Germany and spent the war years in China.

In 1938 I had been invited to the University of Hawaii to lecture on the underseas research I had done for my Masters Degree and to show film of marine life I had made during that time.

In 1940 the Fellowship of Reconciliation, who were also concerned with the fate of the Japanese Americans, and the AFSC sent me back to Hawaii to see what was happening to the 40% of the population of the islands who were of Japanese ancestry, and to see if there was any way in which we could help them. Ruth accompanied me.

As it turned the Japanese Hawaiians were too essential to the economy of the islands (among other things they produced most of the fish and other foodstuffs upon which the islanders lived) to be removed, and so, even after the bombing of Pearl Harbor on December 7, 1941, only a few people of Japanese ancestry were interned. Not one Japanese American was ever convicted of a disloyal act during the war years.

As the war seemed to be coming to a close I discussed the possibility of relief and reconstruction work in Japan with Clarence Picket, then Secretary of AFSC, and suggested that we immediately undertake a training program for volunteer workers. I stressed especially the need for language study as that seemed essential to me and would require a considerable period of time. I knew that there were Nisei college students who would volunteer as instructors. Pickett – though his siter and brother-in-law, Minnie and Gilbert Bowles, had spent most of their lives serving the Japanese people – seemed little concerned, though the desperate situation concerning the European Jews was still too much on his mind.

Floyd Schmoe

As details of the tragic atomic bombing of Hiroshima and Nagasaki began to appear I felt that some expression of regret and shared guilt must be made by Friends, and again opened the subject, suggesting this time AFSC immediately send reconstruction and relief workers to those blasted cities.

When again little concern was expressed by the Service Committee, I determined to undertake a small project, alone if need be, and wrote General MacArthur's headquarters in Tokyo for permission to undertake such a service. I knew that he was concerned because he had already set up an agency called LARA (Licensed Agencies for Relief in Asia) and Esther Rhoads, a Pioneer Quaker missionary and teacher, had been named one of the three Commissioners.

At that time no foreign civilian was given permission to enter Japan unless invited specifically by the Japanese. Esther, through Japan Yearly Meeting, was finally able to get permission for me to undertake relief work. It was already the spring of 1948. Somewhat to my embarrassment I was invited as a "missionary."

A year earlier the Brethren Service Committee, under the imaginative leadership of Dan West, had organized a scheme to get fresh milk to starving and sick people in many parts of the world. It is called "Heifers for Relief" and still functions. The plan is that concerned farmers breed young heifers of good stock and donate them to the committee which then arranges for their distribution where most needed. The operation is not confined to cows or to milk. They also send pigs, chickens, rabbits, goats, even draft animals...whatever is most useful.

I had worked with Dan during the Japanese relocation and we were good friends. In July of 1948 he appointed me "Herdsman in Charge" of a shipment of 250 milk goats out of San Francisco for Yokohama. I would "be required to do the actual work of caring for the goats." There would be three experienced men along to do the

The Years of My Day

chores. I would do the paperwork, oversee the shipment, and attend to the delivery and distribution once we arrived in Japan.

As it turned out my "crew" was a great disappointment. One was a middle-aged evangelical preacher who was taking the opportunity (like me) to get free passage (but for a different reason), another was a seventeen year old boy whose only connection to goats was that his father edited a goat-breeders magazine in St. Louis, and the third was an "experienced" rancher – but an orange grower from southern California. None of us, including myself, had ever milked a goat in our lives and there would be 40 nannies with young kids that should be milked twice each day. Besides that I had unfortunately developed a strong, though misguided, prejudice against goats per se.

The poor animals were penned in groups of about twenty on the open deck of a huge States-line freighter, the M.S. Contest. Sufficient hay and grain was stored in the hold for the voyage. We "herdsmen" would bunk and eat with the ship's crew. It would be a fourteen day crossing. Before we were out of sight of the Golden Gate Bridge my entire crew was seasick in their bunks.

Fortunately I was bunked with the Fourth Engineer, a Mexican American from Arizona, who had been raised on goats milk, and most fortunately he was off watch that first evening. He saw my problem and volunteered to help. Together Tony Lopez and I fed, watered, and bedded 250 bleating white Sannens, Toggenbergs, Brown Alpines, and lop-eared Nubians; and milked more than 40 mothers of young kids who were not yet old enough to relieve their mother of all the milk she produced.

Captain Seaton had ordered that, since there were no facilities for pasteurization, no milk was to be used by members of the crew, so we dumped twenty or more gallons of good rich milk into the sea. Tony however drank all he could hold fresh from the source.

Floyd Schmoe

Much to my surprise I quickly learned how wrong was my superior attitude toward goats. They are highly intelligent and touchingly affectionate creatures. I would place a domestic goat's IQ on par with that of a dog or a horse, and far above that of his relative the sheep, though this may expose my prejudice in regards to sheep.

I became convinced that these goats recognized each of us as persons and read our attitudes and feelings accurately. To me they showed warm affection in many ways such as nuzzling, welcoming bleats, and in the expression of their large brown eyes. Even the newborn kids begged for attention in every way they knew how.

It was not long after departure that we began to experience the joys and sorrows of birth. Most of the older nannies were pregnant – that was part of the program – and a pair of big-eyed, large-headed, wobbly-legged Swiss brown kids were born the first night out. Before they were a day old they had wriggled through the slats of their pen were scampering about on the deck – and before we knew it they had disappeared. The only way they could have gone overboard was through the scuppers, and that was possible, but we continued to search for them, and at Noon found them on the table in the crew mess where Tony had taken them to show off to the men. They were named Ralph and Rachel for Captain Seaton's two children.

Next day twin Sannans were found in a pen and these I named for my twin granddaughters, Mitzi and Mari. All together nine kids were born during the voyage so, although three adults, all males, died during a storm – apparently from seasickness – we arrived in Yokohama with more animals than were visible when we left San Francisco.

I think it was the newborn kids which brought about some welcome, though unexpected, support from both the bridge and the passenger's quarters.

The Years of My Day

As with most large freighters, the Contest carried twelve passengers, which was all that American ships without a Doctor aboard were permitted to carry. Some of our passengers, mostly missionaries, had appeared occasionally on an upper deck to look down on us goats, but not until Ralph and Rachel had invaded their sanctuary did any of them show greater interest in us.

A Mrs. Fisher and her six year old son Sam were among the passengers. Mrs. Fisher is the wife of a Seattle based businessman who heads an import-export business. Mr. Fisher was in Japan at the time and his wife and son were going for a short visit. They came down to the after-deck one morning, Sam to see the goats and Mrs. Fisher to offer her help with their care.

First Mate Thomas also came to help, so, as it turned out, Tony and I had a lot of help with the feeding, watering and milking, in spite of my seasick crew of "herdsmen."

Upon our arrival in the port of Yokohama the goats were offloaded first and placed in quarantine by the Japanese agriculture department. I was housed in an army barracks near the docks and the three "herdsmen" were returned with the Contest.

Fortunately I, having the shipping and registration papers, was permitted time to carry out the formal transfer and distribution of our cargo to its final destination, which was a score of orphanages and tuberculosis hospitals scattered from Hiroshima in southwest Honshu to Sapporo on the northern island of Hokkaido. During the following month I was able to see more of

Floyd Schmoe

Japan than the average Japanese ever sees, though at that time it was not a pretty sight.

In many orphanages children were actually dying of malnutrition and in the refugee camps conditions were as bad for children and adults alike. These were camps for Japanese citizens expelled from China and Manchuria after the war, with no homes or jobs in Japan to which they could return. In addition most of Tokyo, all of Yokohama, much of Osaka and Kobe, and all of Hiroshima still lay in ruin with the survivors living in shacks built from the rubble which lay all around them.

Once the goats were established in their foster homes and presumably making their contribution to the relief and reconstruction of the nation, I was able to negotiate with the occupation government, and the Mayor and other officials of Hiroshima, to bring my proposed "Houses for Hiroshima" work campers and begin building houses the following spring.

I returned home on the U.S. troop ship Fred Ainsworth, well satisfied with my summer's experience.

When word of our project got around, I had quite a number of applications from people of all ages for an opportunity to participate. Some were obviously from "old hands" – former missionaries in Japan who were seeking ways to return – and some were from youngsters who were merely seeking adventure. I chose three people I knew or knew something about. First Rev. Emery Andrews, popular pastor of the Japanese Baptist Church in Seattle with whom I had worked intimately in the relocation centers, then Daisy Tibbs, a home economics major at the University of Washington, and, to complete our American team, Ruth Jenkins, a Sociology major from the University of Arizona.

Daisy was short and black. Ruth (called "Pinky" because of her red hair), is around six feet tall. Together we were to the Japanese – most of whom had never seen a black woman or a redhead – a strange and wondrous sight. Curious bands of children

The Years of My Day

followed us along the street and crowds gathered wherever we stopped, to stare and ask questions. Somewhat to our surprise all the people we met were open and friendly. This was true even in Hiroshima, where we feared that, because of the terrible suffering the American army had brought upon them, there might be demonstrations against and even violence upon us.

It was due largely, I think, to the favorable publicity our little cadre had received by both the local and national press and radio, that our mission was understood and appreciated by the people. In Hiroshima Mayor Hamai of the city, governor Kunose, of the Prefecture, Reverend Tanimoto, hero of John Hersey's powerful book, "Hiroshima," the head of Hiroshima's housing commission, representatives of Buddhist sects, a couple of college presidents, and scores of newsmen and students met our train in the evening of August 3, 1949, and escorted us to a welcoming party and dinner at Kiyoshi Tanimoto's partially rebuilt Nagaregawa Church, where we were to live during the summer.

Next day we met Mayor Hamai and other city officials to arrange for a building site and materials with which to work. We also needed to employ a local architect and master "daikusan" or carpenter since we had no plan to build a western style house in an Asian setting, and that was the only kind of house we knew how to build.

At this meeting we were surprised to learn that the city had already decided what we would build, and where the building should be located. The Mayor suggested we build a children's library in a city park. They had decided that, under the circumstances (and knowing that we could not make any appreciable dent in the housing situation) a "public" building would be more appropriate than a private residence. We agreed that their logic was correct but it did not fit our concern. We had asked for and received money from our friends, with which to build "a home

Floyd Schmoe

for a homeless family." We were concerned. Did they have books for a library should we build one?

Yes, the American Army unit stationed in Kure twenty miles down the bay was being reassigned and had offered the city their camp library of 4,000 books.

We went into a huddle. "Four thousand books, all in English, and obviously titles that would interest soldiers...for a 'children's library'?"

"No," we told the Mayor, "we came to build a home for a family. Perhaps someone else would build a children's library, but we would build a house to be lived in." (Some years later the Mayor of Seattle found money with which the city of Hiroshima built for its children a playground and zoo.)

Our friends from City Hall understood our purpose and would see what they could do to assist us.

We barely reached home before Harry Okamoto, a local architect who had studied at the University of California and spoke English well, appeared at our door with a Japanese carpenter and the owner of a lumber mill.

Harry would donate his services, we would buy our lumber from the millman and we would pay the "daikusan" a hundred yen per day (about 35 cents U.S.) for supervising our work. We would be able to do a great deal of our work under the sheds of the sawmill since the frame of Japanese style houses is largely precut and fitted before it leaves the mill. As the season of heavy rains was just beginning this would be an added advantage.

We went then in Harry's charcoal-burning car to inspect a site suggested by the city for our first house.

It had been an army parade ground at the western edge of the city. Already it had been cleared of debris and a housing development was underway. We would simply add our house to the others and enjoy the advantage of the community bath and laundry which had been built for the new complex.

The Years of My Day

As word spread of our work-camp project a number of Japanese students volunteered to work with us. Tomiko Yamazaki, Yasuko Maekawa, Sumiko Yoshida, Koya Azumi, and Yasuko's younger brother Hiroshi came down for the quaker youth group in Tokyo, and several boys and girls from the Hiroshima University came at irregular intervals or on weekends. These ate with us but returned to their homes overnight. Usually there were about a dozen of us on the job including the Japanese carpenter.

For most of the summer some of us squatted in the shade of the mill sheds with chisel and mallet, cutting mortises and tenons of a fascinating variety, in the ends or sides of 4 x 4 cryptomaria beams (cryptomeria japonica is a common lumber in Japan, with wood similar to California Redwood), which had been sawn to length and marked for us by the "daikusan." At the same time another team would be pushing and pulling a heavy two-wheel cart, borrowed from the mill master, and loaded with timbers. It was almost a mile from the mill to the building site over cobbled streets full of chuckholes, and most days were unbearably hot and humid. It was hard work but it provided much amusement for the locals. "Americans pushing loads just like Chinese coolies… how funny!"

Once the entire frame was stacked on the site and stone footings – which we had subcontracted to a local mason – were finished, we all turned to and put up the frame. It was just like a Chinese puzzle to us but the carpenter had worked many such puzzles. Without a single nail being driven the entire frame of a two-unit house was mauled together between breakfast and supper.

We took a day off by way of celebration. First the local Shinto Priest must be called in to dedicate the new house and a sheaf of rice tied to the ridge pole in token of the occasion. We then all had a hot bath and took the ferry to Miyajima Island for an afternoon's picnic. Miyajima is the site of the famous torii which

Floyd Schmoe

stands in the sea, marking the approach by water to the beautiful Shinto shrine of Miyajima. The island lies in the inland seas about ten miles west of Hiroshima.

Our visit happened to coincide with an annual Shinto festival during which a local god (male) who has, for a season, been on a visit to the goddess of a temple on an adjacent island, returns home in triumph.

For the occasion a huge barge is built and manned by rowers from the home temple. The Royal barge is richly decorated and lighted by hundreds of paper lanterns. The rowers wear only a diaper-like loin cloth, but the divine one (represented by a wooden god), and all his retinue, are luxuriantly gowned.

At midnight the chant of the rowers is heard from far off and the lighted barge appears. It is followed by a flotilla of lighted and decorated boats manned by crews from other shrines. These are local fishing boats decked out for the occasion.

Passing under the great torii the barge is met at the dock by richly gowned Shinto priests of the local shrine and the returning god is carried ashore by his chanting followers with much ceremony.

As the only foreign visitors we were given a place of honor, and later invited by a wealthy Hiroshima lady who had a summer villa nearby, to spend the remainder of the night as her guests.

Although it was already two o'clock in the morning she insisted on serving us tea and sweet bean cakes and even suggested that she do a tea ceremony in our honor. This we declined preferring to get a few hours sleep if possible. I'm afraid our hostess felt slighted; offers of such nature are not usually refused, but we were tired and there was still the day's work to do upon our return home.

When our first house was completed and the papers published pictures announcing that it had been given to the city to be rented at a very low rate to a needy family made homeless by

The Years of My Day

the bomb, the City Housing Authority received more than 4,000 applications.

We were faced with the problem which had caused us concern from the beginning; how to give one family a house, when thousands of other families were equally needy, without causing jealousy or suspicion of favoritism. Even the Mayor, and the head of the Housing Authority, lived in shelters far worse than the house we built.

When the day came we asked the Welfare Bureau to give us 100 names from the most needy of their lists. We placed it in a basket, and before the press and news reel cameras, asked Mayor Hamai's 4 year old daughter to draw a name.

It was the name of a young public school teacher with a wife and two small children. They would pay 750 Yen per month (about $2.00). When I visited Hiroshima 20 years later the children were grown and had left home but Mr. and Mrs. Shimoda still lived in the house which, since the trees and shrubs we had panted had grown up and the house had been well cared for by the Shimoda's and the city, looked better than it did the day we had turned it over to the housing authority.

The city, as they had promised us, had never raised the rent. Such houses in Japan today rent for more than $100 per month.

As it turned out we had enough money, enough time, and enough help to build two such houses of two apartments each, and so house four needy families. We returned home third-class (steerage) on the President Wilson as we had gone over, and promised the people of Hiroshima that we would return next summer to build more houses.

During the winter of 1949-50 I took a job as laboratory technician in the Pharmacology Department of the College of Medicine and at the same time promoted our Houses for

Floyd Schmoe

Hiroshima program so that in the spring of 1950 we had more money and were able to undertake a larger project.

That summer I took only two volunteers from America; Marita Harris, a black social worker, and Bob Yee, a Chinese American political science student – but we had more Japanese volunteers and employed more skilled labor locally. We lived that summer in a large rented house in Koi, a western suburb of Hiroshima, and the Mayor sent his chauffeur every morning to drive us to the job.

Harry Okamoto designed two beautiful little single unit dwellings for us that summer; one we called the "model house" in which we built one hard-floor, "Western room" and a kitchen with stand-up work space, a sink with running water, and a gas range. It still lacked an oven, hot water, or a flush toilet. It was "modern" by local standards. On the outside it is all Japanese with stucco walls and tile roof and, with the garden we planted, a very attractive house.

The other house was tiny and completely Japanese. It was set on a wooded terrace on the side of a hill called Sarayama (Ricebowl Mountain) because it is the shape of an inverted bowl. The top of Sarayama is a public park, but the southern slope was owned by the city. Concrete steps lead up to the little house from gardens at the base of the hill. It looks more like a Japanese tea house than a private dwelling. We also built four more duplexes similar to those we had built the first summer. There was room for several more houses at the same site.

Schmoe Hall, Hiroshima Jogakuin (women's college) Hiroshima, Japan
This photograph of "Schmoe Hall" appeared on the front page of a commemorative pamphlet, distributed at the dedication ceremonies, held on March 29, 1969, of the girls residence on the Ushita campus of the college.
Hamako Hirose, President of the college, said at the dedication, "This fine building, a dormitory for senior girls of Hiroshima Jogakuin, has been built on land donated to the college by Mr. Floyd Schmoe, an American who felt sympathy for those who suffered the destruction of

Floyd Schmoe

> Hiroshima. We have named it "Schmoe House" in appreciation of his good will.
>
> "Mr. Schmoe came to Hiroshima soon after the war and, as an expression of his sympathy, using his own money and labor, and that of others, both American and Japanese, built many houses for survivors of the atom bomb. In the summer of 1952 they built a four-family house on this site which Mr. Schmoe donated to the college. Because of the need for more living space we have, with Mr. Schmoe's permission, taken down the original structure and built this fine dormitory. We wish also to express appreciation to the builders and to Miss Hatsue Yamamoto, who represents Mr. Schmoe today."

In 1951 I did not go to Japan. Instead, Andy took a young architect, Vince Credson, and Jean Young, a Stanford University student, and together with Japanese volunteers, they built a community meeting home and bath, and two more duplexes. The Sarayama project was growing into a sizable community and there was still room for more expansion.

We thought it was time I earned some money. Although Ruth had taken a job in a downtown bookstore she did not earn enough to meet all our living costs.

So, in 1951, with Pete's help (Lyle "Pete" Smith, a pal of Bill's who lived with us for some years) I built a small house on the southwest corner of our Seattle lot, subdivided the land, and sold it even before it was finished. The profits from this transaction gave us some cushion against the next few years, making it possible for me to continue work in Asia. Ruth, however, continued working at the bookstore downtown.

In July of 1952 the Third World Conference of the Society of Friends was to be held at Oxford College in England, and I had been appointed one of the delegates from Pacific Yearly Meeting.

Ruth and I had attended the Second World Conference at Swarthmore College near Philadelphia in 1937 and this was an

The Years of My Day

opportunity not only to enjoy the inspirational programs planned but also to visit England for the first time and to renew contacts with friends, old and new, from many parts of the world.

In 1937 Ruth and I had driven our new Chrysler "Airflow" from Seattle to Philadelphia in four days including a detour and overnight in Yellowstone National Park. It was quite a contrast from the 18 days we spent on the road in 1922.

This time Ruth took a couple of weeks off from her work and she and Ruthanna, who had just qualified for a driver's license, drove with me to Quebec, from where I would travel by ship to Southampton. Returning west Ruth and Ruthanna stopped a few days with Ruth's family in Wichita, then on to Riverside, California for the sessions of Pacific Yearly Meeting held that year at Riverside University. After Yearly Meeting they drove north up the coast to Seattle. On her first overland trip Ruthanna had driven continuously for over 4,000 miles. One hot and windy day across northern Texas she logged more than 600 miles; a record I have never equaled. That was Ruth's second year as Clerk of Pacific Yearly Meeting.

I had a smooth and interesting crossing of the North Atlantic on the old Cunard S.S. Franconia. There were many Canadian and American Quakers on board, all on their way to Oxford, and we enjoyed a number of Meetings for worship as well as social gatherings together. For all the first day we were in the St. Laurence River and Gulf of St. Laurence. Passing through Belle Isle Straight to the north of Newfoundland we immediately encountered icebergs in great numbers. Breathing their cold breath and fascinated by their immense size and weird shapes, we remember the Titanic and were glad that our ship proceeded slowly and cautiously.

In London, at my suggestion, T. Edmund Harvey, looking almost as fit as when I last saw him almost 30 years earlier, had gathered a group of former members of the British and American

Floyd Schmoe

Friends Service Units of World War 1 to a tea at the home of Ruth and Joan Frye. It was a wonderful opportunity to greet old friends and coworkers and exchange reminiscences. The famous sisters Frye were well into their 80's but the old sparkle and enthusiasm had not dimmed. T. Edmund was now Sir Edmund, and still sitting in Parliament. My greatest surprise and joy was to find Rita and Mireille – the Burnand twins we had all loved so much in Paris so many years ago. At last I was able to hug and kiss them both, an experience I would have given a day of my life for in 1919, and still found heart-warming. Rita, now the wife of Fred Page, was obviously quite ill and I was not unprepared to learn of her death a year or so later.

Mireille, now married to Edmund Cooper, was well, and full of life's enthusiasms. Both couples lived at Jordans just outside London, where I visited them again in 1958, though poor Rita had by then passed away.

Oxford, both the conference and the setting, was a memorable experience. I was housed at old Worcester College, originally a Benedictine Monastery. Its old stone walls, three feet thick, had obviously never completely dried out or warmed up since they had been built more than 800 years ago by some forgotten mason.

My room was upstairs of Stair 9. The student occupant was on vacation, but his ancient "scout" was still on duty. Early each morning the wizened old soldier appeared at the door with a kettle of boiling water and a bundle of kindling with which to light a small fire in the open fireplace. It was July but winter lingered on through most of the Summer between those walls.

One of the many strange coincidences of my life was to find myself seated beside the student whose room I occupied that fortnight, several weeks later on a plane out of Calcutta for Hong Kong.

The Years of My Day

We had just crossed over the Bay of Bengal and were high above the hot Burmese hills. The red-headed Scot who was our pilot had warned us with, "Here where the dawn comes up like thunder out of China across the bay," and he was right. The air was rough. While we were making a smooth descent into Rangoon a few minutes later, my seatmate, with whom I had exchanged only a brief greeting, turned to me with a pale greenish face and said, "In weather like that I wish I had taken a ship. I can swim a little but I can't fly at all."

I asked him then where he was from and he said that he was a member of an Oxford University soccer team and that they were going to Hong Kong to play a few matches. When I told him that I had just come from Oxford he asked me where I had stayed. I told him Worcester College. He asked, "What stair?" I said, "Upper 9." He smiled and said, "By jove, my diggs."

Obviously there had been a number of adventures between Oxford and Rangoon. Following the close of the conference, Harold Carson, a good friend and neighbor from Kirkland, and I, did a walking trip through the Cotswalds a few miles southwest of Oxford. Aside from a good soaking in a sudden rain squall it was a delightful stroll through the picturesque thatch-and-stone roofed villages, and the rolling countryside where sheep were our most intimate companions. We had lunch at a quaint Golden Coq Inn in a hamlet with the descriptive name of Bourbon on the Water, and from there took a bus back to Oxford and on to London.

I stopped off at Beconsfield for a few hours visit in the Jordans home of Edmund and Mireille Cooper, and later that same evening took a train for Harwich on the North Sea, where I caught a midnight ferry for the hook of Holland, The Hague, and Amsterdam.

After a day of sightseeing on Amsterdam's canals and narrow streets, and a visit to Marken Island in the Zuyder Zee,

Floyd Schmoe

where the ancient customs and costumes of holland are still enjoyed, I took a train for my first reunion with the people, places and pastimes of the Paris I had loved many years ago.

After Paris there was a happy reunion with my dear Anna Loche (now widowed Anna Dardant), at her home in Couzon au Mt. d'Or on the banks of the Saone River a few miles above Lyon. Anna showed me the ancient Roman ruins; the baths and stone laundry tubs, the church where she and her fathers had worshipped for generations and the e'cole where she had taught generations of village children both before and after the war.

Ruth and I had corresponded with Anna between wars, but we had lost touch during the Second World War. Her husband had died during the war but she was well and happy with her home and garden. Everyone in the village knew and loved Anna and Hélène, her only child, who with her family visited often from their home in Lyon.

Hélène is about the age of our Ruthanna and the two became pen pals. Then when Hélène's Chantel and Ruthanna's Susan were in their teens they corresponded with each other. In 1975-6 Susan spent several months with Bill and Lillian, now living in London, and she was able to visit Chantel and her family in Lyon. After 50 years the third generation of pen pals became real pals, and in the summer of 1977 all of Hélène's family were able to visit us in America.

That summer of 1952 I went from France to Innsbruck in Austria, then over the famous Brenner Pass and down to Venice. Venice was hot and crowded and I spent only one mosquito-harassed night in the "Jewel of the Adriatic," then went to Rome, stopping off overnight to visit the turf of my favorite saint, Francis of Assisi.

After admiring the great murals in the basilica of St. Francis and standing before the tomb of that humble man in the crypt below, I slipped through a narrow gate in the city's wall behind the

The Years of My Day

church and sat on the grass beneath a tall cyprus tree to rest. A narrow trail led down from the postern gate in the direction of peasant cottages in the valley below. While my mind carried me back those 700 years to the time when Francis walked these trails and paused perhaps at this same tree to speak with, and bless, a pair of robins, a small barefoot Italian boy came by leading a sheep by a cord around its neck. He asked me to hold the sheep while he put on a pair of shoes which he had carried around his neck.

Properly shod he entered the gate, and presumably the church, on whatever mission he had. He was not gone long. Returning he removed his shoes, hung them about his neck and thanking me, he took his sheep and disappeared down the dusty trail. Was that perhaps the real Francis of Assisi, incarnate, returning to bless the city of his birth?

Rome was also hot and dusty and hurried. I spent a day wandering among ruins eloquent of past glories and past atrocities; from the great dome of St. Peter's to the gaping wound of the Coliseum; out along the wheel rutted Appian Way past the temple of Mars, to the tombs of the Christian Martyrs and back to the Roman Forum where I lingered so long in the moonlight that I almost missed the midnight train to Bari; where in the early morning I took a ship to Egypt.

We spent most the day in port at Alexandria where we were warned not to leave the docks because of the unrest caused by Nassar's take-over from King Farouk I, who was departing that very day on his private yacht from that same dock area. I did not see the bloated playboy King, but I did talk the sentry at the gate into allowing me out "in order to mail a letter." It took me a long time to mail that letter, and in the meantime I saw most of downtown Alexandria, including a prolonged talk with an Egyptian hustler named "Mr. Johnson" while I rested on a bench in the central square.

Floyd Schmoe

Mr. Johnson professed to know many of the great men and women of the day, including Mr. Einstein, and the Queen of England yet! The conversation was so extended because friend Johnson accompanied me all the way back to the waterfront still hoping I would follow him back to some wonderful "Sooks," where with his good services I could purchase anything my heart desired for almost nothing at all. I was happy that the sentry at the gate had been changed in my absence and also that "Mr. Johnson" was not remembered either and turned back. In the meantime Farouk's palatial yacht had departed carrying the deposed King and his retinue into the luxury of exile.

When I awoke next morning I was paged by George Chidioc and we were at dockside in Beirut. George is a friend of Gordon and Esther, a prosperous then, (now wealthy) Lebanese, who being the owner of a car had volunteered to pick me up. It was a very fine American and, as I learned later, affordable because George, like many other Mid-East business men, invested in a car which is then farmed to a taxi driver during most of the time but available to the owner on demand.

Gordon was the head of the Department of Anthropology and Sociology at the American University in Beirut at the time and he, with Esther and my three grandchildren, had a very nice flat near the campus.

Beirut, in 1952, was a delightful place, especially for those of the university community who could afford to have Palestinian servants, a weekend cottage in the hills above the city or a beach cottage on the seashore. They could swim in warm Mediterranean waters all year and ski in the high Lebani mountains in the winter. They could in fact swim in the morning and ski that same afternoon if the fancy struck them.

I enjoyed Beirut that summer and have grieved its destruction since.

The Years of My Day

One weekend Gordon, Esther, and I drove to Jerusalem by way of Damascus, Amman, and Jericho. In Damascus we walked "the street called straight," visited the great mosque with its tomb containing John the Baptist's head, and had dinner beneath the date palms in the surrounding oasis.

Jerusalem was then divided and visitors were not allowed to pass from the Israeli to the Jordanian sides. We spent an evening at the Ramalla school, established and maintained by British and American Friends over the past years, and next day while Esther and Gordon went shopping, I walked down into the Vale of Kedron, paused at the Garden of Gethsemane, the climbed to the Mount of Olives and sat for an hour overlooking the City of Sorrows. Returning to the walled city by the Jaffa Gate, I found the Mosque of Omar (site of Solomon's Temple) closed. I walked the Via Dolorosa and was sickened to see an old Arab drown a kitten by holding it in the gutter under his foot.

That evening I wrote my mother: "I have seen Jerusalem and now I know why Jesus wept over the city."

From the Jericho road we could look down into Bethlehem but we were not permitted to visit the city because the only road crossed a narrow strip of Israeli territory.

Driving through Amman on our way north the next day we found the city had blossomed out in a gaudy florescence of flags, bunting, and honorific arches. It was all, we learned, by way of a "Welcome home" for the young Prince Hussein, who had returned home from schooling in England. In May of 1953 he would be crowned King Hussein of the Hashemite Kingdom of Jordan. He was only sixteen that year.

But the most unforgettable memory of that desert journey came late in the evening when the setting sun cast black shadows beyond the gold-kissed sand dunes and, except for the narrow ribbon of blacktop which stretched ahead of our car, nothing else was in sight. Suddenly we heard the far away call of cameleers, and

Floyd Schmoe

looking to our left watched a huge herd of wild camels being driven across the sands. We slowed and they crossed the road ahead of us and disappeared over the hills to the east, with the strident cries of the herdsmen still hanging in the desert air.

The breeding of camels, I later learned, is one of the principal occupations of these Jordanian nomads.

From Beirut I took a plane for Karachi, Pakistan. Surprisingly our Pan Am 707 took off to the west and began circling over the Mediterranean. I surmised it was to gain altitude in order to cross the Lebanese mountains which rise immediately to the east of Beirut. Turning back we passed over the airfield and followed the Damascus highway through the Riyaq Pass. There was a glimpse of the Roman ruins at Baalbeck far to the north, a brief sweep of the green Zahlah Valley which is Beirut's "bread basket," and we were passing over the oasis of Damascus, which from the air appears to be more a forest of date palms than a city. Beyond Damascus there is no road, just a web of tracks all running east and west across the flat Syrian Desert.

Gordon had made the overland trip by bus to Baghdad one time and told me that drivers follow a compass course across the sand picking whatever track appears to be the smoothest. This was apparent from the air.

Within an hour the green borders of the Euphrates River appeared, then after brief stretch of sand, Baghdad on the Tigris. We turned south then and, following the river, were over the Persian Gulf in less than an hour.

Looking down on the delta of the river, which below the junction of the Tigris and the Euphrates, is called Shatt al, I was puzzled by a pattern of green, blue and yellow which for all the world looked like the familiar "tree of life" design of a Persian rug. The riddle bothered me for years, for never before or since have I seen a geographical feature which resembled it. More recently I found a photograph of this same scene in an old copy of the

The Years of My Day

National Geographic Magazine and learned that the pattern is formed by the multiple channels of the river as it crosses its delta, and the plantations of date palms which border each stream. Many people consider this the site of the original Garden of Eden.

The Gulf was green with floating oil. Son Bill, who on his job with Continental Oil Company, often visits the area, tells me that such pollution no longer exists, though the number of off-shore oil rigs and loading docks has multiplied several times over since 1952. The oil ports of Al Manamah on the island of Bahrain, and Abu Dhabi on the coast of the United Arab Emirates – large modern cities today – were mud-walled villages then, barely discernable from 30,000 feet in the air.

We turned east over the Gulf of Oman and following a few miles off the baren shores of Iran and Pakistan, reached Karachi at dusk.

I spent that night in a modern motel-type hotel near the airport. Though the room and its furnishings were western, the courtyard just outside my door had a distinctly eastern flavor. Beggars, some blind, some grotesquely deformed, and all clothed in filthy rags, slept on the pavement, and a snake charmer with a basket full of five-foot cobras was camped on my doorstep.

The hotel served a very good breakfast which was fortunate for me because, as it happened that would be my last meal for two days.

After breakfast I took a broken down bus into the city hoping to catch a train for Lahore, a day's journey by train to the north. I had decided to travel overland across Pakistan and India, since it might be my only opportunity to see the vast sub-continent first-hand and up close.

There were two trains per day and I arrived at the railway station too late for the morning schedule.

Karachi is a poor city, though west Pakistan's only port and largest city. I found no taxis or sight-seeing buses and, the day

Floyd Schmoe

being oven-hot, I did not walk far. There were few vehicles of any sort though the streets were crowded with people, few of whom seemed to be going anyplace. Thousands of squatters, refugees from the starving countryside, were living under straw mats or cardboard shacks on the sidewalks. One large modern building was under construction near the railway station, though the tools of construction were far from modern. Men were mixing concrete by hand on the street and women were carrying it up bamboo ramps in baskets on their heads to the fifth or sixth floor levels. Thing which I remember most vividly about the people is that nearly everyone was chewing beetle nut, the scarlet juice staining their mouth and teeth and smearing the sidewalks with their spittle.

I found no place to eat or any food I dared to eat. Most of the day was spent at the crowded railway station observing the people and waiting for the evening train.

Finally the time came and the gates were opened. There was such a rush of people down the narrow platform that the weaker were crowded off onto the adjoining tracks, and the coaches were filled so rapidly that I, not being willing to fight for a place, soon found no place left. When the train pulled out there were people on top of the coaches and clinging two-deep to the steps.

Back in the station a gateman with a minimum command of English informed me that the next day was the beginning of Ramadan, the month-long Moslem fast during which no devout son of Islam is permitted to travel; therefore thousands of city dwellers were hurrying home to native villages to spend the holy days. He directed me to a nearby hotel for the night.

I have slept in many strange places but never one called a hotel that was less comfortable. The room was upstairs over a bazar of some sort. It had no doors or windows as such but stood open to the street on one side and a cluttered courtyard on the

The Years of My Day

other. There was a rope-webbed bed but no bedding. The toilet facilities were a tin wash basin and a hole in the floor at the end of a narrow walkway outside.

On the street side there a fascinating view of life as, unfortunately, so many millions of people of Asia and Africa are forced by poverty and ignorance to live it. Both sides of the street were lined with shacks and hovels in which hundreds of people lived. Two-wheeled, camel-drawn carts carried freight. A young man pushed a handcart on which lay the naked corpse of an old man, and women cooked rice in pots over camel-dung fires. Strangely, from one of these miserable shelters, two little Pakistani girls dressed in spotless starched and ruffled dresses, emerged in the morning to be led off down the street by their father to – I surmise – some religious festival.

I had purchased from a street vendor what I took to be a melon but which, when I opened it, turned out to be some inedible sort of gourd.

The early morning train was almost empty. I had an entire second-class coach almost to myself. A Pakistani student returning from studies in England, was the only other passenger. He apparently slept all day. I never saw him after departure. At the first station stop a food vendor came through the train and I was able to buy some bread, a hard-boiled egg, and a cup of hot tea. This was to hold me for another day and night. I was beginning to know what malnutrition is really like.

It was a slow dusty journey. All day long we followed the great Indus River, passing many cities and town. There were occasional passengers though no one entered my compartment. Gradually the countryside grew more arid and by nightfall we were entering the Sind Desert. It was very hot even with windows open and the small electric fan running. I stripped to my shorts, closed the window against the smoke and dust, and lay sweating on the hard bunk.

Floyd Schmoe

At a station stop sometime early in the night there was a knocking at my window. I opened it to an elongated replica of Mahatma Gandhi who smiled toothlessly and began passing first a small boy, then a smaller girl, into my compartment. These were followed by a cart-load of bundles, baskets, and assorted baggages.

There was a pause, but about the time I had decided that I had inherited a family with all its chattels, my ancient friend appeared at the inner door escorting a young woman covered from head to foot by black veil and loose-fitting burnoose. The baggage was quickly stacking in the lower bunk opposite mine, leaving barely room enough for the boy to curl up at one end. Mama was hoisted into the upper bunk along with the little girl.

Grandpa – who I had now determined to be an ancient servant rather than a member of the family – clambered into the bunk above me and, reaching out with a skinny leg, turned the electric fan (which was now mounted above the door) full upon himself.

So far no words had been spoken to me. As the train moved I began making friendly gestures toward the boy but got little response. Even when I produced and blew up a red rubber balloon and batted it across to him he only stared at me. (I always carry toy balloons in foreign countries for just such emergencies but this was the only occasion I can remember that I got not even a smile in return.)

After a while I began to hear unmistakable sounds of an infant nursing. The mother had a child inside that hot dress of hers where the air must have been stifling. However I never saw the child nor heard another sound from it all that torrid night.

When the old man began to snore I got up and turned the fan toward the mother and children.

Next morning the old man took the children out for a time and returned them looking scrubbed and refreshed. I had slept for

The Years of My Day

a few hours during the night but I do not think the little mother ever left her bunk all night long. I heard her nurse the baby a time or two and the servant gave her, and the two older children, food from a basket. At a station stop we bought hot tea from a vendor who stopped by the window.

About mid-morning we stopped at a larger city and the old man prepared his family for departure. Again I passed the baggage out the window. Just before the train departed he rushed in with a double handful of very sticky dried dates. He smiled for the first time and said, "You like?" and thrust the dates into my hands. I waved goodbye to the children but they did not wave back. I never did see the baby.

We reached Lahore about Noon where I discovered that I could not buy a rail ticket for Delhi because the border wars had stopped train travel. I hailed a horse-drawn taxi and asked to be taken to the airport. My driver did not understand anything I tried to tell him. I might as well have talked to his horse. Finally we set off and I wondered where we might be headed. I was sure it was not in the direction of the airport.

Finally we came to a mission compound – the only place, I suppose, where the cabby knew he could find an interpreter.

The British missionary told me that the airport was some ten miles outside the city and directed my driver to the BOAC downtown office. There I bought a ticket for Delhi. Once inside India I could take train again for Calcutta.

A plane was about to leave but the agent said they would hold it for me and called a taxi – a motor-driven taxi. We set off promptly and promptly ran out of gas. The driver said, or seemed to say, "Not to worry, they are holding the plane." He took off down the road on foot.

About twenty minutes later he returned on a bicycle carrying about a half-gallon of gasoline in a can. Emptying the gas

Floyd Schmoe

into the tank and lashing the bicycle to the spare tire we were off and running again.

A half mile from the gate to the airport the motor sputtered and stopped again. I got out and ran. My plane was waiting, the engines were turning, and the crew was very unfriendly. I could imagine why, but then I was not feeling too friendly myself.

Arriving at Delhi's Palam Airport I was welcomed into India by the meanest customs official I have ever met – Americans not excluded. Sadder still she a rather nice-looking woman. Apparently, as with many Indians at the time, she was nurturing a hatred of all Pakistani, and all things related to Pakistan. The two countries were at war and she was on the front lines.

To open the battle she attacked my intelligence. I had misspelled Lahore on my customs declaration; I had left off the 'e'. I carried a small suitcase and a flight bag, both of which I presented open. She tore out everything in the suitcase and did not replace it. Then she plunged her hand into the flight bag and came out with a handful of very sticky dates. Not knowing what else to do with the mess my Pakistani roommate had given me on the train that morning, I had wrapped them in a scrap of paper and put them on top of the miscellany in my bag. With what must have been the equivalent of at least a sincere "damn you" she threw the dates on the floor and turned her back on me. I have never enjoyed revenge more in my life.

There were other receptions that day with happier outcomes. The airport bus let me off on a street of downtown New Delhi. Walking along in search of a public telephone, an Indian boy dropped alongside and. speaking good English, offered to carry my bags.

I told him that they were not heavy and furthermore, having just arrived, I had no Indian money with which to pay him. He took my suitcase and, smiling, said, "I did not ask you to pay me."

The Years of My Day

He escorted me to a nearby hotel from which I was able to call the Delhi Friends center. The English Friend who was resident said that no beds were available at the moment but directed me to a nearby hotel and invited me to tea the following day.

After a comfortable night, in spite of three huge Brahma bulls, who had bedded down in the courtyard outside my window and snored, I found a young taxi driver who spoke English and agreed to give me a half-day tour of the city at a reasonable price. One of the points of interest was the great Buddhist Temple of Swaminarayan Akshardham. Worship services were under way in one of the halls. I watched for a time while the saffron-robed Priests conducted their ritual. I then wandered about the open court with its life size sculptures of elephants, monkeys, and men, taking motion pictures of the colorful scene. Then came my next adventure.

Out of the crowd barged a huge, white-turbined Sikh carrying a large knife in his belt and a gun on his hip. He must have been either a policeman or a soldier, and I was sure I was to be arrested. I wondered what I had done wrong. I had left my shoes at the gate, I didn't think I had disturbed the worship session, though a few of the monks had looked at me with suspicion. Had my friend from the customs office sent word ahead?

He strode up to me and in perfect English demanded:
"Are you an American?"
"Yes," I replied very humbly.
"Where are you from?"
"Seattle," I said.
He thrust out his hand and said, "I'm from Vancouver." We shook hands.

In mid-afternoon my driver deposited me at Friends Center. Tea was served in a lovely tree-shaded garden, and I was invited to have a nap. Siesta is an institution I have always enjoyed, especially in hot countries, and one to which, since my retirement, I

Floyd Schmoe

have become hopelessly addicted. This one was doubly appreciated.

That evening Friend Baker drove me to the railway station from which I took the 10:00 o'clock train for Calcutta.

In a second-class coach which was often overcrowded, it was long, hot, and often dusty journey. The dust became more bearable because, remembering my night through the Sind desert, I had borrowed from the center, a bed sheet. (I can say "borrowed" because on arrival in Tokyo several days later I donated the sheet to Takeshi and Masa Kobori, my hosts at Friends Center there.)

Calcutta must certainly be the seat of more human misery than any other spot on Earth. Poverty is everywhere palpable. A pilot once told me that Calcutta is the only city that you can smell from 20,000 feet in the air.

My train arrived at the huge Hawrah railway station at about 4:00 o'clock of the second morning. Waiting for daylight I wandered about the station. Some hundreds of homeless people were sleeping on the benches, floors and train platforms. Whole families seemed to have taken up residence there. Several sacred cows, some with calves, also spent the night among the people. On the riverbank in front of the station was a great pile of filthy garbage that had been dumped there, apparently, to be loaded onto barges and disposed of down river. People, rats, "sacred" cows, and a flock of vultures swarmed over the refuse fighting for any edible bit. (I'm sure American garbage would provide a rare feast for the hungry of Calcutta.)

In the street small, almost naked, children followed the wandering cows and scooping up the fresh dung in their bare hands, plastered it against the walls and sides of buildings where it would quickly dry in the hot sun and could then be gathered and sold as fuel.

On a back page of an English language newspaper I read a small item stating that in a certain Bengali village, "it was reported"

The Years of My Day

that "a woman had died of starvation." I had seen the police carry five dead bodies from Hawrah Railway Station that morning and no doubt scores of people were dying of starvation in Calcutta that very moment...but that could be overlooked.

At Calcutta's Dum Dum airport I was turned back from the gate because my "Yellow Book" did not show cholera inoculation. It would be three days before another plane left for Tokyo and I was anxious to quit India. I asked the health officer what could be done. Could I secure inoculation at the airport?

That was impossible but, "for a fee," he could issue me a certificate of inoculation.

I knew it was wrong and that my sins would eventually catch up with me...probably at the Tokyo airport...but at that moment another day in Calcutta seemed to be the worse of the two evils. I paid the 25 rupees and took the yellow slip.

We landed at Rangoon in a tropical downpour which filled the streets curb to curb with muddy water in a matter of minutes; but the airline had offered a quick tour of the city during the two hours required for refueling and servicing the plane and I took it. At our first stop we took off our shoes and rolled up our pants (or held up our skirts as the case may be) and ran up the steps to view the golden domes of the great Shwedagon Pagoda. That was perhaps my second mistake because we returned to the planed drenched and shivering. Before we reached Bangkok I had a fever and was shaking with chills.

Does cholera strike you down with fever and chills, I wondered?

I had asked the stewardess if I could have a glass of cold water. She took a look at my face and reported to the Captain who came back immediately. He had me lie on the floor on a space behind the galley bulkhead, brought me water and a cold towel, and said he would have a doctor see me at Hong Kong.

Floyd Schmoe

At Hong Kong we changed crews and my redhead Scottish pilot took me with him to crew quarters in the Peninsula Hotel where I was put bed in a private room with a servant in attendance. By then I was feeling better and chose to remain quietly in bed.

By morning my fever was gone and, though I felt weak, I was certainly much better. However, after a hearty breakfast in bed, and a bath, I dressed and took the ferry across to Hong Kong (the Peninsula Hotel is on the Kowloon side of the harbor). At Hong Kong University's college of medicine a beautiful Chinese doctor, Alice Chin, saw me, had me say "ah" a couple of times, took my temperature and blood pressure, and said, "Looks like the flu...but it might be malaria." "Take two aspirins, push liquids, stay in bed, and call me tomorrow?" I asked.

"Right on," she said.

By another strange coincidence I was to see much more of Dr. Chin some years later.

Next day I went on to Tokyo but before I arrived the chills and fever were with me again.

I had telephoned ahead from Hong Kong and good friends Takashi and Mrs. Tojo met me in the car. I was quickly put to bed in their lovely home and a Japanese doctor called. Almost immediately he diagnosed the problem as malaria and prescribed medicines which knocked it overnight...a great improvement over the doses of quinine which I took, with less effect, for two years after returning from Europe in 1919.

We brought only one American student to Hiroshima that summer. Dick Hirabayashi met me in Tokyo and several of the "old hands" from Hiroshima joined our group. Late in the season Tomiko, who had been in a service committee work camp in California, returned home and came on to Hiroshima for the last few weeks of our season.

We built a four-unit house at Sarayama bringing the entire complex there to 16 units, plus the community house. Then with

The Years of My Day

some work contracted, we built one small house and another four-unit house on land we purchased adjacent to the Hiroshima Jogakuin in Ushita Valley north of the city proper. Departing from our earlier practice we did not deed this property to the city and did not choose the residents by lot. We placed Hatsue Yamamoto, a local girl who had worked with us several seasons, in the small house as hostess and designated it the "Hiroshima Guest House." It would be available to Americans who, we hoped, would wish to live for a year, or less, in Hiroshima, as "friendly presences" without designated "mission," but free to be part of the community and help out at whatever they saw to do.

The money for our Guest House was given me by an old friend and former classmate at the University of Washington, Alice Franklin Bryant.

Alice had gone to the Philippine islands as a teacher after graduation and there had married the Governor of a province – an American by the name of William Bryant – who was also a plantation owner. When the Japanese army invaded in 1941 they were captured and imprisoned for the duration of the war. Some years after their release the American government gave reparation money to prisoners of war and Alice gave her share of their money to me with which to build a home for a Japanese victim of war.

In the four units of the big house we placed a widow with four children in one, equally needy people in two, and gave the fourth to Masako Okada, her brother and two young sisters.

Masako was a girl of twelve when the bomb fell and her young brother was only an infant. She and her two sisters were at school some distance from the center of the city that August morning and her father and mother were at work. The baby was being cared for by their grandmother. Both her father and mother died in the blast but the grandmother saved the baby and herself from the fire by leaping into the cesspool and drawing some wet

Floyd Schmoe

straw mats over them. The girls were far enough away and sheltered sufficiently to survive.

When we happened to discover the little family in 1949 Masako and the grandmother had managed to keep the children housed in a small shack they had built from rubble and had fed them by gathering clams, oysters and other seafoods from the beach and by planting a small garden. They had a tiny rice paddy and a batch of sweet potatoes beside the hut.

All that Autumn of 1952 we had noticed long trainloads of tanks, trucks, guns, and other "hardware" passing to the west. We knew its destination and said, "Perhaps next summer we will be building houses in Korea."

In June of 1953 I flew to Korea at the invitation of UNKRA (United Nations Korean Reconstruction Agency) and was offered financial support for a relief and reconstruction project in the province of Yongin to the south of Seoul. In December I sent Dr. Joe Alter, of Seattle, James Scharschmidt, of Pasadena, and George Martin, also of Seattle, along with a shipment of food and medical supplies, to open a clinic and build a base camp in the bombed out village of Kumnyangjang-ni and early in the Spring of 1954 Ruth and I went over. With us went nurse Marion Field of Berkley, California. Arriving in Suwon we were met by Joe in an Army Jeep and managed to somehow all pile into and onto it for the hour's drive over very rough roads in Yongin. Here in an ancient cemetery, almost upon the huge grave mound of "Grandma Tiger," (we were told later) the boys had built a large staff house, and had opened, in a village across the river, an office and medical clinic. A local practitioner, a Dr. Lee, and a Korean nurse, Kim Chung He, had joined the staff, along with a carpenter-interpreter, also named Kim. At the staff house we were greeted by a third Kim (none were related) who was to be our cook-housekeeper. Not bothering to remember so many unfamiliar names they became henceforth; Nurse Kim, Carpenter Kim, and Cook Kim. Don Voorhees, from

The Years of My Day

Whittier, who was doing "alternative service" with us, was "Cookie's" favorite, partially because he was the youngest, but mostly because he teased her constantly and she loved it. No one was alarmed when "Cookie" chased Don around the house, waving a butcher knife, and both of them screaming.

The village with the name which means, "Village in the Valley of Yellow Earth," had been a local market center and the home of farmers who cultivated the lands nearby. None were wealthy. There was a brewery for "mool," the crude Korean sake or rice wine, a blacksmith shop, a saw mill which operated only when some farmer felled an apple tree or poached a pine log from the mountainside, a police post, the municipal office, and Dr. Lee. Both the elementary school and a new middle school were on our side of the river. Some of the students were walking eight miles each day to school.

About a half mile up the river there was a large refugee camp, North Koreans who had been driven south by the communists and were still unable to return home.

A narrow gauge railroad ran south out of Suwan, with a rattletrap train which made one round trip each day.

A few months before we arrived the village had been bombed by American planes and largely burned out. It was assumed that a nest of communist troops were holding out there, though this was untrue. The front line was sixty miles to the north.

It was amazing to us how many of the American bombs were duds. Almost every day some farmer dug up an unexploded bomb or grenade. When the police were informed they had a demolition team come down from the Army camp near Suwan and cart it away for safe disposal, but too often some kids attempted the job themselves or the farmer tried to defuse the bomb to retrieve the powder – which was in demand for dynamiting fish in a nearby lake.

Floyd Schmoe

While the boys were clearing a level spot by the river in order to build a playground for the children of the refugee camp they found an unexploded rifle grenade, and one day Joe and I returned from a trip to Suwan and found a dozen houses burning. We hurriedly gathered fire fighting tools. Joe grabbed his medical kit, and we rushed down to help. Some young men had been trying to defuse a large aerial bomb and it had exploded. Six people were killed and several others were hurt. Dr. Lee was already on the job.

There is not much that can be done with axes, shovels, and wet sacks to save a straw thatched house that is on fire but we were able to pull some of the wounded out and give first aid.

That night we witnessed our first funeral, Korean style. Men and women dressed in white sackcloth, the women with their long hair over their faces, sad with professional mourners, formed a long torchlight procession from the village to the burial site above our house. The wailing, dancing, and feasting went on most of the night, and in the morning we watched farm wives come with hand carts or neighbors, to cart their drunken husbands home.

This lost ritual we had witnessed before because it happened each morning following market day.

Market day was every fifth day regardless of the day of the week. Farmers brought their produce; their pigs, chickens, ducks, cows, whatever they had to sell or trade, and merchants came from Seoul or Suwan with more sophisticated merchandise such as shoes, "yardgoods," kitchen ware, medicines, eyeglasses, and bottled goods. The local brew sold by the jug-full and seemed to be the item most in demand. Most of the men were drunk by evening.

On Ruth's first market day she made the mistake of mingling with the crowd in western dress and silk stockings. She was quickly surrounded by farm women who stared unabashedly. Some even crowded her to feel her body and lift her skirts to see

The Years of My Day

what she wore underneath. She made the quickest retreat possible and the next time she went to the market she wore Korean dress.

The dress of both men and women in rural Korea is a long white maternity-type gown, high-waisted for the women and entirely loose for the men. Usually a woman's gown is of finer material than that of the men, and a woman may wear ornaments in her hair. An old man wears a strange, high-crowned hat woven from horsehair. It is a badge of age and respect. Dr. Lee and Mr. Cho wore western clothes. Cho Dong He, though still a fairly young man, was the wealthiest man in his community, his father having recently died and left him with considerable land. He also owned the brewery, and he knew a smattering of English.

Cho had become our contact man with the village and the local government. He lived in an extensive farm compound a couple of miles up the valley but rode a bicycle into town each day so as not to miss any of the action. His wife and numerous relatives and in-laws ran the farm. His oldest son, Cho Sung Ki, spent most of his days with us, helping the boys and learning to speak English.

That summer we built small neat houses for several of the most needy, helped repair an irrigation dam and ditches, repaired the municipal building where we had established a free clinic and a small library, and provided funds, labor, or materials for a number of families who were rebuilding their own homes.

Joe and Dr. Lee, with the help of Chung He and Marion, manned the clinic and the nurses visited several of the nearby villages on a once-a-week round of streptomycin injections for tuberculosis patients.

The American Army supplied us with a Jeep, an X-ray machine, and drugs. I purchased a microscope and two bicycles in Tokyo. That was after the boys had been unsuccessful at teaching Chung He how to drive a Jeep. Digging her, and the Jeep out of rice paddies was taking too much of our time.

Floyd Schmoe

Ruth spent a great deal of time with the women at the refugee camp, providing materials and teaching them to sew and weave. UNKRA had provided us with two Niadau looms with which Ruth was familiar. We also operated a daily milk feeding station in the village at a point nearest the camp. Children, pregnant and nursing mothers, and people who were very old and sick, were given a daily helping of milk which we reconstituted from dry milk provided by the American government. Many people did not like the milk and, fortunately most mothers were able to breast-feed their babies, often until they were three or four years old, and even after a new baby was demanding its share.

One day a sad thing happened in the village. A young woman had twins.

Multiple birth is considered bad luck in rural Korea and at that time one or both such babies was destroyed or allowed to starve.

Ruth and Chung He went to the home as soon as we heard of the twins and talked with the mother. They took clothing, food and other baby things and helped her care for the babies. It soon appeared, however, that she was neglecting them and refusing to feed them. Ruth or Chung He went every day but were unable to help. Within a week both babies died.

The next Summer, 1954, we sent Dr. Hal Lischner to Yongin, where Dr. Lee was still maintaining the free clinic and the T.B. program, and I took Carpenter Kim, and moved into Seoul. Seoul was glutted with refugees and there were hundreds of orphans and widows who needed housing desperately. People were literally living in holes they had dug in the hillsides. Building sites were hard to find and the only one we did find was a garbage dump outside the west gate which was already occupied by a hundred or so refugees, and many times as many rats. In the tent-like huts of straw matting on the dump, rats were literally eating babies alive. Nearly every small child we saw was suffering from

The Years of My Day

rat bites. There was still another problem; in order to build houses we had to displace several families living in huts without being able to find temporary housing for them or assure them that they could occupy the new houses. This matter became so acute that we had to call, reluctantly, upon the police. The whole affair gave me some very bad moments.

And there was still another affair that caused restless sleep. When we managed to push back two or three families and build a two-room house in a corner of the dump area – a house which we planned to use as a community bath and medical clinic eventually but would occupy ourselves during the summer – we looked around for a house-keeper-cook.

On the steps of the compound occupied by Church World Services people, where I went for advice and possible help, sat my problem. She was about ten, though small for her age, and her name was Genius, "Genie" for short. That of course was not her Korean name but that is the name she gave me. In some clairvoyant way she seemed to sense my need. She may have known it before I did, for it appeared she was waiting for me. She had an appealing grown-up look, dressed in a "mission-barrel" western dress, much too big for her.

"I spik Anglish," she said. "I work good. You want house girl."

"I want cook-woman," I said, and passed on into the office of CWS—Korea.

Genie was still by my side. "I cook good. My father cook good. We work good."

An American social worker filled me in. The child's name was Salvation, a name given by, or taken from, the local Catholic Mission. Her father was called simply "Salvation." She was Genie Salvation. CWS knew no other name. And perhaps they would serve my purpose. The father, admittedly, was not too promising, but Genie was truly a genius.

Floyd Schmoe

Letting sentiment overrule good judgement, I said I would give them a trial.

Before I got home they had moved in and were waiting for me, and now there were three of them with all their baggage. The third was a boy, Loyalty, "Loyal" for short, and the baggage was only a few poor bundles. They were ensconced in a small attic over the kitchen, Genie had a fire going in the cooking place, and was waiting at the door with my slippers. I dared the boys (we had added Yoon Gu, a student with a good command of English, to our team as interpreter-workman) to try to get into the house without Genie meeting them at the door to try to take their shoes, or to leave without her help and to take their slippers.

Salvation was a shifty-eyed little man, but Loyal was a promising boy of about seven. Their mother, I learned later, had been Japanese. Salvation when younger had studied art in Tokyo and had met his wife there. When they had been forced, at the close of the war, to return to Korea she had committed suicide. Genie told me that, and demonstrated graphically with a butcher knife how she had cut her throat.

It was evening and I gave Salvation a few hundred whan and asked them to buy food. Genie took the money and when they returned with rice, sweet potatoes, and peaches, Genie carried the change and accounted for every whan spent. We soon found out why she had become the self-appointed treasurer of the salvation team; to Papa Salvation money meant only one thing..."mool." Even so the wiley little tramp had foxed us. The peaches never reached our table but appeared several days later as a flask of very potent brandy.

As it turned out making brandy was just about the only thing Salvation could, or would do. Yet Genie remained fiercely defensive of her father. She admitted that he "had a sick," but she held no blame for him. Genie did all the cooking, all the cleaning, all the buying and still found time to clean our shoes and brush our

The Years of My Day

suits. And she tended little brother like a mother. She even offered to do our laundry and when we would not allow that she quickly found a laundress for us.

This good lady, who promptly appeared at dawn every fifth morning, took all our dirty clothes in a huge bundle on her head and reappeared that same evening with each item spotless, ironed, and neatly folded. We learned from Genie that "our wash woman" ranked "number one" not only with us but above all the other women who washed clothing at the riverbank. This latter kudos was derived solely from the fact that she had soap.

On our first visit to a Korean village we had been puzzled by a rhythmic drumming which often came from nearby houses. We wondered if it was the sound of a loom, or of rice being hulled in wooden mortar. Then one day we looked through an open doorway and saw a woman kneeling before a block of wood over which was spread a folded sheet or dress. With round wooden sticks she was beating the cloth vigorously to the rhythm of a softly hummed tune. This was the way Korean housewives "iron" their clothing, and since they – both men and women – wear white almost exclusively, they have a great deal of ironing to do. Like housewives everywhere their work is never done. (I have since observed this same method of ironing clothes in African villages.)

While gradually easing the squatters back from our building site we had a high retaining wall of stone built along the lower property line so that the ground could be filled and made level. Almost directly above this 8-foot wall we built a two-unit house, Korean style.

Where our first house – which was built for public use – had a board floor, this one, which was to be occupied by two refugee families, had an "ondle" floor.

The Koreans had invented "radiant heat" even before the Romans, and most country houses still have "hot floors." Winters are severe in Korea and fuel is scarce so they must conserve heat wherever possible. A mud-walled, thatch-roofed house is well insulated, especially since it often has few or no windows, and it is doubly snug because all the heat from the kitchen fires, which usually goes up the chimney, passes beneath the floor of a Korean house.

Traditionally the kitchen is at one end of the house and a couple of steps lower than the living room floor. Cooking stoves of mud are built on the living room side with the flues passing beneath the adjoining floor to be vented through a chimney at the far end of the house. This is the "ondle" floor.

In villages old men and children spend a great deal in the open hillsides gathering any scrap of fuel that can be found. Forests are all public owned and it is not permitted to cut trees but they may be stripped of the lower branches. Fallen twigs, brush and even weeds can be gathered, and these are carried home to be stacked outside the kitchen for fuel. One of the most common sites on country roads, or mountain trails, is a child, an old man, or even an ox, loaded down with a bundle of twigs or sticks several times their own size.

Where no such fuel is to be found rice straw is burned. Old men or women may sit all day during the winter on the floor of the kitchen tying bundles of straw into tight knots and feeding the cooking fire, over which a large pot of rice or beans is constantly cooking. Outside the kitchen there is certain to be one or several kimchi jars. "Kimchi" is second only to rice a dietary staple and large quantities are made each autumn to be stored in tall stone jars for winter use. It is a sort of sauerkraut made from chopped cabbage, radishes, turnips, and red peppers, placed in jars and allowed to ferment. Kimchi jars can be smelled from afar and only one born to the diet can enjoy it. With the red peppers (scarlet festoons of which drape every Korean farm house, and which are eaten raw as well as forming the fiery backbone of kimchi) Korean food would make even a Mexican weep. Only the Thai enjoy hotter viands. The

The Years of My Day

size of a Korean family can be judged by the number of kimchi jars outside the door.

Our "wall house," unfortunately, turned out to be misplaced for even before it was occupied, a torrential rainstorm one night sent floods of muddy water surging down the hillside above us which undermined our wall and left half our new house sagging over empty space. It was no consolation that a score of other houses on the same hillside were also washed into the valley that night.

There was a team of Church of the Brethren relief workers in Seoul that summer and since we had a surplus of money and they had a surplus of hands we cooperated on four other projects. For a small organization of war widows we built a sort of retirement home about a mile outside South Gate, and a similar one outside East Gate. These were large houses accommodating 15 or 20 persons who lived cooperatively on public welfare.

Also on a hilltop a couple of miles beyond East Gate we built an orphanage for about 50 homeless children which had been gathered together by a young Buddhist monk.

One of the Brethren boys was interested in the use of earth as building material and suggested that we experiment with a "rammed earth" structure. We put him in charge and with all the children carrying clay up the steep hill from a pit at its base, and with the help of the young monk, they built the big house. It was square, about 30 feet on a side with walls two feet thick of compacted clay mixed with straw. This was roofed over, partitioned, and the outer walls stuccoed with lime mortar. Before we left in October the children had moved in, justly proud of the house they had built.

Under Dr. Kim's leadership we experimented that summer with another form of specialized housing. A doctor at Severance Hospital had told us of the need for small isolation houses for TB patients who often lived in poorly ventilated rooms with their

Floyd Schmoe

families. Under these conditions, along with poor nutrition, there was the constant danger of the spread of the infection.

Kim, working with Dr. Arnold, designed a one-room cottage which could be prefabricated in the mill yard, carted to the patients home and assembled in a day's time. So successful was this project that Mr. Kim continued to build TB isolation huts after we closed our work in Korea.

We also contributed the funds with which the Brethren team built a dozen small houses for refugees at Taegu, and the Friends Service committee built sixteen at Kunsan. We considered that a very good summer's work.

In 1956 the French and English bombed the city of Port Said, making some 4,000 families homeless. The unhappy incident left me with the feeling that again innocent people had been made to pay dearly because of political differences which, in no immediate way, concerned them, and over which they had little or no control. I consulted President Nassar's government to see if we might help in some small way with the solution to their problems.

The Egyptian government under Mr. Nassar had earlier undertaken a program of agricultural expansion whereby the pressure on the cities could be relieved and the food supply augmented. Settlements had already been made and oasises extended westward into the Libyan desert, and plans for the high dam at Aswan were well underway. It was Nassar's thought that these refugees from Port Said could best be resettled on the land, and he looked toward the Sinai oasises. At El Arish some 40 miles east of Port Said there were some ancient walls and a few Bedouin camps. Before World War 1 the British army had built a military base there and they had bored several more deep wells. These had supported a few acres of dates and figs, but during the Israeli-Egyptian war of 1956-57 these wells had been sabotaged, the pumps carried away and the bores filled with rubble. Now in 1957 the Egyptian Ministry of Agriculture was clearing the wells and

The Years of My Day

expanding the irrigated lands. It seemed a good site for the resettlement of the Port Said refugees and they could use some help.

I went to Cairo in 1958 to visit El Arish. With the small amount of money we had about all we could do was to buy some pumps and nursery stock. Dates and figs were available locally, but citrus fruits and apricots came from Lebanon. A nursery was established to supply the settlers.

Before I left Africa I took some time off to explore the Nile Valley. One evening I took the "White Express" upriver from Cairo and stopped off the next day at Luxor. After visiting the great temples of Aman at Karnak and the ruins of Luxor, I was put across to the west bank by an Egyptian boatman who handled a sail with greater skill than I have ever seen before or since. His boat was a crude affair with a ragged lanteen sail on a stubby mast, but with a fair upriver breeze against a 3 or 4 knot current he sailed straight across the quarter-mile wide river and made his landing as neatly as if by motorboat. A battered old Chev was waiting which took me the few miles into the wadi where many of Egypt's kings, and at least one queen, were buried.

On a sunny afternoon there can be few hotter spots on Earth than this "Valley of the Kings." After walking only a few hundred yards from the parked car I was relieved to dive down the first open tunnel I came upon. Even inside the rock cavern of Ramses VI's tomb the air was stifling. I did not stay long.

I spent more time in the nearby tomb of Tutankhamun for there the mummy and many of the treasures of the boy king remained on display. Earlier in the Cairo Museum I had seen more of his "goods and chattels" including the magnificent gold mask which became so admired when exhibited in America in 1978.

From Luxor I took the train on next day to Khartoum in the Sudan, and spent the night on a Nile River barge which was serving as an annex to the overcrowded hotel. Actually I spent only part of

Floyd Schmoe

the night for I was awakened about 2:00 a.m. driven across the river on the only bridge which spans the Nile above Cairo, through the ancient mud-built city of Omdurman, and far out into the desert to a military air strip to wait for the London to Nairobi plane which would arrive at some uncertain hour. The chill of that desert night contrasted with the heat of the previous day marked perhaps the greatest range of temperatures I have ever experienced in so short a time.

From Nairobi I took a native bus across the great Serengeti plane to Arusha in Tanganyika (now Tanzania). I was met there by that wild man of east Africa, Ax Nelson, and driven to his home on a coffee plantation at the foot of Mt. Kilimanjaro. Ax has climbed Kilimanjaro more often than any other man.

The bus ride was memorable. Actually it was an ancient truck with jerry-built board seats, which provided second class accommodations in back. There was a driver and helper in the wide cab up front, and this I found was "first class." There was also "third class accommodations on top of the truck. Out of Nairobi's market place at six in the morning, we were well filled with men, women, children, chickens and baggages. I was the only white and I rode second class.

There was no fare differential. Where you rode, I discovered, was at the fancy of the driver. When, at the first village, all second-class seats were filled, the driver came back, selected the prettiest young woman, and put her between himself and his helper up front, and when the next second class passenger boarded, he chose another pretty girl. That filled first-class. All other passengers rode third-class if they could find room.

I sat next a tall, light brown young Masai woman with a year-old baby boy. By way of congeniality I offered to hold the baby when his mother appeared tired, and we got on well. I got a bit worried however when at our noon lunch stop the mother handed the baby over to me, disappeared into the bush and had

The Years of My Day

not yet returned when all others were assembled and the driver started to go. At the last minute however she came running.

Nearing Arusha in the afternoon we encountered a sudden downpour of rain and in the midst of this were flagged down by a group of Masai herdsmen carrying spears. They were stark naked, their bodies glistening from the rain. Once crowded aboard they unfolded thin red blankets which had been folded and carried in their armpits to keep them dry. Properly half-clothed they did not appear nearly so fierce.

My week with the Nelsons on Africa's greatest mountain was exciting. The first evening Ax killed a six-foot green mamba at the door of the little guest house where I was to sleep. The venom of these snakes, it is said, is so virulent that, if bitten, there would not be time enough to administer an antivenom even though one was at hand. Fortunately for the field workers who, barefooted, are exposed to them, neither the green nor the black mamba is very aggressive. This is not true of the spitting cobra, which is also found in the area and which can blind a man with its venom from ten feet away. Another mamba was killed while I was there but I saw no cobras. This "spitting cobra" is the snake which, in South Africa, is called the "spy slang." It is perhaps the most feared snake in Africa.

One evening Ax and I took a two-man mountain tent and drove to the 5,500-foot level where we camped upon the rim of one of the several secondary craters of the great volcano. It was over the road, negotiable only by four-wheel drive vehicles, and to the look-out point, which had been carved out of the lower slope jungle on the occasion of the visit of Princess Elizabeth. She had been camped at this spot six years earlier when news came of the death of her father and she was rushed back to London to become Queen of England. Although we got very little sleep (what with the mosquitos and a family of colobus monkeys who inhabited the huge wild fig tree under which we had pitched our tent, and which they claimed was private property) it was a night not soon to be forgotten.

The floor of the crater, some five hundred feet below us, is about three miles across flat and marshy, and the home of a wonderful collection of African birds and animals. This is the reason the Princess and her party had been brought here. During the evening we counted a herd of more than a hundred buffalo, thirty-some elephants, several family groups of giraffe and scattering of wart hogs. There were bands of baboon all over the place, and many birds, from the beautiful crested crane and the ugly marabou stork, to a host of smaller birds. With binoculars we could see flocks of yellow and black weaver birds and their bulky globular nests in the trees, and the black tick birds which provide insect control for the buffalo and giraffe.

There was only one easy trail out of the crater, a deeply worn track made by the elephants who sometimes during the night climb out and descend to the shambas of local farmers where they raid their patches of corn. Several times during the night we heard the distant sound of farmers beating on drums, or pans, and shouting, to drive the animals from their fields.

We pitched our tent just above this trail and, although I did not hear any animal pass during the night, tracks in the wet earth next morning showed that several had, including a leopard. Although more people are killed in Africa by leopards than by lions or elephants, I would rather sleep by a passing leopard, whose mind, undoubtedly, is upon other matters, than to meet one on the trail.

A few days later Ax and Mrs. Nelson drove me back to Nairobi in their Volkswagen Bug. We took a roundabout route, often cutting cross-country in semi desert areas. It was a rough trip, not only because of the cramped space of a VW, but because Ax drives at the same speed through the bush as he does on paved roads. At one point we stopped to watch a pair of giraffe feeding

The Years of My Day

on some flat-topped acacias. Strangely the 2-3 inch needle-sharp thorns do not appear to bother them. While we watched, the male, who must have stood close to 14 feet from toe to knobby horn, leaned down to watch us. Somehow it seems a bit of an embarrassment to have a 14-foot giraffe stopping to look through a VW window at you.

Later, in a grassy area we came upon a pride of lions who had killed and partially eaten a zebra. Now they were sleeping, their tight round bellies exposed to the sun. Although we stopped within 20 feet of them, they paid no attention to us. Not until Ax gave a beep on the horn did the black-mained male lift his head to look at us. Then he yawned and went back to sleep.

Driving at 40 mph on a dirt track we almost collided with a pair of sable antelope, the only ones I have ever seen in the wild. They are among the largest of the great family of antelope; and because their long backwards-curving horns make them desirable trophies to sportsmen, they have become a rare species.

From Nairobi I took the narrow-gauge, one-a-day, train across the Rift Valley to Kisuma on Lake Victoria.

In the Rift the train passes close to the shallow, brackish Naivasha Lakes, where shell-pink flamingos feed in such numbers that, from a distance, they appear to be a rose-tinted cloud.

I spent the night in Kisuma, then went by bus to the Friends Mission some 20 miles north of Kimosi, where I had friends. Next day I flagged down a bus on the road west to Kampala, the capital of Uganda. This bus was crowded and again I was the only white aboard. We stopped once for lunch at a tree where Margoli women were selling various native foods, including fresh milk direct from a nanny goat tethered to the tree.

Later we came to a sudden stop and the driver scrambled out to kill an eight-foot python which was, to its misfortune, trying to cross the road. It was brought aboard, still squirming, and

Floyd Schmoe

deposited beneath the driver's seat. Large snakes provide juicy steaks and roasts in that part of Africa.

I visited Makerere College in Kampala and talked with people in the Geography Department about what I might see and expect to experience on the voyage by river boat down the Nile. At the rest house, where I spent the night, I met the pilot of a private plane who had just flown in from Addis Ababa in Ethiopia. He told me that he had flown over a herd of migrating elephants in northern Kenya which were walking south in a file which he estimated to be near 10 miles long.

From Kampala I took a bus north to Lake Kyoga, then west to the town of Mesindi. Again I spent the night in a comfortable government rest house, where at breakfast I met the radio operator of the Lake Albert steamer on which I would begin my long trip down the Nile River system. He drove me in a company Land Rover to Betuabi where the B.S. Speke berthed. On the opposite side of the dock, half awash in reeds, lay the remains of the African Queen which had been used by Humphrey Bogart and Katherine Hepburn in making the film of the same name.

We loaded some 1,500 Sudanese natives here, seasonal workers from the Uganda cane fields, who were returning to their villages downriver; along with a whole truckload of elephant ivory, which an officer of the ship told me was legal, and was headed for Amsterdam where it would be turned into billiard balls, or Hong Kong, where pretty beads or figurines would be carved from it. At that time for a $75.00 license fee, you could shoot a bull elephant just for the tusks which were worth $100.00 each.

The Speke took us only a day's journey to Pakwach, at the foot of the lake, and there we transferred to a stern-wheel, shallow draft, river boat. While we changed boats a half dozen elephant fed in the tall grass only a couple of hundred yards away on the opposite bank of the river.

The Years of My Day

I had a second-class cabin on a double-deck barge lashed to the port side of the steamer. There was a first-class barge on the starboard side on which several missionary families, and a few colonial-type Englishmen were ensconced. They allowed me to take afternoon tea with them, but for the rest of the time I drank Nile River water and ate bananas and mangoes with the Sudanese and Indian families who were my shipmates.

Our power boat also pushed six barges, six abreast in front of it on which rode the 1500 field workers and considerable freight and livestock.

On that first day on the upper Nile I saw my first Congo Pygmies, my first crocodile, a pair of rhinoceros, and more than a hundred elephants. I had started counting elephants when I first came on deck and by eight o'clock, I had seen ninety and had lost count. It was a dry season, the water was low, and the animals had come down to the riverbank to eat and drink.

Because of the low water and the crooked narrow channel, and also because of our unwieldy tow, we ran aground a number of times. Because of the difficulty of steering, which was impossible by rudder alone, our power boat had twin diesel engines and a split stern wheel. An engineer sat between the engines with his hands on two throttles, reversing one and gunning the other on command from the wheelhouse, in order to turn our flotilla around sharp bends.

The fat, good natured Sudanese river pilot allowed me in the wheelhouse where I had a better view of the passing scene.

At one point where the river curved sharply to the right a huge bull elephant stood at the water's edge. As we headed straight toward him he raised his trunk, flared his huge leathery ears, and trumpeted his defiance. Boldly he stood his ground until the leading barges grounded within fifty yards of where he stood.

Floyd Schmoe

Then, having stopped the monster, he turned and ambled leisurely up the bank. It took us an hour of backing and twisting to haul the barges out of the mud.

There were no towns or villages along the river because during the annual floods the stream is miles wide but during the dry season when the river is low the young people bring their herds of long-horn cattle and camp on the riverbank. We made a number of these mud-bank landings and always there was a crowd of people waiting. The boat came only once every fortnight but they seemed to know exactly when it was due. At these stops we offloaded a few people and loaded a small amount of such products as reed mats, elephant ivory, and dried fish.

At every stop our Sudanese passengers would swarm ashore to cut grass for their goats, buy chicken and fish for their food, and bathe in the river. Local people came to bathe themselves and their children also because only between the boat and the shore were they safe from the giant crocs. I had seen many along the way and one that I would have sworn was 20 feet long, although it is rare that a Nile River crocodile reaches 14 feet in length.

We had now left the Bantu people of central Africa behind and the Pygmies of the Congo, and were in the land of the Nilotic tribes; the tall, slim Nuer, Dinka, and Shilluk, who are herdsmen like their southern cousins the Masai. These are the people who cover their bodies with ashes and stand for hours on one leg while watching their grazing animals. For this reason they have been called the "heron people."

At Nimule just over the border into the Sudan we made a "mud bank landing" on the east shore and although no one bothered to tell me, I soon got the message that this was the end of the line for most of us. Looking ashore I saw only a low storage shed and a naked African woman with a fat little baby boy, equally naked. She was cooking some posho (ground corn) over a small

The Years of My Day

fire. Sound of a great many people came for the distance and many of my fellow passengers headed in that direction.

I followed the crowd and came upon a huge market area. There was no town or village but hundreds of people had gathered to sell, barter, or buy an endless variety of produce. Displayed upon the bare earth or in rude shelters of brush or reed mats was everything literally from bananas to brides. There were herds of cattle and donkeys, a few camels, and many goats and sheep. One man had two young ostriches no larger than game cocks. Also there was an abundance of a sour-smelling home brew, and although no one appeared drunk there were many whose enjoyment of the occasion was obviously enhanced by the liquid refresheners.

As In similar situations all over the world, many young women were on hand for no better reason than to be seen, and many young men were there to see.

I walked back to the river still with no idea how I was to continue my journey.

The young mother was feeding her child. With nothing better to do I held the baby while she pushed corn meal mush into its mouth with her fingers. The boat with it now-empty barges had departed and no other vessel was in sight.

After a time a large, badly used, American car appeared and the fat Sudanese driver indicated that we were "Juba" bound. I recognized a German-speaking man with a blonde young woman (obviously not his wife) who I remembered having seen earlier on the first-class barge. They were occupying most of the back seat so I got in front with the driver.

As I was preparing to leave the young mother brought her baby, his face still smeared with mush, and thrust him into my arms. When I tried to return him she turned her back and indicated that I was to take him with me. I have never understood why. He appeared healthy and well fed. Perhaps she felt he would have a

Floyd Schmoe

better chance in life with the white community, I have no idea, but I could imagine what American immigration officers, or even my wife, would have to say should I turn up with a black child in my baggage. I had to sit him on the ground and leave.

We traveled all afternoon through high bush country, sparsely populated with only a few poor villages, and at nightfall crossed over the river on a small man-powered ferry into the walled city of Juba.

It was dark, the city seemed to be asleep, and I was tired, so I went directly to the river and aboard the next steamer. A small cabin was assigned to me on the second-class deck and when I awoke next morning we were moving silently downriver in a narrow channel lined on both sides with tall papyrus reeds as far as one could see.

We were entering the Sudd, a thousand square mile swamp into which the great river entirely disappears and from which only a small fraction of its waters ever escapes.

It is said that virtually no Nile River water from the snowcapped Ruwenzori and the great lakes of central Africa ever reaches the Mediterranean Sea. That which is not lost to evaporation in the swamps and deserts of the Sudan is absorbed by the Egyptian and Libyan Sahara, and only the cool water of the Blue Nile fresh from the Ethiopian highlands remains to fill Lake Nassar and irrigate the fields of Lower Egypt.

There were no elephants here, nor any of the zebra, giraffe, or antelope of the high plains, but crocodiles and hippos were still numerous, and bird life was abundant. Herons, egrets, crested cranes, storks, and a dozen other long-legged waders speared fish and frogs in every shallow; a variety of ducks and geese, swam with white pelicans in spots of open water, and huge flocks of various insect eaters swarmed starling-like over the marshes. For most of the day we followed a network of unmarked channels that only an experienced pilot could know but occasionally we crossed

The Years of My Day

large open areas like lakes within a swamp. Even here there was a mass of floating vegetation, chiefly the blue-flowered water hyacinth, and occasionally denser moss composed of many varieties of plants, and even shrubs and small trees, that appeared to be islands until pushed aside by our vessel. There were sometimes such swarms of small flying insects that they appeared to be clouds floating over the swamp.

In the evening we came to solid ground and stopped to load firewood for our boilers.

I could see by the mountains of logs that it would be hours before the job was done so I took off on a path leading inland and came upon a cattle camp where a dozen or more young herdsmen, both men and women, had settled their cattle for the night.

They had built smudge fires to drive off the swarms of insects, some had covered their bodies with ashes for the same reason, and some had built slightly elevated sleeping platforms of tree branches beneath which they made smudges of dried cow dung in order to get some relief from the gnats and flies. A girl was shaking milk or cream in a gourd to make butter which it appeared was used both by the men and women for cosmetic purposes more than food. Returning to the river I met a young woman on the trail. She was, except for a few strings and ear ornaments, totally nude, and at the same time totally innocent of the fact. We slapped hands, as I had observed was the custom of the Dinkas, chatted briefly, she in her strange language of deep-throated gutterals and tongue-twisting clicks, and I in my strange American dialect. Neither of us understood a single word the other spoke, yet we communicated and parted, I'm sure, good friends. At least I shall always remember her as a beautiful and warm human being.

On board again – while a gang of men, both local wood cutters and our crew – were still loading firewood, I selected a slim branch to be carved into a walking stick and souvenir of the occasion. Later when I approached the piece with my pocket knife I discovered that it was ebony. Imagine burning ebony as fuel: to me, a forester and naturalist, it seems almost as irreverent as burning Egyptian mummies in the fireboxes of locomotives, as the English are said to have done on occasion during the early days of Anglo-Egyptian railroading.

After two days and two nights of churning through matted vegetation and unmarked mazes of the river called the Bahr-el-Jabel by the Sudanese, we came at last from out of the clouds of insects and endless stretches of papyrus, into the well-defined channel of the Bahr-el-Abid and the border town of Malakal.

Malakal, with its donkeys and veiled women, its mosques and minarets, at about 9 degrees North Latitude, marks not only the transition from swamp to arid land, and black to brown people, but more dramatically, the southern reach of Islam.

Here for the first time is heard the Arabic language and the call of the muezzin, and here for the first time on my voyage I met a Catholic missionary.

She was a tiny German nun in starched white cap and she spoke English. She met each boat from the south, she told me, in order to buy fresh fruit and vegetables from the surplus that might be carried by passengers. Only dates, figs, and olives grew in the area and she and her brother and sister missionaries craved the bananas, mangoes, and sugar cane from upriver. Sometimes, she said, she was able to buy melons, but there were none on our boat. She went ashore quite happy however with a basket load of mangoes and bananas.

At the town of Kosti the following noon we were once again at railhead, and likewise at the end of navigation on that stretch of the mighty Nile. For more than a thousand air miles (almost 2,000 by the way I had come) there had not been a bridge, a paved road, a railroad, or an airport. Not since I had left Mombasa and Lake Victoria railroad at Kisuma had I heard the wild scream of a steam locomotive.

The Years of My Day

There were rapids in the river below Kosti and the Gebel Aulia Dam which diverted water into a huge irrigation project of the Sudanese government known as Gezira, where is grown the finest "Egyptian" long-staple cotton and, perhaps, the largest plantation of sugar cane in the world.

The train for Khartoum was scheduled to leave at 1:00pm but at 4:00 there was still a long line at the station's ticket window and I was at its head. The problem was that I had only American money, Egyptian Pounds, and Thomas Cook Traveler's checques, and the Sudanese Railway and Steamship Company would not accept any of these as legal tender.

After a long debate, aided and hampered in turn by impatient volunteer interpreters, it had been decided by the ticket agents that they would issue me a ticket (worth $3.00) and send a police officer with me to the capitol, where a bank would honor my travelers checque and the officer would return with the proper moneys to Kosti. In addition I would of course pay the wages, round-trip fare, and necessary refreshments of the police escort. This had been agreed upon by the agents but not by me; and that was what was holding up the train which was long ago loaded up and waiting.

Finally, with the people behind me in line grumbling with rising tempo, and the engineer of the train tooting his whistle threateningly, a Sudanese gentleman stepped to the window and, judging from his intonations and "body English," told the assembled agents that, "This is no way to treat a visiting foreigner, even If he is American," and "by the beard of the prophet" he would not tolerate it longer. With that he paid my fare to Khartoum and we were on our way.

It was an all-night journey, and crowded into a compartment for eight with about ten other Sudanese who had no intention of sleeping, I got very little rest.

Floyd Schmoe

At the station in Khartoum I waited for my friend who took his time emerging fresh and well-rested from the first-class sleeper, and offered to repay him in whatever way possible. Instead he shrugged the matter off and took me to breakfast at the best hotel.

I spent the day in the capitol lolling on the first green grass I had seen for ages in a park overlooking the junction of the Blue and the White Nile Rivers, visiting with professors and students at the university where we discussed the wildlife of the river and the swamps and examined specimens of rare fish which were displayed in the small museum of the Department of Biology.

I spent the night in a comfortable bed, complete with mosquito tent, which was placed for me in the quiet inner court of a small hotel on the riverbank – since all the rooms were already filled. The atmosphere and balmy air was reminiscent of Hawaii.

The train for Wadi Halfa followed the river valley all the following night and I got only glimpses of passing villages, fields of sugar cane, and groves of date palms. My second-class coach was not crowded and I had an entire compartment to myself. It was very hot and dusty but I slept well. In the morning I was awakened by total silence. The train was not moving, no one was talking, in fact, as I discovered presently the entire coach was, except for me, completely empty.

Reaching for my shoes beneath my bunk I found them half full of sand, with sand covering the floor of the compartment. I went outside and although my watch said it was six o'clock it was still almost as dark as night. We were only a few miles out of Abu Hamed, where the railway leaves the river valley and cuts straight across the Nubian Desert, while the river with its cataracts swings far to the west, and we were stalled in the midst of a dust storm.

The temperature, I learned later reached 126° that day and the visibility was about 100 feet. Most of the passengers of the

The Years of My Day

train were huddled in the lee of some sheds, their turbans wrapped around their faces, simply sitting it out.

I walked the length of the train. It was completely deserted and even the engine had vanished. Near where the engine should have been was a small telegraph shack with a sleeping operator slumped over the table. He greeted me in English and when I asked how long these storms might be expected to last he said, "Allah only knows." (The engine, I learned later, had been taken ahead to break through the drifts of wind-blown sand.)

On my way south some weeks earlier we had crossed this desert and I had noted these isolated stations with only a telegraph office, a water tank, and a dome-roofed hut for the station master, his family, and often, I noted, a few chickens in a pen and lop-eared Nubian milk goat. Now I knew why theses dry oases were placed at intervals all across the 300 mile stretch of sand. They were to supply water and communication for stranded trains and manpower to shovel out sand drifts.

Fortunately I had brought some dried dates, some bread and cheese, and a couple of boiled eggs from the hotel in Khartoum, for the only other food I found to eat was a stalk of sugar cane given me by a fellow refugee, and we lay there for 30 hours.

At Wadi Halfa at the head of Lake Nassar on the border of Egypt, the boat had waited for us, and I was soon well fed, and comfortably ensconced in a reclining deck chair, drinking tea and enjoying an informative conversation with a black American professor of anthropology, who earlier had been upriver studying the cultures and art of those Nilitic tribes I had found so fascinating.

He told me among other things that Dinkas, one of whose young women I had fraternized with on the trail from the cattle camp a few days earlier, had a custom, still practiced, whereby, the son of the chief buried his aging father alive in order that there be no break in the line of succession.

My friend was also most helpful when, in mid-morning, the lake steamer stopped at the great temple of Abu Simbil and allowed us an hour to visit this magnificent temple which Ramses II had carved, during the 12th century B.C., into a mountainside in honor of Ra, the Goddess of the Sun; and the smaller temple nearby which he later constructed in honor of his wife, the lovely Nefrere.

In the main temple, where at the far ends stands a colossal statue of the Goddess holding the round disc of the sun above her head, there is not a square foot of the walls or ceiling which is not covered with the sharply incised pictographs which tell the life story of the great Pharoah – undoubtedly "in his own words."

This was March of 1958 but the high Nassar Dam at Aswan was already under construction which in time would bury Abu Simbil beneath 70 feet of Nile water.

Crews of artists, and engineers were already at work copying the carvings for restoration and laying out the work of carving the great cavern from out the rock to be transported and reassembled on high ground. I am told that the now completed work is an amazing job of engineering and artistic salvage. Much of the multi-million-dollar cost was provided by the United states through UNRWA.

Arriving at El Shallal near the high Aswan Dam, and much in need of a proper bath, I took the overnight train for Cairo.

There was one more adventure to be anticipated before leaving the land of the Pharaohs; I wanted to spend a night in the desert, and I chose to spend it on top of Cheops pyramid at Giza.

A few days later Esther and I called up the Captain of police responsible for security at the Giza area and asked for permission. After introducing myself as a writer I said, "We have what may

The Years of My Day

seem to you a foolish request." His prompt reply was, "I will not consider any request from you as foolish."

He said that as far as he knew no one had ever slept on top of the pyramid, but if that was my wish, I had his permission and protection.

That same evening Esther, the twins Mitzi and Mari, ten-year-old Jay, and I returned with a canteen of tea and our sleeping bags and climbed to the top, almost 500 feet above the surrounding desert.

As we started up several local guides came screaming but we continued to climb. When they scrambled up to stop us we referred them to the Captain of Police and they finally allowed us to proceed. These men make their living escorting tourists into the burial chambers and occasionally to the top and they are very jealous of their profession.

The so-called "Great Pyramid" was built by a little known Pharaoh named Cheops some 3,000 years before Christ. Huge blocks of stone, more than a million of them, the largest 8 x 8 x 8 feet, were quarried from the cliffs beyond the river, ferried on barges upriver, then by manpower alone, transported more than a mile over the sand and up ramps to construct what was for 5,000 years the largest and tallest man-made structure on Earth (it is said that King Cheops even sold his daughter into prostitution in exchange for stones with which to build his pyramid). One hundred thousand men, mostly slaves, labored over a period of 20 years to construct this monument to one man's vanity, a precisely engineered pile of rock covering 13 acres of land and rising 150 feet higher than the dome of St. Peter's in Rome.

I doubt if we were the first to spend a night on its top, and certainly we were not the first to reach its summit. Some 30 feet of the peak has been stolen and tumbled down for use in construction of other buildings, and all the smooth limestone facing has been carted away. This leaves a flat, but not smooth,

Floyd Schmoe

space at the summit about 30 feet square. On these sandstone blocks have been carved the names or initials of the Kilroys of the ages. Caesar had been there, and Alexander the Great. Napoleon Bonaparte climbed it in 1798 and watched his soldiers use the Sphinx for target practice.

It was not the ghosts of these men that kept me awake most of the night however, but the hard, uneven rock, and the howling of jackals who lived in the scattered tombs which surround the pyramid on all sides. Also, in the middle of the night, a face appeared over the rim of rock and said that he had been sent by the police to protect us from robbers. He was another of the disgruntled guides and we spent a half hour convincing him that we had no desire for his protection.

For me the crowning experience was the sunrise over the wide mirror of the Nile and the shadows of the three great piles which stretched for miles into the empty western desert, then raced inwards toward where I stood, as the red disc of the sun climbed higher into the morning sky.

It was my plan to spend the following night within the Parthenon atop the Acropolis in Athens, but the Greek police were not nearly as cooperative as the Egyptian Captain in Cairo.

I did spend two exciting days in Greece, however.

A Greek student who lived for a time at Friends Center in Seattle while attending the University of Washington, had given me the address of her family in Athens and promised to write them about me.

My plane arrived at about nine in the evening so it was rather late when I arrived at the door of her home, having checked in at a hotel earlier.

I found only an old grandmother at home, the rest of the family having gone to the theater. Grandma neither spoke nor understood either my English, or my worse French or German, but she called in a young man who did. By then the father, mother and

The Years of My Day

a sister had returned and I was received most hospitably. We made plans for a day picnicking and sightseeing next day. They had a beach cottage near the temple of Poseidon which stands on the very tip of the Attica Peninsula.

We visited the imposing ruins situated on a high cliff overlooking the sea, enjoyed a solid picnic lunch of goat cheese, bread, wine and fruits at the cottage, and in the evening drove back to Athens in a round-about way past the plains of Marathon. I found that they did not own the car but rented it just for the occasion. My friend's father was a professor of mathematics at an Athens school, but I am sure the family had better use for their money than to spend so much entertaining an almost unknown visitor. I did appreciate it.

I spent a second day with my friends seeing the art antiquity of Athens then flew on to Geneva. An incident remains in my memory. At the temple of Poseidon, as at all similar sites, there was a sign warning against the defacing of structures and objects which I read, while the guide proudly called our attention to the initials of the poet Lord Byron scratched boldly into a marble column.

Crossing over the Alps on our decent into Geneva I was anxious to look down on the Matterhorn but my Greek seatmate had drawn the curtain of the window and was sound asleep, so I walked aft and was looking through the small round portlight in the door when a Stewardess came and stood beside me. As we returned to my seat she said, "Some passengers thought you were going to attempt to jump out."

After a day in Geneva during which I attempted to buy a Volkswagen but could not find one that would meet the American requirements, I went on to Lyon for a brief visit with Anna Dardant; then still having several days before my schedule flight from London to New York, I went down to Nice and the French Riviera. Then on to Barcelona, Spain, where I spent a day.

Floyd Schmoe

My plane from Barcelona was turned back by violent thunderstorms over the Pyrenees delaying my arrival in London.

When we put down at Heathrow Airport I had less than an hour to catch my BOAC flight to New York. Since my bag was not yet offloaded I appealed to an Airport attendant in BOAC uniform.

She listened, then said, "Then let's get cracking." She took me back to the plane, grabbed the bag as soon as it appeared, commandeered an airport bus, and the two of us rode the two miles from the BEA to the BOAC terminal. There she put me through the long lines and onto the bus for my New York flight.

I told her she had saved the reputation for British womanhood for me and that then and there I was forgiving the rudeness I had experienced (or imagined) on the plane out of Calcutta.

In 1959 my New Year's resolution was: Enough of trying to DO good, let's concentrate on BEING good. This difficult program would keep me at home and it would not exclude doing something I had long wanted to do – that was to write some more books. For almost two decades, all during the war and during my work in Asia and Africa, I had spent more time away from home than at home, and during this time my family had perhaps needed me most. Although Ruth had done a wonderful job as head of the household, which both the family morale and the family economy gave evidence of, the strain had taken its toll and she was not in good health.

The children were all married and had homes of their own, we would both be eligible for Social Security benefits within a few months, and time was passing.

We decided to make profit from our adventures by writing a book about them. I took a quote from the book of Job and called it, *From Walking To and Fro Upon The Earth*.

The Years of My Day

Thinking it as well to start at the top when seeking a Publisher, I sent an outline and a couple of sample chapter to Harper & Brother in New York.

Much to our joy a letter soon arrived signed by Elizabeth Laurence, Editor. She wrote, "We find your material interesting, but feel that you have undertaken too much ground for one book. We would suggest that we try to make a book from your third chapter, titled, *A Year In Paradise*. If this idea appeals to you we would like to see an outline of your material." Before the year was out we had a beautiful book in which I had condensed our experiences of ten years on the mountain into a story of the four seasons in Paradise Valley. The book is one of my best, due in no small part to the skillful editing of Elizabeth, and is at the moment of this writing going into its fourth edition.

Having left the Park Service in 1928 and returned to the University where I did my Masters Degree in Marine Biology, while teaching ecology at the College of Forestry, I was now more interested in the world of the sea than that of the mountains, and so proposed to Harper's (now Harper and Row) that we do a book on Puget Sound.

With the encouragement of Elizabeth I decided to build a small houseboat and while living on the water write the story of the Puget Sound waters. I would put a window in the floor, and a door, so that we could sit at home and look out (down) into the waters about us, and we could, with scuba gear, go and come from our house directly into the underwater world. I worked up an outline and again Elizabeth scaled down my dream. When the book was published in 1964 the title had become, *For Love of Some Islands* (the San Juans), and "The Houseboat With a Basement" was only one of the chapters. (Both *From Walking To and Fro*, and the Puget Sound book still simmer on a back burner of my mind where from time to time I add to or stir up the contents.)

Floyd Schmoe

Between books opportunity came for a third trip to Africa. The 1961 Tri-ennial meeting of the Friends World Committee was set to meet at the friends Mission in Kenya and I was named one of the delegates from Pacific Yearly Meeting.

By chance I discovered that a round trip ticket to Johannesburg in South Africa cost only a few dollars more than a ticket to Nairobi in Kenya so I decided to make the tour. This would be my first crossing of the Atlantic by air, a journey which would, because of the peculiar geography of this small globe, take me not only from continent to continent but from Arctic to Tropic. On the round trip I would cover more than 30,000 miles, fly over 25 countries, and cross the Arctic circle and Equator twice. In fact, on the great circle route from Seattle to Amsterdam we crossed the Arctic Circle over Greenland twice each way, and since Kimoso lies directly upon the Equator I crossed that imaginary line many times. In going from the Mission at Kimoso to the mailbox on the highway you cross the Equator twice.

In 1961 I could have flown jet planes all the way, but Canadian Pacific Air was still flying four-engine propeller-driven aircraft on their Vancouver to Amsterdam route and these made stops for passengers in Edmonton, and for fuel in Sondre Stromfjord in Greenland. In Edmonton I could visit with Esther and her family for a half-hour, and in Sondre Stromfjord I could see more of Greenland and get a breath of Arctic air beneath the midnight sun. I chose the slower plane.

Because Air Canada had the Vancouver-London franchise, CPA was forced to fly into Amsterdam and ferry London passengers back from there.

At Heathrow I was met Edmund and Mireille Cooper and taken for an overnight visit with them at nearby Jordan's. Next day I flew on a Sud-Afric jet from London via Rome and Khartoum to Nairobi. Passing over France our pilot, an Afrikaner from Cape Town, took us within a few thousand feet of the summit of Mt.

The Years of My Day

Blanc, and later almost as close to Africa's second highest peak, 17,000 foot Mt. Kenya.

A week later, flying south from Nairobi we flew directly over the ice-filled crater of 19,340-foot Kibo – which is the local name for the higher of the two summits of Mt. Kilimanjaro. We were so close that I am sure we could have seen climbers had there been any on the summit at that moment, and, on the south slope I could clearly see the Ngurdoto Crater where three years before Ax Nelson and I had slept beneath a wild fig tree.

In Salisbury, Rhodesia (editors note; now Zimbabwe) I began to feel the social pressures and fears which existed, unfortunately, between me and my black brothers; pressures which were non-existent in the Nuhr and Dinka villages of the upper Nile, vaguely felt in Nairobi, but here in prosperous and "modern" Salisbury, clearly evident, yet still only a hint of what I was to see and feel in South Africa and again in the Congo and Nigeria. In Johannesburg ("Jo-burg" to the locals) people live in two separate and most unequal worlds, and most people, both black and white, appear to be unaware of the existence of any world other than their own.

The intelligent and educated man who served my room at the Salisbury Hotel, replied to my question on social affairs evasively and escaped our conversation at the first opportunity, but the native people I tried to talk with in South Africa refused even to look at me and had no answers. In booming Lagos on the coast of Nigeria however, I was treated with something midway between scorn and condescension, which perhaps served me right, having had the misfortune of being born "colorless," but which was equally distressing.

One of the most frequent adventures in travel to a foreign country (where you, not the country is being foreign) is occasioned by ignorance of language. One happened to me on a train between Pretoria and Johannesburg. Two ladies sat in a seat behind me and

Floyd Schmoe

talked loudly and without end in a language totally unfamiliar to me. By then I knew enough Afrikans to know that that it was not, and neither was it an African tongue. It was many minutes before I heard a familiar word, then one or the other said "tuppence" and I realized they were speaking English.

It was an all-night flight back from "Joburg" back to Brazzaville across the wide Congo River from Kinshasa (then still Leopoldville); along the Zambezi, which shone like a silver ribbon in the moonlight far below, then over the grasslands of Zambia where countless fires burned (as I later learned) in an attempt to clear brush and improve grazing as well as destroy the habitat of the tsetse fly, and finally for hours over the black jungle night of the Congo, which was blacker still the next day as Dag Hammarskjold died in an airplane crash near Elizabethville (now Lubumbashi).

The Congo between Brazzaville on the north bank and Leopoldville (Kinshasa) on the opposite bank, appears to be five or six miles wide though still 300 miles from the sea, and on the morning I crossed it was so completely blocked by floating vegetation that our ferry appeared to be plowing a furrough across a busy plain rather than navigating a deep river.

I saw little of the city because I went directly to a hotel down-river from the ferry landing which is operated by a number of Protestant missions as a rest home and way station for traveling missionaries, and where I was warned not to enter the city because of attacks on Europeans by black nationalists who were taking revenge on any white man they met in retaliation for the mistreatment of blacks by the Belgium government. On my way back to the ferry next morning I stopped at a sidewalk café for coffee and felt, or imagined I felt, the animosity of the people who served me. Most of the customers were black.

Back in Brazzaville I went immediately to the office of Air France to catch the first plane for Lagos. It was dark when I arrived

The Years of My Day

and it, I was told by waiting passengers at the airport, was 24 hours late.

At Lagos I took a decrepit taxi into the city after first buying hors d'oeuvres for the car in the form of a few gallons of gas.

When I reached my hotel, not over five miles distant, I was charged the equivalent of twelve dollars. This I considered robbery, but not being able to reason with the driver in a language he could understand, I took him to the hotel manager, a Swiss lady, who assured me that because of inflation that was not an unreasonable fee. I wonder what taxi fares are in Lagos now.

The terrible tribal wars in the eastern province of Biafra were sputtering to a close, money seemed to grow on trees, the harbor was being improved, tall buildings were going up, roads paved, everyone you met had something to sell, from fish to Fords – the town was booming – I wanted out.

It was my dream to visit Timbuktu on the lower Niger in Mali. At the gateway to the desert, the southern terminus of the yearly salt caravans, the camel market of the Sahara; Timbuktu seemed to me to be at the ends of the Earth, and I wanted to be able to say, "I have been there." But I could find no means of transportation and it was almost a thousand air miles away. I settled on Kano instead.

Kano, in northern Nigeria, is similarly situated, at the edge of the desert, a camel and cattle market, at one time the largest city in all of Africa and today the largest city built entirely of mud in all the world. Perhaps I should say built "almost" entirely of mud, for if I remember correctly the tall minaret of the mosque is constructed of stone, though I cannot imagine where it came from. I saw nothing but a flat wind-swept plain in all directions.

There was a small tree-shaded motel near the airport where I spent the night and where I met a young couple – people like me who had strayed from the beaten paths in search of adventure along the byways.

Floyd Schmoe

After breakfast the three of us rented bicycles, employed a young Nigerian guide, and spent the entire day roaming about the entire city.

It was perhaps three miles from our hostel to the gates of the walled city and this was, like the dry lake beds of California, as flat and as hard as a billiard table. It was also the market place, and this was market day. Perhaps every day was market day there. There were herds of longhorn cattle similar to the cattle I had seen along the upper Nile, herds of camels with many spindley-legged calves, smaller flocks of fat-tail sheep, lop-eared goats, and sleepy donkeys. Never, even on the Texas ranges, have I seen so many animals. Apparently they were all for sale. Groups of desert men were camped with their herds and everywhere selling and bartering was taking place. Conspicuous among the men were many blue-gowned and blue-skinned tribesmen of the nomadic Tuareg, camel breeders of the desert who traditionally wear clothing of indigo-dyed cotton cloth. The men wear veils over their faces, whether, being Muslims, from religious custom or as protection from the sun and sand, I do not know. In either case their skin has become dyed blue from the clothing they have worn since birth combined with, apparently, a total absence of facilities for bathing, or aversion to it.

Inside the city we found other men dyed an even deeper shade of indigo blue, and when we came upon an open area of steaming vats which emitted acrid fumes we saw the reason why. It was a dye works where the indigo plant is processed for its violet-blue dye, and where in other pits cotton cloth was being dyed.

Men, naked except for a loin cloth, treaded the cloth in the vats like men tread grapes in France for wine. Only the color and the smell was different.

The third product, aside from livestock and the dye industry, appeared to be ground nuts.

The Years of My Day

I saw no area of cultivation but there were, in a certain area, mountains of peanuts, bagged and stacked in pyramidal piles as large as three-story houses.

Where they were grown and how they were shipped, and for what purpose, I never learned. Our guide did not know. Of course peanut oil is an important article of world trade but there appeared to be no factory and no road, railroad, or other means of transport, within hundreds of miles.

We found no food for sale which we cared to encounter and no water to drink. The day was hot, the streets dusty, and we were thirsty. At last we found a small shop selling bottled drinks. We chose an amber fluid in Coca Cola bottles but without the Coke cap. It was not cooling, but it was wet. The taste may have been from tea or coco, or both, we never determined. We decided we had best return to the hostel by the airport, and thought it wise to send word ahead so that a meal might be arranged.

At the mosque we inquired if there was a telephone and were told, surprisingly, that the Sultan had a telephone in the palace. It was the only one in the city.

The palace was also built of mud, but huge and pink-tinted; quite imposing.

Armed sentries at the gate gave us permission to enter and a turbaned servant showed us the instrument in a large reception hall. We reached someone at the inn and arranged refreshments, then started home.

Outside the gate we saw a crowd gathered around a snake charmer, who with his assistant, a small boy, perhaps his son, was exhibiting his charming ways.

Within a ten foot circle, which no one encroached upon, were six or eight big cobras coiled with heads erect and forked tongues flicking. Among these the bare-legged man and boy walked without fear, sometimes stepping over a serpent or standing, back turned within a foot or two. There were other

Floyd Schmoe

snakes in a large, narrow-mouthed basket, which the man took in his hands and exhibited to the people. Some he held to his face and pretended to kiss.

While we watched we heard our guide calling us and turned to see him struggling with several other young men at the edge of the crowd. We thought they were trying to steal his bicycle, but discovered that they were rival guides who apparently thought he had invaded their turf, and were beating him.

When the three of us foreigners, one a girl, approached, they let our guide go and we returned to the inn.

At midnight I caught an Air France plane for Rome.

Home in 1961 we considered another book. I still wanted to do the Puget Sound story, but I had also become fascinated by the fate of the sea otter. Once these intelligent animals had lived by the hundreds of thousands all along the rugged shores of the north Pacific from Japan, to Alaska, to Mexico. Vitus Bering, the intrepid Danish explorer who in 1740 had headed a Russian expedition to Alaska, had discovered these animals, these "sea bears" as the Russians called them, and had taken a few pelts with him back to Moscow.

When the Moscow fur merchants saw them they drooled. Such soft fur, such thick pelts, they had never seen. They wanted more.

A larger expedition was fitted out for the following year and this time Wilhelm Steller, a German naturalist, was taken along as physician and naturalist. Steller was the first man to study the habits of the sea otter and discover that they were of the order Mustelidae - relatives of the weasels and river otter – and not related to bears. Steller and Bering became very well, not to say intimately, acquainted with the animals, when later shipwrecked on an island, now called Bering Island, at the western tip of the Aleutians, almost in sight of Russian Kamchatka. There they had to

The Years of My Day

eat foxes and sea otter in order to stay alive. In fact Bering died that winter.

Other expeditions followed, other nations joined the hunt, and in less than a hundred years the sea otter was almost exterminated.

Fortunately, for those along the coast of the Monterey Peninsula in California, another lust took over. Sea otter hunters left the coast in search for gold in the mountains, and a small band of sea otter survived.

It is an amazing animal with an intriguing history, and I suggested to Buz Wyeth, who had taken over at Harper's upon Elizabeth's retirement, that we do either the Puget Sound story featuring the killer whale, or the Big Sur story featuring the sea otter. He opted for Big Sur, and since he would be the publisher I let him have his way. Puget Sound could wait.

William Matchett, professor of English at the University, told me of his friend Dryden Phelps who had a summer cottage on the Big Sur coast, and wrote us a letter of introduction.

Ruth and I drove south, called upon Dryden and Margaret Phelps in their rustic cottage perched a thousand feet above the beach on Partington Ridge, and were offered the use of the cottage for the summer. Dryden took me to the beach and introduced me to the otter. I was immediately entranced by the spectacular setting, the unique community of plants and animals, and the historical background of the area. My enthusiasm has never dimmed. Few places on Earth offer as great a feast of nature as this bit of Earth, called by the early Spanish-speaking settlers of Monterey, "The big country to the south."

We made many trips during every season of the year, camping, hiking, spending days and nights observing the life of the shore, the beach, and the sea. There were not only the small colonies of otter, but there were passing whales, porpoise, seal, and sea lion. There were kelp beds with a whole world of plant and

Floyd Schmoe

animal life associated with them; and on shore the coyote, rabbit, ringtail cat, deer, and even wild boar, which had been introduced by sportsmen long ago. Bird life, both land and marine, is equally abundant. There may even be a few California Condor left but we were not fortunate enough to see one.

In March of 1969 I made what I thought would be my last trip south. Ruth had suffered a slight heart attack and was under medical care. She did not feel well enough to accompany me, but we had no premonition of further trouble. I was to fly down and rent a car in Monterey. My sister and brother-in-law, Inez and Earl Voorhees, with daughter Karla would drive up from their home near Los Angeles in their house car and we would camp in it. We had two exciting days together and found new and useful material, but when I returned to Monterey I had word that Ruth had suffered another heart attack and had died. It was late afternoon and there was no plane until Noon of the next day. I went to the beach and sat in the sunset. Almost every day I had written Ruth, as for more than fifty years when away from home I had, and that evening I wrote her again. I would not mail, she would not read it, but I felt that she would know.

This is what I wrote: Monterey Bay, March 16, 1969

My dear Ruth: I have just been told of your death. May God give you peace and joy. As I wait for the first plane that can take me home to Seattle where all our children wait and mourn, I feel I must talk to you. Yesterday when I thought that you were safe at home I wrote a letter which you will not receive. Today, though I know that you have gone, I write again. Yesterday I told you that I love you. Today I love you even more. I am certain that you will understand.

The Years of My Day

We knew each other and loved each other for more than fifty years. Now I shall miss you greatly though we can still communicate in spirit. Love does not die.

Everyone who has known you has become a better person because of knowing. Nothing speaks more truly of you than this. I, I am sure, would be far less than I am had we not met and loved. Your children – our children and our grandchildren – who were your greatest joy, could not have been the wonderful people they are had you not bore and mothered them. Your loving spirit will stay close to us all.

Here by the sea, warm in the spring sun, I sit and wonder: Will I ever know you in this way again? Will we as individuals and as family ever be part of another and a better world? This is the eternal hope of mankind – but is it a hope born only of human desire?

Life, ongoing, expanding, ever-renewing life, is without doubt the greatest gift of God to man. We as individual persons are only a minute part of the marvelous whole, yet in living we become involved in the entire creative process. Death is an inseparable part of life so in dying we only rejoin the past in order to remain one with the whole.

What my human emotions tell me I want to believe, my reason tells me may not – in the light of truth – be the highest good. For men to retain their individuality after death to Earth could, I suppose, actually hinder the creative process. To give our faulty, though cherished, personality that it might return to its Divine Source, and thereby enhance the totality of life, would seem to be the greater good. Only thus, perhaps, could we Earth-tried spirits become an enriching part of the eternal whole – becoming one again with the Giver and Creator of all. That seems to be the rational point of view and I am trying now to be rational, difficult as it is.

But whatever the eternal plan, I have faith that it is right.

Floyd Schmoe

So I sit here by the sea in the sunset and I wait. For the moment I can only wait. Flowers bloom around me. Their sweet scent bless the air. A hummingbird flits from blossom to blossom of a eucalyptus tree nearby, and a family of sea otter are playing and feeding in the surf. Each is living its own span of this amazing thing we call life. Theirs is a far different manner of life from ours, yet it is still essentially the same stuff – part and parcel of the divine whole. I say Goodbye my love, but only for now.

Floyd.

The Years of My Day

In 1958 Donn and Ruthanna had purchased land with a magnificent view of Mt. Rainier and Lake Washington on top of Finn Hill, three miles north of Kirkland, and in 1963 we had helped them build a large and unique house which Jerry Vanslyck had designed in the Frank Lloyd Wright style.

Then Ruth and I decided that we would like to live nearby to enjoy the children as well as the view, and Don offered to help us build an apartment adjacent to the big house. So in 1967 we sold our home of many years on the west side of the lake and moved into the Finn Hill complex almost directly across the lake.

Ruth had done a great deal of the work on the house and its furnishings, as well as the planning. She had woven fabrics for upholstery, purchased rugs and furniture, and helped me do all the shoji and other interior work. She and Ruthanna had done all the inside paint jobs. She had enjoyed all this, but it may have been too heavy a load. As it turned out she had only a year to enjoy her new house.

Rod, who was only 7, was spending nights with her while I was away. That morning, March 15, 1969, they had finished breakfast and Rod was ready for school. Ruth cleared the table and sat down to write a card to me. In the middle of a word she slumped over the table and died. Rod called his father and mother and they tried to call me. All day they tried but even the California State Police were unable to locate us, though we were never out of sight of the highway, which follows the beach all along the Big Sur coast.

When I arrived home the following afternoon all the family were there. I have never appreciated or loved my family more. Still my bed was a lonesome place that night.

On August 17 Ruth and I would celebrate our 50th wedding anniversary. We had planned a family gathering. Now Ruth could not be there in person but we felt she would be close to us in spirit,

Floyd Schmoe

so we went ahead with the plans. When the day came all the children and grandchildren (with the exception of Esther's Jay) returned and we had a wonderful weekend together. As I remember it August 17, 1969 was a Sunday, as August 17 fifty years earlier had been. Actually Ruth and I had been as close as two people can be for more than fifty years, for we had been engaged more than a year before we were able to marry in 1919.

Even with the family close, with many good friends and neighbors, and with two books ready for publication (I had condensed my Pendle Hill lectures of 1965 into a small volume titled *What is Man*, which was published by Voyagers Press, Tokyo in 1970), I felt a great loss and empty void in my life.

Ken was aware of this at dinner one evening and he and Agnes suggested we go on a trip to S.E. Asia. Ruth Karen was finishing two years with the Peace Corps as a nurse in rural Thailand and Ken and I would go out to visit her and escort her home. It was an exciting prospect. I could visit friends in Japan and Hong Kong again, and see more of Thailand and Cambodia, and show my favorite places to Ken and Ruthie. I could also visit Tomiko Yamazaki, our first and most enthusiastic Japanese "Houses for Hiroshima" volunteer.

I had loved and admired Tomiko from our first meeting on a volunteer work project at a Tokyo orphanage in 1949. She had managed most of our business affairs in Japan for 20 years and we had kept in touch since our last visit in 1956. In 1952 Tomiko had come to America to take part in an American Friends Service Committee work camp and had visited our home, so Ruth and the family had come to know her and to love her. Also Ruth had gone with me to Korea in 1955 and going and coming we had spent time in Japan.

Now I was very lonesome without Ruth and I had discovered that I was not only poor company for myself but a reluctant cook and housekeeper as well. I wondered if Tomiko,

The Years of My Day

who had never married, might consider coming to America and sharing her life with me. She would not "replace" Ruth either in my home or my affection, but she would fill a special place of her own; be an added bonus to my already full and satisfactory life.

I have never measured success in terms of money or property, fame or public acclaim, but rather in terms of friends, family, public service, and work accomplished. I feel my life has been full and, to me, highly successful. Certainly I have not accomplished nearly all that I would like to do, and what I have done has always been with the help and support of many others. Also there is much more that I hope to do, God willing; and I intend to keep busy as long as I live.

I wanted to ask Tomiko if she would help me carry on.

Without telling anyone why, I went to Tokyo a week before Ken was to leave. I would spend the time with Tomiko and meet him when he arrived. We would then go on together to meet Ruth K. in Bangkok.

I found Tomiko the same sweet person we had known twenty years earlier and we spent a happy week together. I asked her to meet me in Paris in the spring of 1970 and she agreed to give the matter a lot of thought.

At the Bangkok airport Ruthie was waiting for us and took us to a hotel with a swimming pool. That evening we had dinner at a large hotel with table set near a pool with an inner courtyard where fountains, greenery and beautiful costumed Thai girl musicians and dancers accented a lush tropical atmosphere. On the next day we sampled typical Thai food at a public market and found it "hotter," if that is possible, than Korean kimchi. We took the "long-tailed" boats on the muddy Chao Phraya River, visited the Wat Arun (Temple of the Dawn), and the Royal Barge sheds where several huge ceremonial barges are kept between festivals, and another was being built with all the dragons heads, gilt and decorations, the craft could carry. Ken was especially fascinated

Floyd Schmoe

with the long-shafted outboard motors which zip the slim river boats about the harbor like so many water bugs. Actuallly they are rebuilt automobile engines mounted on a gimbal at the stern of the craft with a long shaft which puts the spinning propeller six or eight feet behind the boat to kick up a "roostertail," like a miniature hydro foil.

On another day we took a wood-burning train for about three hours across the lush countryside to the famous River Kwai, then by local motorboat down river to visit the cemetery where hundreds of Allied POW's, who died while working on the railroad, are buried. We also visited the ruins of the ancient capitol where the remains of great brick towers and temples remind one of the Mayan ruins of Yucatan.

Flying directly from Bangkok to Hong Kong on a Cathay plane we had passed high over the northern hills of Viet Nam in a matter of a few minutes but during that brief time I saw two military planes far below dropping bombs on Communist villages. We would not, of course see the dropping bombs, but the white puffs of the exploding bombs which followed the low flying planes like a string of dots and dashes were unmistakable.

Returning home we flew farther south via Air Burma and stopped off in Phnom Penh, Cambodia.

From the capitol we took of Air Cambodge's three planes, an ancient DC 3, and flew north an hour's flight to Siem Reap to visit the great ruins of Angkor. The huge temple (Wat) at Angkor, though said to be the largest religious structure in the world makes up only a small part of the remains of what was once a great city covering some 60 square miles. With a rented car and driver-guide we spent all day exploring the hundreds of ruins with their amazing and unique architectural forms and artistry. Much of the ruin has been skillfully restored but more remains in the grip of the jungle which can, if allowed its way, submerge even the largest structures in the matter of a very few years.

The Years of My Day

Returning to Siem Reap we flew over the shallow basin called Tonle Sap, which in the dry season covers about 100 square miles to a depth of only four or five feet, but when the Mekong river is in flood becomes a sea covering almost 800 square miles with a depth of 40 or 50 feet.

From Phnom Penh we flew Air Viet Nam to Saigon, and from there, by Air Cathay again to Hong Kong.

While waiting in the terminal at Saigon a young Japanese man walked up to me and bowing said, "I congratulate you."

"What for?" I wanted to know.

"An American Cosmonaut has just set foot on the moon." He replied.

It was July 21, 1969.

I was with Inez and Earl in California several months later when a telephone call came through from Tokyo. Tomiko said, "I'll meet you in Paris next February."

"Do you mean we can be married in France and you'll come home to Seattle with me?" I asked.

"Hi," was her simple reply. There was not much more to say.

I reserved a room at the small Dues Continents Hotel close by the ancient church of St. Germain des Pres and left for Paris via Edmonton.

I arrived a day early. Tomiko's plane was due in at ten the next morning. About nine I called the Paris office of Japan Airlines and asked when the flight was due. A girl said they are arriving at this moment.

I caught a Metro train to the Invalides Station, and an airport bus to Orly Airport. She had caught a skiers' charter loaded with young Japanese skiers headed for the French Alps. It took an hour to unload them and their mountains of skis and baggage. I met Tomiko just as she came through the immigration check.

Floyd Schmoe

Next day we went to the American embassy to inquire about the marriage procedures. After considerable inquiry we learned that to marry under French law we would have to "post bans" with the Catholic Church and wait forty days at a fixed address. It was cold and snowing, and we had no desire to spend forty days in Paris during March snowstorms. I went to Friends Center and asked advice. They sent me to a lawyer. The lawyer said, "Ce impossible. Go back to America to marry."

"Perhaps." we said, "it would be easier in Holland. The Dutch are Protestants." I went to the Dutch Embassy. The sentry at the gate did not understand my mission but passed me on to the imposing structure across the large courtyard.

There was no one at the door. It was not locked. I entered and found myself in a large, beautifully furnished reception hall. Soon a young lady came down a broad marble stairway and, speaking French, asked what I desired.

I asked, "Do you speak English?"

"But of course," was her reply. (The sentry at the gate did not even understand les inglais.)

After I had explained our problem she said: "But you have come to the wrong place. This is the home of the Ambassador. You must go to the Chancellery." And she gave me the proper address.

At the Dutch Chancellery, a beautiful secretary who, of course, spoke English, listened to my story most sympathetically but had not the slightest idea how two people, neither of them citizens of Holland, might contrive to commit marriage in her tidy little country. "However," she would telephone The Hague and make inquiry. This she did. Someone there suggested we try England. "You can get married in three days in England," they said.

We decided to try Portugal.

At the American Embassy in Lisbon a friendly and sympathetic under-Secretary said, "Go home and get married. It will save you a lot of trouble."

The Years of My Day

I wrote Esther. She wrote back" "Come to Edmonton. You can buy a license here and get married the same day."

We went to Spain, made a short visit to Morrocco, returned to Spain and took a train for Barcelona, then to France for a day in Carcassonne, and on to Nice for a week along the French Riviera including a glimpse of Italy at San Remo. From Nice we turned north to Chamonix and the French alps. We found the same small hotel, and the same room with a balcony looking out at Mt. Blanc, that I had stayed in on a visit more than 50 years before. It was directly over the bar and I remember that it even smelled the same.

One day we took a bus through the Mt. Blanc tunnel, crossing the border of Italy thousands of feet below ground, we went on the ancient Roman city of Aosta, and back to our hotel the same evening.

The next day we took a narrow gauge train through the 500 foot Col des Montets and down to Montreux at the east end of Lake Geneva. All day we traveled through snow and Alpine forests where only the previous evening we had lunched among beds of daffodils and beneath palm trees at Aosta. It was not Italy which gave the contrast but the south slope as opposed to the north.

At Montreux we boarded an express train which carried us swiftly along the north shore of the lake past the picturesque Castle of Chillon, through lovely Lausanne, and into Geneva.

I had developed a severe headache due the glare of sunlight off the snow, so we did not go into the city, though there would have been time for a brief visit before our train to Lyon was to depart. Instead we had tea and rested in the station.

While waiting I noticed a pretty Asian girl who appeared lost or bewildered and thinking she was Japanese I suggested to Tomiko that she ask if we might be of assistance to her.

The girl was Vietnamese and did not speak Japanese or English so we did not communicate well. We hope she managed.

Floyd Schmoe

Our train reached Lyon late in the evening and we went directly to our hotel. Next morning Jeanne, Anna's sister, called to say that she would come by and drive us out to Couzon au Mont d'Or to visit Anna.

It was a joy to see my old friend again though she had aged and looked tired. The next day we returned to Paris.

Unfortunately the weather had not improved greatly, though the snow had gone and the marronier (horse chestnut) trees were in bloom – much to Tomiko's delight. There was new green grass in the Luxembourg Gardens and some days were sunny. We spent hours wandering the streets of the Latin Quarter, finding familiar faces and remembering past times. I had spent many months in Paris after the Armistice in 1918 and it was good to be back. I was unable to find the Atelier of the Academy Julian where I had studied sculpture – the entire street seemed to have vanished.

Tomiko had never been to Paris but she had a better memory than I of places we had read about in French novels, or had seen in French films. Near the place of St Michel, we discovered the tiny "Rue de Chat Qui Peche" leading down from Elliot Paul's beloved Rue de Huchette to the river.

We visited the Louvre and Notre Dame, bought violets on Rue de Rivoli and lily of the valley on May Day. One night we went to L'Opera to see Tosca again - I had seen the great opera first from the Royal Box of Warsaw's beautiful Opera House when, in 1919 we had gone to Poland with a trainload of relief supplies; and Paderewski, then Premier, loaned us the Royal Box for the evening. On May 7th we returned to Amsterdam and flew home. In Edmonton next day with Gordon and Esther, Mitzi and Gerry at our side, we were married by a magistrate who was barely convinced that it was us and not Mitzi and Gerry that he should be uniting in Holy Matrimony.

The Years of My Day

Donn, Ruthanna, and Ken met us at the Vancouver airport and soon we were safely at home on Finn hill where all the family met us and took Tomiko into the arms and hearts.

In a cold dark room of our small hotel in Seville at Easter time, Tomiko and I had read the galley proof of my book, "What is Man," and in the early summer a thousand copies arrived in a huge box from the publisher in Tokyo. I spent much of the summer selling it. I consider it my most important work to date, though a sequel to it, which I shall call, "Why Is Man," will, I hope, be more important.

In 1971 we bought a small camper and in August Tomiko and I drove to Saint Mary's College, near Oakland, to attend Pacific Yearly Meeting.

Ruth was clerk of FYM for two terms and we had both been active in the organization since its formation in 1946. Now Tomiko found friends and interesting involvement also and we seldom miss the annual sessions.

From St. Mary's, in 1971, we went to the Big Sur to continue my study for the new book, which was published in 1975, in an attractive paperback edition by Chronicle Books of San Francisco. The title, "The Big Sur: Land of Rare Treasures," is fitting, for no area on Earth, so far as I have discovered, is richer in the abundance and variety of fascinating life forms than this rugged 100 miles of California coastline.

On September 21, 1975, I reached my 80th birthday. Since never in my life had I been given a birthday party I decided it was about time I gave one for myself.

All my wonderful family; Tomiko, Ruthanna, Agnes, and some others baked apple pies, and more than a hundred of family, friends, and neighbors arrived to share my happiness. Bill came from London, and Esther, Gerry, and Mitzi came from Edmonton. All the children, including Pete, shared in presenting me with a fine

Floyd Schmoe

color television set which has given us many hours of pleasure and instruction.

I decided that this party was such a success that I shall have one every five years from here on. Next year I will be 85, and I am looking forward to another great celebration...hopefully with apple pie.

I have on occasion declared that my criteria for a high standard of living are: clean sheets, hot running water, flush toilets, and apple pie, and I have boasted of the fact that in certain areas of the world I have, I believe, been the first to introduce this great American delicacy to the grateful populace.

1976 was a memorable year not only for the nation (our 200th anniversary) but also for me and my family. Bill "borrowed" a "hunting lodge" on the River Carry in the Highlands of Scotland and invited the entire family over.

This "lodge," it turned out, had 14 bedrooms, ten baths, a larder stocked with beef and game, a bar stocked with everything else, a station wagon, and resident hosts. Each bedroom was a period piece. Mine had a delft blue china toilet and wash basin, in addition to matched chamber pots in a commode beside the bed – a redundance that may have been appreciated by heavier imbibers than us.

Scotland was beautiful in June with rhododendron in full bloom, but England was dry and hot that summer.

On our way back to London Lee, Lori, and I stopped off at Lake Windermere for a days' cruise, then down to Lancaster for a visit to Swarthmore Hall, and the George Fox country. The young Friends who do the annual pilgrimage call it the "Fox Trot."

Tomiko stayed in London where she enjoyed the shopping, the restaurants, and the theater, then came directly home to her cats; but I stopped off in Hamilton, Ontario, where triennium meetings of the Friends World Committee were being held at McMasters University. From there I went directly to North Pacific

The Years of My Day

Yearly Meeting in Oregon and, with only a day in between, on the Pacific Yearly Meeting at St. Mary's. The extra day was spent at a Schmoe family reunion on Mt. Rainier...and when it was all over I was spent.

The reunion attended by some 80 Schmoes also celebrated the 50th wedding anniversary of Earl and Inez Voorhees who were married on Mt. Rainier in 1926.

The 1977 yearly meeting was held at Chico State College in northern California – St. Mary's having undertaken a summer session. Tomiko and I flew down. The living conditions were good and the meetings stimulating. Though the weather was not as hot as we anticipated, it was still uncomfortable in crowded rooms. Outdoors, surrounded by almond orchards, it was quite pleasant.

The 1977 Schmoe reunion was held near Newburg, Oregon and we did not attend.

In 1978 the reunion, largest to date and with more than 100 relatives attending, was held at a campground in the Cascades on the shores of Rimrock Lake. Bill's family came over and Esther was down. Next day I went to Whittier College for yearly meeting. Tomiko felt more like resting at home.

We had good sessions in a comfortable atmosphere, which were highlighted for me by the Author's Tea on afternoon, an innovation I had suggested and organized to introduce a new book by Margaret Simkin which the Friend in the Orient Committee of Yearly Meeting had sponsored and underwritten. I had worked all year on the editing, publication, and promotion of this book and had drawn the maps and chapter decorations for it, so I was happy to see it in print, and happy with the reception given it. Naturally Margaret was highly pleased also, for it was the personal story of the more than 20 years she and Robert had spent in S.W. China before and during the revolution.

The day following my return from Whittier we took off for a week's cruise to Alaska. Bill, Lil, Lori, Ken, Liz, and Pete, Ralph and

Floyd Schmoe

Ruth all went. We had two staterooms on the Alaska Ferries flagship COLUMBIA and were very comfortable. We were going only to Sitka and Skagway, and I had been over all the area several times before in the LINDA, but it was fun to be with family on a more leisurely voyage.

During turn-around at Skagway we had four hours so we chartered a six-place Piper Cherokee with Ben Lingle, seasoned "Bush Pilot," at the controls, and flew over to Glacier Bay. Pete, Lil, Lori, and Liz remained to shop and sightsee in Skagway. The story of this adventure, as I wrote for the local newspaper, follows:

When, in the autumn of the year 1792, Captain George Vancouver with his ships DISCOVERY and CHATHAM sailed down Icy Strait in what is now south-east Alaska, he passed on his starboard side a great wall of moving ice which probably stood two to three hundred feet high and stretched for fifteen or twenty miles. Today, less than 200 years later, a wide bay opens to the north and, lying deep between the rugged Chilcat Range on the east and the high Fairweather Range on the west, extends for more than 50 miles inland. This is Glacier Bay.

In August of this year (1978) I, with a number of my children and grandchildren, took the Alaska State Ferry COLUMBIA on a week—long cruise to Skagway. During the four hour turnaround at Skagway we chartered a six-place Piper CHEROKEE and with veteran flyer Ben Lingle as pilot, flew over the bay and its fringing glaciers.

Several glaciers extend down the eastern valleys of the Chilcat while a thousand square miles of snow and ice mantles the summits and upper valleys.

At the Rainbow Glacier clouds filled the summit pass, but at the next, the Davidson, there seemed to be a hundred feet of open space. We decided to try a passage. So steep is the fall Of the Davidson that we were able to fly up its canyon only by a series of looping spirals. With our wingtip sweeping the tumbled ice on the

The Years of My Day

upper pass, banking almost against the sheer rock cliffs on the turns, and passing high above the glacier on the lower pass provided some of the hairiest flying I have ever encountered.

Near the summit we flew close to high ledges and glacial cirques where white mountain goat grazed. I counted several bands of up to 20 each. Only the eagle and the hoary marmot keep them company.

Slipping through the pass we appeared to have less than fifty feet of clear air either above or below us.

Dropping down the west slope the mighty Muir Glacier extended for as far as we could see, and across the green waters of the bay Mount Fairweather rose more than 16,000 feet in icy splendor.

After circling the upper icefields for half an hour we descended the Muir and crossed its lower cliffs at close range. Ben thought the noise of the engine would cause ice to fall. None did but the hundreds of floating bergs which filled the water below the face of the ice indicated that this is happening constantly.

On this drifting ice in Muir Inlet we saw hundreds of basking seal. Such a population, along with a herd of fifty or more humpback whales which inhabit the bay during the summer months, and the great flocks of marine birds, testify to the abundance of fish which populate the icy waters.

My fascination with Glacier Bay at the moment is due to the fact that I am engaged in writing the history of the Puget Sound basin. From geological and ecological evidence is apparent that Puget Sound was formed by the same forces which are now shaping Glacier Bay and similar areas in S.E. Alaska. In fact what we observed from Above Glacier Bay this summer is, without doubt, almost exactly what we would have seen had we been able to look down on Puget Sound fourteen or fifteen thousand years ago.

On our return to Skagway we found all the high passes blocked by clouds, and so were forced to fly

Floyd Schmoe

some 30 miles to the south in order to pass over the Chilcat and return up Lynn Canal to our waiting ship.

*Publisher note: In order to preserve Floyd's drawing superimposed on the previous piece of writing, we have elected to use a scan of his original typed version. This is how it appeared in his own typed, hand-bound edition of this book from 1979:

> When, in the autumn of the year 1792, Captain George Vancouver with his ships DISCOVERY and CHATHAM sailed down Icy Strait in what is now southeast Alaska, he passed on his starboard side a great wall of moving ice which probably stood two to three hundred feet high and stretched for fifteen or twenty miles. Today, less than 200 years later, a wide bay opens to the north and, lying deep between the rugged Chilcat Range on the east and the high Fairweather Range on the west, extends for more than 50 miles inland. This is Glacier Bay.
>
> In August of this year (1978) I, with a number of my children and grandchildren, took the Alaska State Ferry COLUMBIA on a week-long cruise to Skagway. During the four hour turnaround at Skagway we chartered a six-place Piper CHEROKEE and with veteran flyer Ben Lingle as pilot, flew over the bay and its fringing glaciers.
>
> Several glaciers extend down the eastern valleys of the Chilcat while a thousand square miles of snow and ice mantles the summits and upper valleys.
>
> At the Rainbow Glacier clouds filled the summit pass, but at the next, the Davidson, there seemed to be a hundred feet of open space. We decided to try a passage. So steep is the fall of the Davidson that we were able to fly up its canyon only by a series of looping spirals. With our wingtip sweeping the tumbled ice on the upper pass, banking almost against the sheer rock cliffs on the turns, and passing high above the glacier on the lower pass provided some of the hairest flying I have ever encountered.
>
> Near the summit we flew close to high ledges and glacial cirques where white mountain goat grazed. I counted several bands of up to 20 each. Only the eagle and the hoary marmot keep them company.
>
> Slipping through the pass we appeared to have less than fifty feet of clear air either above or below us.

The Years of My Day

Dropping down the west slope the mighty Muir Glacier extended for as far as we could see, and across the green waters of the bay Mount Fairweather rose more than 16 000 feet in icy splendor.

After circling the upper icefields for half an hour we descended the Muir and crossed its lower cliffs at close range. Ben thought the noise of the engine would cause ice to fall. None did but the hundreds of floating bergs which filled the water below the face of the ice indicated that this is happening constantly.

On this drifting ice in Muir Inlet we saw hundreds of basking seal. Such a population, along with a herd of fifty or more humpback whales which inhabit the bay during the summer months, and the great flocks of marine birds, testify to the abundance of fish which populate the icy waters.

My fascination with Glacier Bay at the moment is due to the fact that I am engaged in writing the history of the Puget Sound basin. From geological and ecological evidence it is apparent that Puget Sound was formed by the same forces which are now shaping Glacier Bay and similar areas in S.E. Alaska. In fact what we observed from above Glacier Bay this summer is, without doubt, almost exactly what we would have seen had we been able to look down on Puget Sound fourteen or fifteen thousand years ago.

On our return to Skagway we found all the high passes blocked by clouds, and so were forced to fly some 30 miles to the south in order to pass over the Chilcat and return up Lynn Canal to our waiting ship.

The Years of My Day

The Overflow Bin

Incidents and observations overlooked along the way and thrown in here as supplementary reading. Optional of course.

Floyd Schmoe

As soon as I had finished college and got an appointment with the National Park Service, we began to save toward the education of our children. We set up a special bank account for the purpose.

One afternoon in 1921, while working as a guide on Mt. Rainier, I was assigned a small party to the Ice Caves of the Paradise Glacier. Among others in the party was a large friendly man by the name of C.B. Voorhees from Kenosha, Wisconsin. With him wre a teenage son (later to be Congressman Jerry Voorhees of California) and a younger daughter. During the leisurely four-hour hike we became quite well acquainted. I remembered later that he had shown unusual interest in my work at the College of Forestry, and in our plans for the future. Before parting, after the trip, Mr. Voorhees asked if Ruth and I would have dinner with the family at the Inn that evening.

During dinner he told us that he was Vice President of the Nash Motor Company (now American Motors), that he was concerned with helping young people with their education, and he asked if we would allow him to help with my plan to do my final year of forestry at the New York State College of forestry at Syracuse, where I could get courses in Ecology not then available at the University of Washington. He offered to pay what additional money we would need.

They were leaving the next day but he asked us to think about it and let him know. It was a rare opportunity which we decided to accept on condition that the help be in the form of a loan to be repaid with interest after I had graduated. Mr. Voorhees agreed to that and I signed a personal note providing $100 per month for the coming year.

When, a year later, we were back on the park with a job assured, we wrote Mr. Voorhees that we would like to begin paying off the debt.

The Years of My Day

He returned the note marked "Paid," and said he would be happier if we paid what we owed into a savings account for Kenneth's education when he was ready for college. This we did, and by the tine Kenneth entered the University the account amounted to some $2,000.00, which, as I've said, none of the children have ever needed. We have used it, however, and more, to aid a number of Asian and African students who have come to America to study.

Floyd Schmoe

Poland Adventure

In the Spring of 1919 with the war at an end and a year of service behind me, I applied for release and return home. Ruth and I had plans to marry in August and I was anxious to see her. However a million or more Americans were equally anxious to leave France by the first available ship and there were not enough ships. Most of the great transatlantic liners had either been sunk or converted into Army transports. On these the soldiers, rightfully, had priority.

I reasoned that if I came down from the Verdun where we had been building refugee housing, and waited in Paris, I would have a better chance of getting out.

Arriving at our hostel at "90 Boul Mich," Joe Marvel, Chief d' Equipe in Paris asked me if I would "tend the store" while he took a long delayed vacation in Italy. I had little better to do so I agreed. It proved to be an interesting experience. The Peace Negotiations were underway at Versailles and the city was full of fascinating people. It also gave me an opportunity to study sculpture for a couple months at the nearby Academy Julians, attend opera twice a week, and meet a lot of famous people. Among artists was the great American sculptor, Lorado Taft, and the popular Swiss painter Eugene Burnard, who was also father to the beautiful Burnard twins. They lived just across the street from the hostel, and invited us for Sunday luncheons.

There were guests for dinner almost every evening, mostly visiting British or American Quakers, or the French girlfriends of the fellow residents at the hotel. Most of these were men and women staffing the Paris office of the Service Committee, but there were always transients like myself. Often we invited visitors to speak to the group following dinner. Jane Addams was in town, an observer of the Peace Conference, and with her Jeanette

The Years of My Day

Rankin, Congresswoman from Montana. Jane Addams was famous as head of the Hull house in Chicago, a pioneer social service institution, and Jeanette Rankin was the only woman member of Congress. She also held the distinction of casting the only vote against America's entry into the war, and of becoming (some 20 years later) the only member of Congress to vote against entry into the Second World War. We enjoyed a delightful evening with the two great women. Many years later, on the 100th anniversary of Jane Addams' birth, I was asked to represent Friends at a Seattle dinner commemorating the evening, and Jeanette wrote me recalling that evening in Paris.

It was during the Paris sojourn also that the call came for volunteers to convoy a relief train of the Hoover Commission from Paris to Warsaw and as a consequence I became, for a brief time, a prisoner of war.

In May of 1919 Poland was still fighting for her life against both the Germans and the Russians. In addition there was an epidemic of Typhus and widespread starvation. Four of us who were waiting in Paris volunteered to go.

Prisoner of War

On Monday evening we reached the town of Kreuz in eastern Germany and found ourselves on the front line between the armies of Poland and a German army of the so-called Spartacist Movement which did not recognize the Armistice or any authority from Berlin.

Machine guns were set up, our locomotive taken away, and German soldiers with fixed bayonets and huge police dogs began patrolling our train. For more than a week we were not allowed to leave our coach. Our French porter, who wore the uniform of a French soldier, disappeared, but we found him the next day hiding beneath a pile of dirty sheets in the linen locker. Our cook was

Floyd Schmoe

allowed to bring food to us and the Captain was allowed to return to Berlin in order to find some way of rescuing us.

After several tense days in which every one of our cars was broken into and searched for contraband, and we were searched, the Captain returned with an engine and train crew, and we were allowed to "retreat" toward Berlin. However at Landsberg we met the armed trains of Polish General Haller, who was returning his trains and equipment back to Poland from their operation with the Allies on the Western Front.

The General had armored cars equipped with artillery, and machine guns did not require "permission."

He allowed us to join his army, but because of our problems to the east he turned south and we entered Poland by way of Silesia. But our problems were not over. At the border our German crew shifted the engine to the rear, pushed us across the line, and took off.

Again we sat under fire from both sides while our Captain went on into Warsaw with General Haller to arrange for a Polish engine and crew to come retrieve us.

For ten days we had been virtual prisoners of war, enjoyed very little sleep, and had not been out of our clothes for two weeks.

I remember the field of red poppies which covered the marshy Silesian plains, but I do not remember our arrival in Warsaw, where we were met by a brass band and given garlands of flowers by Polish girls, and speeches by the mayor and other government officials. I slept through it all and only awoke about Noon the following day when we were parked in the freight yard of a Warsaw railway station, and our train was being unloaded.

On our second night some Polish Red Cross girls invited Olin Hadley and I to attend the opera with them. They had the loan of the royal box for the evening.

The Years of My Day

After the opera – a beautifully-staged presentation of Verdi's Tosca – we offered to see the girls home, but they declined, saying, "It's late, and you have farther to go then we have."

When we were unable to secure a "Trotsky" (the horse-drawn equivalent of a taxicab), I said to Olin, "it's only a mile or two. Let's walk."

We had arrived at the opera house by a round-about way in order to pick up the girls at Red Cross Headquarters, but we thought there was a shorter way home. After walking for almost an hour in what we supposed was the right direction and not finding the station, we had to admit that we were lost.

The city was full of soldiers, for Poland was still fighting the war on two fronts – the Germans to the west, and the Russians to the north and east. Soldiers with rifles and bayonets directed traffic in the streets. There were stacked rifles in the aisles of the theater, and I had seen a soldier walking in the park with his wife and a baby. There was a rifle thrust into the baby carriage alongside the child.

At 1:00 am however the streets were empty and the only people we saw were people, mostly Polish soldiers, in bars. Finally we entered one and, not speaking Polish, we made an inquiry in French. We got only stares. We then tried English, and failing that, attempted German. No one understood German but they recognized the language. They did not however recognize the Quaker gray uniform which unfortunately was the same color as the German uniform. They became suspicious and hostile. We hurried on.

At another bar we found Polish students who understood German. "Wo ist der Bohnhof?" we asked.

"Welcher Bohnhof?" they asked. (They said there were six.)

We did not know which station but explained we had arrived "nach posen" – by way of Posen. They showed us which way to go.

Floyd Schmoe

After a short walk we came to a dead end. There was a high wovenwire fence around the railroad yard and the station was on the opposite side. The fence seemed to extend for miles in either direction, so we climbed over.

No sooner had we dropped down inside the yard, than a soldier came running. He had a rifle with fixed bayonet and was screaming which we assumed meant "hand up." Our hands went up, high up. He understood no English and we did not dare try any German. He marched us to the command post in the station and the C.O. recognized us and put us to bed.

I have seen La Tosca twice since then under more normal circumstances, but never a finer performance.

The Years of My Day

Flying

The Glacier Bay flight was only my most recent experience in "the great blue yonder." In France in 1918 we were stationed near airfields on at least three different occasions so I had the opportunity of seeing a great deal of aerial activity including several combat actions. On Sunday afternoons, or at other times when not otherwise engaged, we would hang around with the fliers hoping for an invitation to go out on an observation or a practice flight. Some of the fellows managed to get out with British or French fliers but I never did. When at Sens one morning while we were having breakfast a Polish pilot in training at the nearby French field crashed his old biplane trainer just outside our door and died before we could get medical aid to him. I lost some of my enthusiasm for flying.

However, when in Washington one day, on National Park Service business, I went over to what was "Hoover Field" alongside the Potomac River and bought myself a half-hour's sightseeing flight over the city. It was my first visit to the capitol and I was curious to see it from the air, but it was mainly a desire for the experience of flying that hooked me.

In 1924 airplanes had not improved much over the Jennies, Sopworths, and Spads of the war years.

This was a Fairchild monoplane with wings hinged to fold back along the fuselage for ease in storage. The leading edge of the wing was attached to the airframe with an ordinary barndoor hasp and staple secured by an ordinary padlock. This device was just beside my right foot as I sat beside the pilot, and all during the flight it jiggled violently. I think I spent more time watching that padlock than I did looking at the capitol, the white house, and Washington's soaring monument. I could well imagine what would happen if that little padlock jarred loose and that wing folded back.

Floyd Schmoe

Twice I have flown through violent electric storms, once over Missouri and again in the vicinity of Mt. Kilimanjaro in east Africa. Lightning appeared to surround the plane with its forked tongues and even the air inside the cabin seemed to be charged with high voltage electricity. Both times were at night, which added to the drama.

In such situations I am reminded of a story Ruthanna told when she was flying as a stewardess with United. On a dark night a starboard engine flamed out and had to be shut down. A couple of nuns were sitting on that side and one had her face glued to the window peering intently at the crippled engine.

Her companion asked, "What do you see out there?"

The answer was, "Three Ave Maria's and a Te Deum."

My first overseas flight was in October of 1946. I was trying to get permission to enter Japan for the Houses for Hiroshima project and when it was not forthcoming I applied to the University of Hawaii for a teaching assignment. Dr. Harold St. John, head of the Botany Department, wired me that he had an opening for an instructor, if I wanted to come immediately.

Ken, Ruth and I were building a small brick house on East 135th Street which we had already sold and had to finish. However it was almost finished and Ruth and Ken could make out. I looked for passage but no seats were available. Then I got word that the Matson Steamship Company was applying for permission to open an air service to Hawaii and were making a test run within a day or two. If I flew down to San Francisco I might get out with them.

They had borrowed an old DC-4 transport from the Army and were taking crew members only, but they finally consented to allow me to go along. It took most of the day and the "bucket seats" were far from comfortable. The male crew members and a number of the stewardesses were playing cards most of the way, but I found little to do. However at sunset as we were nearing the islands, I witnessed the most spectacular cloud formation that I

The Years of My Day

have ever seen. We were flying at only about 10,000 feet and came into an area of thunderheads scattered a few miles apart over a wide area. The tall cumulus clouds stood like marble columns from far below to high above us as we flew in clear air between. Then the setting sun turned each into a pillar of shining gold. It was as though we were entering the "Pearly Gates."

It was 1953 before I first crossed the Pacific by air. Now we fly nonstop in nine or ten hours but on that first flight in an old Constellation we made three stops between Seattle and Seoul, and spent a total of twenty hours.

The weather was beautiful and the scenery along the rugged Alaskan coast was spectacular. In the vicinity of Mt. Fairweather all the mountain peaks were snow covered and broad glaciers extended from their summits clear down to the sea. Nearing Anchorage the huge mass of Mt. McKinley (Denali -ed.) loomed dead ahead.

We stopped briefly at Anchorage for refueling then took off down Cook Inlet racing the rising sun. We were still fairly low when we crossed directly above volcanic Augustine Island and looked down into the smoking crater. Crossing the base of the Alaskan peninsula we passed over Katmai National Monument with its Valley of 10,000 smokes. Most of the craters and steam vents have cooled during the years since 1912 when Mount Katmai exploded blowing several cubic miles of earth high into the sky and scattering dust and ash over practically all the North American Continent.

From the air the burned-out valley looked more like the dead surface of the moon than the raging inferno it once was.

Coming out over Bristol Bay we turned southwest along the north rim of the Aleutian Islands.

Several of the volcanoes were smoking and tall. Fuji-like Shishaldin sent a plume of white thousands of feet into the air.

Floyd Schmoe

We touched down at Shemya Air Force Base 1600 miles further out, then turned south for Tokyo.

An hour out of Shemya Captain Cox came into the cabin and I asked him if they would be contacting the Coast Guard weather ship on station "Papa," still some 500 miles to the south. He thought they would and I asked him if he would say "hello" for me to my friend, Engineering Officer Lieut. Robert Lee.

I had talked with Bob's wife Catherine the evening before and she told me to tell her husband, if I should see him in Tokyo, that they had a new baby daughter.

About half an hour later Captain Cox came back into the cabin and said, "We have Lee on the phone. Want to talk to him?"

The Coast Guard cutter was far below and not in sight, but Bob's voice came out of the void as if he were in the next room. He said he had been in the shower when the intercom blared, "Lieutenant Lee, report communications immediately." Fearing a possible emergency he rushed topside with only a towel around him. Later I did see him in Tokyo, fully dressed.

Soon we were over the green mountains of Hokkaido where, for some reason which I never learned, a flight of Japanese jet fighters joined us and escorted us into Tokyo's Haneda Airport. Tomiko was there to meet me and the next evening I went on to Korea – however, we never saw the place on that flight.

At that time Kimpo Airport near Seoul was not lighted and had no ground control. A violent thunderstorm was raging and after circling the airport for an hour without making contact we returned to Tokyo.

Flying out of Korea a month later I spent an even more hectic night.

UNKRA, the United Nations agency which financed our work in Korea, had their headquarters in Pusan at the southern tip of the peninsula, and being there on business I arranged with Air CAT (Civilian Air Transportation) to fly from Pusan to Iwakuni – an

The Years of My Day

American Air Force base near Hiroshima. The plane was to leave at 6pm, or 1800 their time.

I went to the airport in time and was not thrilled to observe that the only aircraft on the field was a dilapidated C-37, undoubtedly one of Claire Chennault's fleet of reclaimed "Flying Tigers" which I had seen, flat tired and rusting, on the Hong Kong airstrip a year before. There was no sign of a crew.

About 7pm a jeep dashed up in a cloud of dust and four people sprawled out.

The American Pilot and American Co-pilot had both taken on more liquor than they could carry. The Korean purser looked scared, and the Japanese stewardess was flippant and slaphappy. I was the only passenger.

After considerable stalling I was permitted to board and we taxied to the end of the runway.

Again a delay. It was dusk by now but still very humid and hot and the cabin of the plane was like an oven.

Finally the engines were revved up and we started to roll. Just then a blue military police jeep roared out onto the field and blocked our take-off.

The purser, who didn't speak English, appeared more frightened, and the Japanese stewardess, who spoke little English, did not know what the trouble was. The pilots did not leave the cockpit, but argued with, and cursed the police out an open window. Finally the pilot left the plane, with engines still running, and went with the police.

It was after ten o'clock before we finally got off.

Although I was in a poor frame of mind to enjoy it, the two hour flight was quite pleasant. The stewardess went to sleep and the purser went forward. For an hour the sea of Japan was black below us until the lights of Japanese cities began to appear. We crossed over Shimonoseki, the gateway to Japan's inland sea, then followed the southern coastline of Honshu to Iwakuni. I was

Floyd Schmoe

fascinated by the unbroken chain of lights which fringed the coast in an unending lacery for the entire distance. It was like a closeup view of the Milky Way.

It was after one o'clock when we reached Iwakuni. The last train had left for Hiroshima, and the only waiting room was a barren barracks with no place to pie down and nothing to eat. The flight crew had disappeared and the station master, if there was a station master, was nowhere in sight.

I caught the first train out at 6:00 am.

On the flight home from Tokyo that Summer I retraced the "great circle" route with but one memorable incident. Shemya was a bare rock of the Semichi Island group a few miles east of the 3,000 foot crest of craggy Attu, westernmost of the American Aleutians; until the Army flattened it to a single runway only a few feet above sea level.

As we approached Shemya for our first service stop I saw that only the tip of Attu stood out like an island in an otherwise unbroken sea of clouds. No other land as in sight. With ground control, and, I hoped, an abundant store of experience and good judgement, our pilot plowed a furrow in the upper surface of the fog bank directly over the runway a few hundred feet below, then pulled up and circled for a landing approach.

Returning we entered the cloud and in a moment touched down. So dense was the fog that I did not see the runway until we touched it and I was looking intently. Later, talking with one of the ground crew about the problem, he said, "Oh, we always bring them in...we have to. There's no place else to go." Then he added, "we don't always bring 'em in right side up, but we bring 'em in."

Beginning with that 1953 crossing, I have flown the Pacific some 20 times and have always been able to sleep peaceably most of the time.

Once I flew back from Tokyo by way of Wake Island and Honolulu. That is a long flight, even by modern jet, and the only

The Years of My Day

memorable incident I recall was the approach to Wake, which first appeared far below as a tiny atoll of three islets enclosing a lagoon of the bluest water I have ever seen.

While other passengers were drinking coffee and liquors in Pan Am's Quonset hut, I walked to the beach and sat meditating on the awful carnage which had taken place during the recent war on these now so silent and peaceful shores. While the air base was being constructed, the Japanese navy and air force, on their return from Pearl Harbor, launched a violent attack which the Americans withstood, but with heavy loss of life. On December 23, 1941, after prolonged bombing and shelling, the Japanese succeeded in landing an attack force of more than 1,000 men, and Commander W. S. Cunningham, U.S.N. was forced to surrender. Some 1,600 surviving American Marines were taken prisoner and shipped off to China and Japan. The Japanese then fortified the island and it was not recaptured until Sep. 4, 1945, almost at the end of the war.

The beach was still littered with the wreckage of war and I was sitting the rusted hulk of a Japanese landing craft.

The hour passed before I knew it and I would have missed my flight except that a steward came in a Jeep looking for me.

Floyd Schmoe
Unfinished Business

Although in the more than four score years that have been mine, I have accomplished far more than I ever dreamed in my youth, there are many things which I wish I might still be able to do, and several that I feel that I must, if possible, accomplish.

For my many mistakes I must take full blame (unless ignorance is a valid excuse); but for my "good deeds" I must surely share credit with many people.

First my father and mother who, though they may have lacked in skill and experience, never faltered in concern and love. Mother was deeply religious and held an unfailing trust in Divine guidance. I'm sure her prayers for the blessings of God on her son were heard in Heaven long before I was born, and continued until the day of her death. She believed firmly in teaching and even more in the importance of example.

Sometimes her teaching – hours of bible study on a Sunday afternoon when all the other children were skating or playing baseball – was more than I could probably absorb, but it has paid dividends in later years. And an example she set of kindness, honesty, industry, and concern was unfailing both in the home and in the wider community.

Father was not religious. He only tolerated the forms and trappings of religion, though he held to the basic principles of honesty, decency, and fair play. He went along with mom largely out of respect and love for her; and later in life he did turn more toward the life of the spirit. He supported Mom wholeheartedly in her concern for and the guidance of their children.

Mom, I believe, though she loved us equally, held special, secret wishes for me. She encouraged my small talents at art, my love of nature, and my urge for learning. She hoped that I might become a minister, or a missionary, or at least a teacher. I never

The Years of My Day

shared any of these hopes, and though I did at last enter the teaching profession I drifted into it more by chance than by intent.

It was my ambition to be a big game hunter, an explorer, and an adventurer. This was when I read Teddy Roosevelt's stories of Africa and the Amazon, Robert Perry's conquest of the Arctic, and Vilhjalmur Stefansson's life with the Eskimo.

Later, after reading John Muir, John Burroughs, Henry Thoreau, and Ernest Thompson Seton, I was convinced that I should be a naturalist.

When I met Ruth Pickering, while still in high school, I knew almost immediately that I had found a kindred soul. Though deeply involved in her study of the piano she still had room in her heart for love and beauty wherever she found it, and that she found something she loved and appreciated in me was a blessing for which I shall always be grateful.

Through Ruth it was that my third great treasure could come into being – our children, our grandchildren, and now already our great grandchildren.

There have been many others as well; teacher, neighbors, friends, even some chance acquaintances, and of course the great souls of history who, though I never saw or knew them in person, have had powerful influence on my thinking and my life. Some, like Jesus of Nazareth, who perhaps never even learned to write, taught profound truth and a livable philosophy, Plato and Aristotle who taught and wrote, and the wonderful Francis of Assisi who lived his simple way of love and compassion for even the birds and the beasts as well as for his fellow man.

Artists; the unknown Egyptian and Greek sculptors, the great medieval and Renaissance painters and sculptors. Michelangelo, da Vinci, Goya, Van Dyck.

And of course the great men and women of recent days, some of whom it has been my good fortune to know.

Floyd Schmoe

I have spent many happy hours in The Louvre, the Metropolitan, London's Royal Gallery, and many other museums, absorbing the beauty of their creations. The most compelling reason I have for a visit to the Soviet Union would be to see the great hermitage of Leningrad. I levied for several months near the Luxembourg Gallery in Paris, where there were at that time some of the most exquisite marbles I know. I dropped by frequently and never tired of seeing them.

Poetry, although it was mom's favorite art form, never quite captured me, although I find that a few of the great poems speak to me. Bryant's Thanatopsis, quoted in part earlier, and Burns' To A Mouse, though at opposite ends of the spectrum, are my two favorite poems. However the first poem which really gripped me, aside from the 23rd Psalm, was Scott's Lady Of The Lake, and that was because when we built the new house on the Davis place about 1900, Dad, at Mom's urging, no doubt, extended himself to the extent that the door purchase for the front entrance bore a long pane of glass on which was etched a reproduction of the famous painting by Sir Edwin Landseer, "A Stag At Bay," and Mom read Sir Walter's poem to me. I have no ability at writing poetry myself, though I have felt flattered when some reviewers have labeled bits of my prose "poetic."

My proudest accomplishment, aside from our children, has been my books. None have yet approached the levels of sensitivity and excellence I admire in Burroughs' *Wake Robin*, or Thoreau's *Walden*, or even the intimacy with the wilderness which Ernest Thompson Seton displayed in his stories of birds and animals. It was an early edition of Seton's Lives of The Hunted, given me by my boyhood companion "Spider" Jones, that most inspired me not only to observe but to write of the wilderness world.

More like Thoreau and less like his friend and neighbor Ralph Waldo Emerson, I am inclined to write of actual experience in the wild than of my philosophies derived from that experience.

The Years of My Day

Certainly Henry was capable of sensing and expressing the deeper implications of life as amply demonstrated in his *Walden*. And it is my ambition to obtain to something of that mastery.

I have attempted it only in my book *What Is Man*, and a sequel I am at present writing and which may be called *Why Is Man*.

My first published book, which was also my most ambitious undertaking, was the result of my preparation for my job as park naturalist on Mount Rainier National Park. It is titled *Our Greatest Mountain* and was published by G.P. Putnam's Sons, New York, in 1925. Stephen Mather, first director of the National Park Service, wrote an introduction to it.

I had lived and worked on the mountain as guide, Park Ranger, and Park Naturalist for only a few years and much of the material was taken from previous studies already in print. However it has all been verified and assimilated through my own observations and experience.

In it I made perhaps one real contribution to the enjoyment of nature in that I classified the alpine flora according to association, color, and sight, rather than by the elaborate and highly technical keys employed by professional botanists. This made identification easy even for amateurs.

I wrote the 350 page book largely during the winter of 1924-25, often with baby Esther on my lap. Four feet of snow surrounded our Longmire Springs house that winter and there was little else to be done. Occasionally I was called out to repair a down telephone line, search for an overdue snowshoer, or shovel snow off the roof, but mostly my time was my own.

During publication the following year I had occasion to become quite well acquainted with George Palmer Putnam, the President of the publishing house that had been established by his father and brothers. Later he was to become better known during the tragic experience of his second wife Amelia Earhart. The fruitless search for her and her navigator, who were lost on a

Floyd Schmoe

round-the-world flight in 1937, brought financial ruin both to Mr. Putnam and his publishing company.

In 1925 Putnam lived with his first wife, a sister of the famous oceanographer William Beebe, in a luxurious New York apartment overlooking Central Park, where I was entertained one evening at dinner. This I believe was one of only two times that I have been served dinner by a liveried butler. G.P. also took me to a meeting of the Explorers Club where it was my pleasure to meet such famous men as Carl Akeley, African explorer and taxidermist of the American Museum of Natural History, Roy Chapman Andrews, who discovered Dinosaur eggs in the Gobi Desert of China, and Peter Frauchen, the Arctic explorer who amputated part of his own frozen foot while on a crossing of the Greenland Glacier.

Putnam also published my second book, *Frozen In*, in 1930.

The company had a series of "Boys Books by Boys," which had grown from the publication of the story by his own son, David Binney Putnam, who had gone on the Arcturus Voyage of his uncle Wiliam Beebe. David later accompanied two arctic expeditions, partly finance by his father, which resulted in the books, "David Goes to Greenland," and, "David Goes to Baffin Land."

The series also included two books by Bradford Washburn, who is now Director of the Boston Museum and famous as a mountaineer. Also included is a book by Paul Sipe, the Boy Scout chosen to accompany Admiral Richard E. Bird on his 1934 expedition to explore the Antarctic continent.

In 1929 a 13 year-old Seattle boy named Clarke Crichton signed on the trading schooner Nanuk as a cabin boy. On the same voyage 16 year-old Marion Swenson, daughter of the owner, was to go along just for the fun of it. Swenson traded in furs along the Arctic coast of Siberia and this voyage was planned to require only four months time. Actually the vessel was away more than a year, and two men lost their lives in the adventure.

The Years of My Day

That summer the ice closed in early off the North Cape, and the Nanuk, along with a Russian freighter, the S.S. Stavropol, were frozen in for the long Arctic winter.

However, because of the two youngsters who should be in school, and the value of the cargo, Mr. Swenson chartered a plane out of Nome, Alaska, to bring Clarke and his daughter, along with some of the most valuable furs, off the stranded vessel.

The first flight, with Arctic bush pilot Frank Dorbondt at the controls of his ski equipped monoplane, was successful, and Clarke, along with a few bales of Arctic furs, were safely landed at Nome, 500 miles away. Marion elected to remain with her father and await a later flight.

On the flight out of Teller a few days later, Carl Ben Eielson, Chief Pilot and General Manager of Alaska Airways, with his mechanic Earl Borland, ran into a blizzard over Siberia, were diverted from their course and lost. This was on the morning of November 9, 1929.

There followed a three month search in which dog teams from the Nanuk and Stavropol, many native, and flyers from three nations became involved.

On January 25, 1930, the wreck of Eielson's Hamilton monoplane was discovered some ten miles inland and 80 miles to the west of the stranded Nanuk. The wreck was buried deep in frozen snow and it required weeks of digging to find the bodies of the two airmen who had been thrown more than 100 feet from the plane. Apparently they had flown full speed into the earth and during an arctic white-out and had died instantly.

Of course all this made daily headlines in Seattle newspapers and I had followed the story with interest and concern.

When the 13 year-old boy, Clarke Crichton, Jr. arrived home in Seattle just in time for Thanksgiving (1929) his picture was on the front page of the Seattle Post-Intelligencer along with a story of his

Floyd Schmoe

six-month adventure and news of the still unsuccessful search for the missing flyers. I sent the clippings to George Putnam suggesting that it would make a good book in his series.

He wrote back immediately, saying, "Get the story."

I was only teaching half-time at the college of forestry then, so I had leisure to do free-lance writing. I was able to locate Clarke easily and found him living with his mother nearby the campus. He was quite willing to cooperate but before we had actually begun to put the story together Putnam sent a telegram saying, "Marion Swenson doing story of Nanuk adventure, stop. Essential we beat her to publication, stop. When can you get manuscript to us?"

The wire arrived on a Sunday. On Monday I hired a stenographer, took Clarke out of school, and we sent he book to New York on the following Saturday.

Clarke and I talked and compared notes each morning. I dictated during the afternoon. Next morning we went through the story, rewriting and adding to it. There was quite a lot of research to be done, especially on the geography of the area and the people involved. Clarke was not of much help there. He did not remember names or places. It had all been a wilderness of snow and ice to him. He had only a few snapshots of himself and the ship. He had no real concept of the geography of the area.

Fortunately Ruth's sister, Rachel Chance, and her family were living and working at the time in arctic Alaska and they had written long letters telling of their surroundings and the life of the native people. They were on Kotzube Sound some 600 miles to the east but in the same latitude and in a similar climatic zone.

Also the native Alaskan and the Chukchi of Siberia are similar and closely related people, so I already felt quite familiar with the area and the manner of life of its people.

I was pleased when Putnam had the story checked by Harold McCracken of the American Museum of Natural History, and he found not a single change to suggest. Dr. McCracken was

The Years of My Day

biologist who had been in the area that same summer on a study of walrus and knew the Siberian Arctic well. The check cost me $100.00 but I felt well satisfied.

I also felt satisfaction in being able to do a 40,000 word book in six days and have it published by an internationally known publishing house. The book remained in print longer than any of my other books, and perhaps paid better, even though I split the royalties with Clarke. My final royalties check came from Putnam's London branch more than ten years after publication.

I was not satisfied that Putnam gave me no credit in the book. It should have been titled, *Frozen In*, by Clarke Crichton, Jr. as told to Floyd Schmoe," for Clarke did not write a single word of the manuscript. However it is likely that David Putnam, Deric Nusbaum, and the other young authors of the series had a lot of help from their fathers and mothers also.

The only place my name appears in the book is on the map, which I drew, and which was used as end papers.

My picture appears on page 85 with a sled dog, a picture posed in Paradise Valley. Some of the pictures of Clarke were also "faked" on the Wowona, a sister ship that laid up on Lake Union, and at Sand Point Naval Air Station where we found planes similar to those used in the rescue.

Recently (1978) a story of the Nanuk adventure was written by Robert J. Gleason, and published by Alaska Northwest Publishing of Anchorage. Gleason was a wireless operator on the Nanuk, a good friend of Clarke and Marion, and the hub of all communication during the long hunt for the flyers.

It pleases me that Gleason's book, titled, *Icebound in The Siberian Arctic*, does not differ in any material way from our story written almost 50 years earlier.

He is fortunate in having "been there" and having diaries, ships logs, and many splendid photographs, none of which I had.

Floyd Schmoe

My next book was *Wilderness Tales*, a small volume of nature stories and original drawings, published in the same year (1930) by the University of Washington.

While still Naturalist with the National Park Service I had written and illustrated a weekly column titled *Nature Notes*, which was published by the Stockton (California) *Record*.

Now at the university with time to spare, though I was carrying on the program of the Academy of Science, as well as working toward my Master's Degree, I gathered about 50 of the best of these essays for this little book, and the following year made a collection of those *Nature Notes* which dealt with plants rather than animals. This I published under the title, *Cattails and Pussywillows*.

Both volumes, though they barely paid their way, have since become "Collector's items," and may well become worthy of a new edition at some future time.

Things got more involved in the latter half of the 1930s; my teaching was occupying more of my time, we were building the big house, and the children were growing up. Also the Second World War loomed closer and closer and my involvement with the American Friends Meeting and the American Friends Service Committee was taking more and more of my time and energy. I did not attempt another book until after the war.

With the completion of the Sinai "Wells For Egypt" project in 1958 Ruth and I felt it was time to retire, or at least "shift gears" from public service to catch up on some of the things "left undone." She wanted to take up weaving and I wanted to spend more time writing. We had also sold the "big house" since three of the four children had married and gone to homes of their own, and 14 rooms were a bit more than we required or cared to maintain.

The extra space had been well used during the war years, however, providing shelter for Japanese students and many visitors. At one time, so many refugees from the War Relocation

The Years of My Day

Centers, and the Civilian Public Service Camps were around that there was seldom a time when I did not harbor an extended family. Our own children had made such people feel so welcome that sometimes they even dropped in unannounced. I remember that one Sunday morning we woke up to find 16 extra people for breakfast, all of whom had arrived after Ruth and I had retired on Saturday night.

But in 1958 the war was over and we had done what we could to help pick up the pieces, so when I came home from Africa that Autumn I sat down to write some of my adventures. I was to title my first volume, as I believe I have written earlier, *From Walking To and Fro Upon the Earth*.

In the book of Job, chapter 2, verse 2, the Lord asks Satan, "From whence cometh thou?" And Satan answered the Lord and said, "From walking to and fro upon the Earth, and from walking up and down in it."

Then, as you remember, the wily old devil, admitting that he knew of poor Job's problems, proceeded to bad-mouth him still further.

Even though I had never had such poor relations with the devil I still thought the quote would make a good title for my book, and perhaps I may yet use it.

However, the book that resulted was limited to, *A Year in Paradise*, which Harper and Brothers, in New York, published in 1959. The book has this year (1979) been reissued by the Seattle Mountaineers Press, in a fourth edition.

My Masters Degree was taken in marine biology, a subject I had found of increasing interest after moving back to the Puget sound area, and the San Juan Islands in the upper Puget Sound had appealed to me as the ideal setting for a story of popular interest on local marine life.

Floyd Schmoe

So during the next year we built the "Sea Monster," with its window on the deep side. I wrote the story, and labeled the manuscript, *Houseboat With a Basement*.

The book, also by Harper's, came out in 1964 under the title, *For Love of Some Islands*. It was edited, as was the Paradise book, by Elizabeth Lawrence, now Elizabeth Kalashnikoff of Deep River, Connecticut.

I think Elizabeth is responsible for the title, and I liked it on sight. The "basement" concept was good but limited to what could be observed from the "basement window," and the story had to be much more comprehensive than that. Life on shore and on the beaches, the marine birds and marine mammals, our experiences as a family afloat and as part of the marine community; and our adventures while diving below the surface and flying above it...none of this could be seen through the window and none could be left out. So, *Houseboat With a Basement* became the title of only one chapter, and *Love...* became the story.

The book presently in the works – *Peter Puget's Sound* - will be an expansion of the endless story of life on, in and around, this beautiful sea, of which Captain Geroge Vancouver, in May of 1792, drew a map and labeled it "Puget's Sound."

The Years of My Day

> ### A YEAR IN PARADISE
>
> In 1979 The Mountaineers Press published the fourth edition of my most popular book *A Year in Paradise*. Harper's had done two editions in hard cover in 1959 – 60 which sold well and brought favorable comment from the reviewers and its readers. William O. Douglas, Hal Borland, Donald Peattie and others did splendid reviews in national periodicals, but Harper's decided not to keep it in print.
>
> In 1968 Charles E. Tuttle Co. did a third edition in both hardcover and paperback which sold out in three seasons.
>
> Due to the careful editing of Elizabeth Lawrence of Harper's the book had few errors and most of these were caught in the second printing. However, one glaring typo on the very first page survived all three editions; Rainier spelled Ranier.
>
> The Mountaineer edition corrected that.
>
> So my favorite book has finally grown up and I hope it will have a long life.

Books

My next book proved to be the most difficult to date. All the others had been on subjects with which I had enjoyed considerable contact and had already a considerable store of knowledge. In fact they were pre-mix concoctions, but *The Big Sur* had to be created from scratch.

We had driven California Route 1 south from Monterey to San Luis Obispo a couple of times and had been greatly impressed by the grandeur of the setting, but I knew little of the detail which comprised the scene.

Buz Wyeth, a distant cousin of the three generations of painters by that name, had succeeded Elizabeth Lawrence as

Floyd Schmoe

Managing Editor of Harper's (now Harper and Rowe) and I suggested two titles to him; one a story of Puget Sound which would be an extension of the San Juan story, and the other an ecological study of the Big Sur, with the small colony of sea otter resident there as the central attraction.

Buz opted for the Big Sur and otter, so Ruth and I planned a visit to the area.

We realized that there was much that was unfamiliar to us and the book would require a great deal of research, but I thought we could do it in a couple of years.

I proposed to title the story, *The Big South Country*, since that would be a literal translation of the hybrid Spanish name.

Actually, as it turned out, the area was a richer mine of jewels than we had imagined and the deeper we dug the richer the lode turned out to be. It was almost ten years from our first visit to publication of *The Big Sur; Land of Rare Treasures*, and Ruth would not live to see the finished product.

I have earlier mentioned our first summer when we lived in the charming Partington Ridge cabin of Dryden and Margaret Phelps. The following summer we borrowed a trailer-camper and, at the invitation of Bob Freeman, then the supervisor of the Julia Pfeiffer Burns State Park, made our headquarters beside the Range Station which was perched on the very rim of the little cauldron-like, near-landlocked bay which I call Waterfall Cove in the book.

Around our camp grew young California laurel trees whose spicy odor added flavor to the moist sea air, and between our tent and the ranger station was Bob's pile of fireplace wood in which lived a family of friendly pack rats.

The firewood was also laurel – called myrtle in Oregon – which provided me with an ample supply of whittling material of the rarest sort.

Ken and John Carson accompanied us on this trip and their rock climbing and scuba diving abilities aided our exploration.

The Years of My Day

    Together Ruth and I made at least a dozen visits to the area, managing to be there for a week or two during each season of the year.

    I had gone alone in the winter of 1969 because of Ruth's illness and the trip was cut short by her sudden death.

    In August of 1971 Tomiko and I bought a self-contained motor camper and drove to yearly meeting at St, Mary's College. After the sessions we went on to the Big Sur for a couple of weeks, where during delightful weather we, on a combined honeymoon and field trip, completed my research for the book. However, along with editing and rewrite, it did not reach publication until the Spring of 1975, and then not by Harper's but by Chronicle Books of San Francisco.

    Chronicle Books, a subsidiary of the *San Francisco Daily Chronicle*, are publishing a series of similar books featuring west coast regions, and have expressed interest in my book on Puget Sound.

    Since I was not satisfied with their sales efforts with the Big Sur book, I have given an option on the Puget Sound book to the Seattle Mountaineers Press. It is my hope also that they will undertake a reprint of the San Juan book.

    The Puget Sound story will take much less effort than the Big Sur story did. I have known the Sound country for sixty years and still live on its shores. I did much of the work for my master's degree in the San Juan Islands, and for several years the family spent each summer cruising Puget Sound waters in our LINDA. With Bill or Ken I have covered it all at low altitudes by plane and have spent many hours below its surface in scuba gear or my underwater observation post on Minnesota Reef. The problem is largely one of making the ecology of the area come alive for others. This will be done not only in words but in pictures, both photographs and pencil sketches.

Floyd Schmoe

There are some things which cannot be photographed. The ancient glaciers and the ancient men and animals most notably. Tomiko and I have however come close to these scenes of the "long past." I, by last summer's aerial survey of Glacier Bay, Alaska, which just now is re-enacting the history of Puget sound glaciation of 10,000 years ago, and our recent visit to the mastodon dig at Sequim, Washington, where the remains of ancient elephants, and artifacts of ancient people are being unearthed. I have also examined a number of ancient kitchen middens along the shores of the Sound. These are the "garbage dumps" of the first "Puget Sounders," men whose ancestry came across the Bering land bridge (which in Miocene times connected America and Asia), then moved southward with the caribou, the musk oxen, the mammoths and the mastodons, as the ice melted and vegetation reclaimed the land.

From a painting by C.R. Knight, Chicago Museum

Scratches from the mastodon bones found at Sequim, and flint tools associated with them, are good evidence that these men either killed the giant beasts or finding them mired in a giant swamp, salvaged the flesh and carried it to their camp (which was likely only a mile or so away on the shores of Sequim Bay).

Some years ago in a midden on the west shore of Similk Bay, a few miles to the east, I found a beautiful arrow point of snow

The Years of My Day

white quartz. The point was broken, either during its manufacture or use, and it had been discarded just as we toss our worn out or broken tools and utensils into our trash piles.

Most of the garbage of these ancient people is more recent than the prehistoric elephants, but the fact that a bone spearhead was found embedded in a rib bone of a Sequim mastodon proves that men did dwell on these shores that long ago.

The second book I presently have underway is a sequel to *What is Man* that seeks answers the age-old question; What is man's Destiny? It may be titled *Why Is Man?*

Of course I know there is no definitive answer to the question though many people have proposed answers.

Or, perhaps we should say, there are many answers but no great agreement on any one answer.

Still it is a legitimate question which no doubt every thinking person has at one time or another asked of himself, if not of others. It is my purpose to find as many of these answers as I can and from them, and from my own inner search, formulate an answer which, at the moment, satisfies me. (I say, "at the moment," because it is more than likely that even after I have reached some conclusions the question will persist and other, perhaps better, answers will later evolve.)

It is recorded in the Bible that Job (chapter 7, verse 17) asked the question, "What is man?" perhaps more of himself than of others, and it is also recorded in the Bible (Genesis 1, 28) that God created man and admonished him to "be fruitful and multiply, and replenish the earth, and subdue it, and have dominion over...everything that moveth upon the earth."

This would seem to be a direct order from the creator and answer enough, even for Job, as to why man was created and what his job was to be.

It does not appear, however, that this answer satisfied Job and it does not satisfy me.

Floyd Schmoe

It depends entirely upon how you define dominion. If by dominion God meant concern for, and loving care of, "all the beasts of the field, the birds of the air, the fishes of the sea, and all creeping things," that is good enough, but that is not the way man has defined it.

Man, since he became man, has assumed a superior attitude toward his fellow creatures and has used them as he saw fit. He has enslaved, abused, destroyed, tormented and killed (even for his amusement) millions of sensitive and intelligent animals which he has considered "lower" than himself. Today, as the greatest predator Earth has ever known, he actually breeds animals that he might then kill and devour them by the millions each day, though God in the same breath that he gave "dominion" also said, "I have given you every herb bearing seed, which is upon the face the Earth, and every tree, in which is the fruit of a tree yielding seed, to you it shall be for meat." (King James version.)

For me to preach this "gospel," when at best I am a vegetarian only between meals, as many people are pacifists only between wars, is, I know, hypocrisy.

My problem and my excuse is that I have never lived in a family or a society of vegetarians, and I have never felt free to inconvenience others, even my wife, with my "fads and fancies." I remember my mom once said, "If I knew how to make good gravy out of potatoes I would be a vegetarian."

My objection to the use of animal products as food or clothing stems entirely for moral rather than dietary reasons, and I think it had its beginnings in my horror, as a small child, of the slaughter of domestic animals on the farm.

Mom did not like it either and for that reason she asked me to kill the chicken, which at least once a week, we were to have for dinner. To catch it fighting and screaming for its life, to chop off the head and see the blood spurt, then to watch its dying struggle in the blood-spattered snow, literally made me sick.

The Years of My Day

Although, like most farm boys, I liked to hunt rabbits and squirrels, and to catch fish, I never enjoyed seeing them die, and I came to view the entire livestock industry as cruel and repulsive. Male hogs had to be castrated, and I had to hold them while Dad slashed away, and they struggled and squealed in agony. Cattle had to be de-horned, branded and dipped in stinking chemicals. Even the little lambs had to have their tails cropped, and some people cropped their horse's tails.

I liked meat, and I still do. And I am sure it provides good food for the human body. Even human meat would be good food for humans and there have been many men among our ancestors who enjoyed it. I never met a cannibal, but I once knew the son of a cannibal and he was a nice fellow with a college education.

It is not the eating. It is the killing. And for that reason I now deplore all hunting and trapping as well. Still I find it impossible (or inconvenient) to be consistent in the practice of what I preach. I still use milk and eggs, and wear leather shoes freely. We have spent at least two million years developing a carnivorous society. I doubt if any of us could change it in our lifetime, but I do look forward to enlightenment (perhaps within a thousand years).

Actually, the entire population of Earth could live well, even better, in today's world, without meat, and milk, and eggs, and leather. There are adequate, often superior substitutes for all of them, and they are cheaper. The acre of grass that produces the pound of beef, that feeds a man less than a week could, if properly cultivated, produce enough vegetable food to feed that same man a month, and most likely he would live longer.

All that is grist for another book, which I may or may not write, but which, if I do write it, I will title, *God's Mistake*.

The mistake obviously is noted in the same first chapter of Genesis where it says, "Let us give man dominion over…"

I'm not God, but I believe I would have said, "And let man share Earth with all other men and with all his fellow creatures." I

Floyd Schmoe

believe my good friend Francis of Assisi would have said the same thing also.

There is another matter – now that I am in the mood to criticize the creator – another thing that I would have done differently.

I would have made some basic changes in the structure of man himself. Certainly he is not the most perfect thing imaginable. Many birds and animals, even many insects, are superior to man in many respects. Some are more graceful, some more brilliant, many are stronger or run faster, or swim better. Man, like my Oxford friend, can swim a little, but he can't fly at all. I resent that. I'd love to be able to fly like a bird.

There are some animals that even live longer than man, and many that have fewer diseases and bad habits. I know of no animal that habitually destroys itself with drugs, which spends more effort (or represented by money) on weapons of destruction than upon the means of health and education, or that enslaves other animals and uses them for its own pleasure and profit.

Even the human body could stand some improvement. It is said that a renowned surgeon, when operating before a class at Columbia School of Medicine, opened the abdomen of a patient, exposed the diseased organs, shook his head and mumbled, "Any plumber could have done a better job."

Since the Creator had all power (otherwise he could not have invented life in the first place) why did he not make man like he made the flowering plants; to live for his season, to blossom and bear fruit, then simply without disease or pain to fade away and thereby enrich the soil that the next generation might "bear fruit more abundantly"? "It wad frae monie a blunder free us, a foolish notion." (Robert Burns)

Simply to look like a rose, and smell like a rose would save the female of our species billions of dollars and years of time. And

The Years of My Day

why does a rose have more right to beauty than does a man, or a woman?

Sex is another problem for mankind. Flowering plants invented sex and they still handle it far better than animals do. One problem was (and it's simply a matter of design) sex somehow got mixed up with the function of elimination, and what should sex, essential to reproduction, have to do with elimination, which simply a matter of garbage disposal?

Too bad, isn't it, that I was not consulted.

I know, of course, that writing books will not change the world. There may be many other writings that are more effective, but there is a job to be done. It will take the skills and efforts of all right thinking people and it will take time. Writing books may be my best contribution at the moment.

With all the evil things which man does, from dropping bombs on innocent people, to mass suicide in the name of religion, right down to the murder, rape, and dishonesty of simpler souls. There is cause for pessimism, and I am often pessimistic, though only for the short run...say a million years or so, I am optimistic.

I see both good and evil in the world and see man as involved in both. But good is creative and evil destructive, and construction dominates over destruction. In other words good is cumulative while evil fades away. It must be so, otherwise we would all still be savages. But it takes time and it takes effort. If I can do only a bit more good than bad, and my children can do it a bit more, given time...given time...

"...Thy will be done on Earth as it is in heaven." And, "given time" Earth will become heaven. It must, we have no other (at least so far as I can see).

Floyd Schmoe

Sunset and evening star, And one clear call for me!
And may there be no moaning at the bar,
When I put out to sea.
  Tennyson.

The Years of My Day

End Of The Journey

The final chapter of my story – a journal recounting the scenes and adventures encountered during this incredible journey – is yet to be written. On September 21 of next year, the year 1980, I will be 85 years of age. A number of my good friends and "fellow travelers" on this somewhat hazardous journey through life, have reached that milestone but few have traveled far beyond it.

My mother and father however each were given near five additional years of life and each lived it to the full. Mother reached the end quietly and in her own bed, on October 31st, 1954, at their retirement home near the Friends Meeting House in Newberg, Oregon. She had likely attended Meeting for worship on the previous Sunday. She was 98 years, 6 months old.

Father survived only a year and a few weeks longer. He died in the Newberg Hospital with his much-loved daughter-in-law, Tracy, as his nurse, on November 19, 1955. He was 90 years, and 5 days of age.

Mother's father, Jesse Moon, had died at age 70, and my father's father, Ernest Schmoe, was 72 when he passed away.

If, as a result of an easier life, better medical care and perhaps, better nutrition, my father and mother survived almost 20 years longer than their fathers, my generation can expect a similar bonus, then we may each expect to live to be more than 100 years of age. I'm afraid however that life expectancy may be subject to the laws of diminishing returns, so that even a five year gift of time, with each generation, would be as much or more than one could ask.

So if by God's love I am permitted to celebrate my 90th birthday, I will do so with joy and thanksgiving, and invite all my friends and family to share that joy, and if by the same grace I am permitted to 95 I feel sure that I shall be blessed enough. Beyond

Floyd Schmoe

that, even at our present stage of care and life support, I fear I may become more of a burden to myself and my family than a joy, and that is a situation I would deplore.

So (with the poet William Cullen Bryant) let me, when my "summons comes to join
The innumerable caravan which moves
To that mysterious realm, where each shall take
His chamber in the silent hills of death,"
I will go, "not like the quarry-slave at night
Scourged by his dungeon, but, sustained and soothed
By an unfaltering trust, approach" my "grave
Like one who wraps the draperies of his couch
About him, and lies down to pleasant dreams."

At this point may I permitted to outline my understanding of the human destiny as I, at present, somewhat dimly perceive it?

Life as we know it on Earth – and to date life is not known to man on any other planet of this vast universe – is an amazing and marvelous phenomenon, even to those of us who have experienced it. That the simple inorganic elements, many of them literally as common as the dirt we walk upon, the air we breathe, and the water we drink, could in some miraculous way, come (or be brought) together in such a manner that the combination would become (or be created) into a living organism – even a single living cell – with the capacity to grow and sustain, even to multiply and perpetuate itself, is a marvel beyond my understanding, or the understanding of even the most astute biologist I know.

I accept this gift of life with humility and thankfulness. Whether it is a gift of God or a gift of nature is to me of no concern, for, to me, nature is simply the Creator's **modus operandi** – his way of conducting the orchestra.

The Years of My Day

The human animal, man ("man," the word is a generic term, neither male nor female), then becomes only the top figure of the divine Totem Pole (life) which is in itself a rare work of art.

And as all works of art inherit and express much of the soul of the artist, so life inherits some of the divinity and some of the majesty of its divine creator.

And, to me, it follows, that if life itself is of the divine stuff, and man, being alive, has inherited something of this divinity, then *all* life is of the divine and divinely sacred. For life, of whatever form, is of the same stuff still.

Trained in the scientific school of today I like visible, tangible evidence of truth. Since I see no such evidence of a physical, corporeal, personal state of being, either on this Earth, or another, following life here, I neither believe nor disbelieve in a life after death.

Men love life and long for a continuation of life but it may be simply because of this longing and this hope that we have "invented" hope and expectations, and even images of such an immortality. I do not know, and I know of no one who knows, but I also hope, and I continue to seek evidence of that hope.

And I do find evidence, richly circumstantial if not empirical, that life is in its essence immortal, though all living things are patently mortal.

The real stuff of life (the divine spark which kindled the inorganic mass into a living organic creature) seems to be, like light, heat, electricity, or atomic radiation, a form of physical energy, and such forms of energy, we have discovered through the laws of physics, though they can change or be changed, even by such simple processes as filtration, into what appears to be entirely different forms (such as solar energy in the form of light changed into heat, or electricity) cannot be destroyed.

Then, it would appear, that the organic creature (man), like a burning coal, might appear to be consumed, but is actually only

Floyd Schmoe

transformed into another form of the same energy (in this case the burning coal, into heat or light or both) and in truth still exists....is in fact immortal.

This is, I submit, circumstantial evidence of the immortality of life (or if you like, the human soul) but there is more.

Nature is, in its fundamental principles, logical. Nothing comes from nothing, and something is not, and cannot, become nothing. What is *is*. Old Marcus Aurelius (121-180), though no physicist, knew that much.

Logically it would seem foolish, therefore unnatural, that any living organism – which even in its most primitive form is the product of millions of years of evolution – would be allowed to lose itself through death and decay.

One of the essential characteristics of life – of even the simplest living cell – is its ability to reproduce itself and thereby carry on its race. This is in itself a form of immortality, not for the individual but for the species. And it may well be that individual man, regardless of his desire for immortality as an individual, is, like the individual cell, expendable, though an essential step in the continued life of the race of mankind.

The cell dies but the tissue lives and grows. Individual man dies but the life he had becomes the matrix of life eternal. It is quite possible for the individual (much as longs to retain his individuality, to be known as he was known and to know others as they were known) to become, like dead tissue in plants, as enemy of growth, a deterrent to the evolution of the species.

So not knowing, and therefore not convinced, of my personal immortality, I am convinced and satisfied to accept the immortality of life. And whatever the plan, whether oblivion and total forgetfulness or "a more abundant life" in a better world time without end, I am convinced that it is good, and that to make some contribution to the greater good is the destiny of man.

The Years of My Day

I ask myself, as every man must himself, who is God? What is God?

It is an impossible question, useless to ask for no man has the answer. Still it should be asked by every man for upon the answers he builds his life.

In seeking my answers I listen to those of others. Mother taught us that God is love. The Bible tells us that God is Spirit, that God is light, the light that is the light of life. It refers to God as the Father, the father of mankind. These are not definitions. These are metaphors. A definition limits, and God cannot be limited. A metaphor, though it does not tell us what a thing is, it tells us what it is like unto.

George Fox once said: The Bible says this, the bishops say that, but what doth thou say?

I like to start with spirit, the spirit of love. Love is creative, and the greatest creation I know is life. Life is the one miracle that I see most clearly.

It may be boastful but I see mankind as the ultimate creature, the high mark of creation.

So then I have spirit, and I have light, and I have love, and I have life, and I have man...and none of these I call God.

But altogether they represent God. God is bigger still but my concept of God is not great enough to fathom that.

Mohammed, the prophet of Islam, said, "There is one God. Allah is God. There is no other." Perhaps his answer is as good as any.

Floyd Schmoe

The Last Chapter

Since this is the story of a life-long journey, which obviously is not over yet, it would appear that the "Last Chapter" must, necessarily, be written by another. This, therefore, is only the scenario of my "Last Chapter."

I have said that there is unfinished business, things I yet hope to do, and the "hope," the wish, may well father the act.

One of my Professors at Syracuse remarked in his retirement, "I have found that the way to keep from growing old is to always have something exciting to do tomorrow."

On this earth there is always so much to be done, so much to be seen, and so much to be learned, that I have no fear of running out of something exciting to do for all the 'tomorrows' that may yet remain.

There is a story of an old priest who at ninety years of age set out on a journey around the world. When a friend asked, "Father, why does one of your age wish to undertake such a journey?" He replied, "I do not have many years left to live on this earth, and when I go to heaven and the Good Lord says to me, "My son, what did you think of my little world down there?" I'd hate to have to reply, "I'm sorry, Lord, but I never really saw it."

This coming Summer Esther, and Rod, possibly Lil and Lori, and I are making plans for a week of leisurely cruising along the old canals of north England. I'd love to do the same some summer in Holland and France.

Rod and I plan to go by train north across Norway to the "land of the midnight sun," then south again across Sweden, Finland, and Denmark. By then I will have had glimpses, at least, of every European country. I have crossed Asia across its southern borders but there is still a vast interior and northern area little known to me. And I have never even touched South America.

The Years of My Day

First, however, I want to spend time among the islands of the southern Pacific and explore Indonesia. Australia has not appealed strongly to me though glimpses of the Great Barrier Reef and the vast "Out Back" would fascinate me.

New Zealand's spectacular southern "Alps" are without doubt of great beauty, as are the high Andes. I want to visit the legendary Vale of Kashmir, then being in the vicinity, I'd want to cross over the famed Khyber Pass, and get a glimpse of the high Himalayas from the back side. I'd fly up to Nepal also, where I have friends, and see Everest, the top of the world.

Actually there are many places much closer to home that I have not seen, and scores of places well known that I would love to see again.

I plan to visit the "old home place" at least once more, though few of the familiar sights, and fewer still of familiar faces, yet remain. Of Prairie Center, only the Quaker Meeting House still stands, and it is at some distance removed. The high wire fence which houses the Sunflower Ordinance Plant, present occupant of my birthplace, skirted the cemetery which remains the only familiar ground left.

I want to go canoeing again in the Ozarks and hunt arrowheads along the Neosho, though my old friend Spider Jones will be there only in memory.

I have given up hope of visiting Antarctica, though it's still possible, and a trip to the moon, which is still possible, is I'm sure beyond my means.

Some of my children or grandchildren will do it and I plan to watch them, via celestial TV from the comfort of my eternal home "over there."

There are many books to be finished – this and the Puget Sound story – and at least one more to write. *Why Is Man* may be my last, and I hope to make it my best.

The Years of My Day

Stories Forgotten or passed by along the way which now seem not to fit any other category or sequence and are therefore heaped together in the catch-all corner of the book

Floyd Schmoe
Rainier

During the two seasons I served as a guide on Mt. Rainier I made 14 summit climbs but never as head guide. Hans and Heinnie Further were the only summit guides at that time and the younger guides at that time went only as assistants.

The ascent of Rainier, though a long hard grind by any standard, is, during fair weather, only that, a long hard grind. We used the old Gibraltar Route those days, and although there was always the danger from falling rock as we made the traverse across the face of Gibraltar it was a danger that could not be avoided nor anticipated. We were lucky that no one was hurt (the following season, however, Hans did have a man killed by a falling rock from Gibraltar, and the search was begun for safer routes).

We left Paradise Inn usually early in the afternoon in order to complete the four or five hour climb to Camp Muir at the 10,000 foot mark before dark.

After a good meal and a few hours rest at Muir we would leave at about 2:00 am in order to reach the summit and return, if possible, soon after noon.

At 1:00 pm the sun would strike the face of Gibraltar and the ice would begin to melt. This would loosen the stones, which were our chief hazard.

I only had one real close call on the summit. Hans had taken about a dozen climbers that day and three assistant guides. The party was too large, and for that reason not only unsafe, but slow.

We had reached the summit late, and Hans was descending too fast. At about the 13,000 foot elevation, while crossing the steep snow dome above the area of open crevasses, someone near the end of the line slipped and slid under those in front. Soon the entire group were sliding toward a huge crevasse a few hundred feet below. Wes Langlow and I were anchoring at the end

The Years of My Day

of the rope. We dug in with our heels and our ice axes and the rope broke. We did not have the fine nylon ropes, as strong as steel, that are now available.

Wes and I simply sat there in horror as the mass of human beings slid and tumbled toward that open crevasse. There was nothing we could do to stop them.

Fortunately the upper lip of the crevasse – a bergschrund, more technically – flattened off, and at this shelf, by some miracle, the group piled and came to rest. (A bergschrund is a crevasse on a steep slope where the upper lip stands much higher than the lower, forming an ice cliff. In 1929 another guide, in a similar accident, lost a party in this same area. One guide and a member of the party died.) While Wes and I still sat on the snow 100 yards above, Hans stood up out of the tangle of bodies, ordered the others to their feet, and started off along the upper edge of the crevasse without looking back.

It was on a later trip that I gave Ruth a bad scare.

Coming down from a summit climb it was the duty of an assistant guide to remain behind at Camp Muir in order to fold and hang blankets, put cooking gear away, and tidy up the cabin for the next party of climbers.

On this trip we had a young girl of about 17 who became sick during the night and was left at Camp Muir. On our return she appeared recovered and joined the descending party.

It took me about an hour to set the camp in order. I then took off running and sliding down the Muir Snowfield in order to overtake the party which I could still see far below.

It was only by chance that I noticed something strange a hundred yards or so off the trail to my right and stopped to investigate. It was this girl lying in the snow unconscious. She had become ill again and fallen behind. Strangely she was not missed until the party arrived at Paradise Inn more than an hour later.

Floyd Schmoe

I was able to half-carry, half-drag her down the slope. Ruth, not knowing that I was to stay behind, had watched the party return and noticed that I was missing.

She started up the trail to find me and we met at the edge of the snowfield.

By then the girl had recovered enough to walk with Ruth and I on either side, and soon a rescue party came hurrying up to meet us. The girl's father gave me a ten dollar tip when the party left next day.

Tipping was not expected by the guides, but on one other occasion I was given a ten dollar bill. This time also I had earned it.

A wiry little grey haired English woman turned up at the Guide House one day, asked for the Chief Guide, and stated that she had come to climb Mount Rainier. Hans questioned her – she had climbed her whole life. She walked miles each day at home in England, a hike to the summit of Rainier posed no problems for her.

She admitted to being more than 70 years of age.

Mountain guides soon learn that there are some people who cannot be persuaded that some mountains may, just possibly, be unclimbable to them, so often we would send an extra guide along to return the climber from his point of surrender, or we would try to persuade them to try an easier climb first, "just to limber up." On the summit climb we would leave dropouts at Camp Muir, but if they insisted on going beyond that point and failed, either a guide had to return with them or the entire party had to abort, since there was no other place of safety. On more than one occasion summit guides have literally carried or dragged exhausted climbers the last few hundred yards to the crater rim rather than disappoint the other climbers.

Our little English lady, in spite of her years, (or perhaps because of them) was not to be dissuaded, so Hans suggested she

The Years of My Day

first climb our "miniature Matterhorn," Pinnacle Peak, "in order to get in shape for the longer ascent."

She finally agreed to this and I was assigned to be her guide.

We set out early in the day and she proved to be a delightful companion, and an amazingly strong climber as we crossed the canyon of the Paradise River, crossed Mazama Ridge, and made the long climb from Reflection Lake to the Pinnacle ice field.

Even after scaling the Pocket Glacier and Pinnacle, and a bit of lunch, she looked up at the sheer cliffs of the Pinnacle and said, "Shall we go?"

I have scaled Pinnacle at least 50 times, but I have never lost respect for that last 500 feet of rock. We roped up and I went ahead for a firm belay. She scrambled up like a teenager. Near the top, however, she showed signs of fatigue and I had to help her for the long reaches from one firm foothold to the next. I was below her pointing out each step and handhold. Sometimes she was literally in my arms as I helped place and hold her hands and feet.

We reached the top by noon and rested. I feared the descent more than I had the ascent, but we had to descend.

Again I was amazed as that little old lady scrambled down that rock. Of course I kept a firm anchor above but even a single misstep could have injured her severely.

When finally we returned to Paradise Valley we were both exhausted but proud of our success. She did not however mention a possible attempt on Rainier, and as she went down the next day she gave Hans a nice new ten, "For that lovely lad."

Floyd Schmoe

I was past seventy when I made my last ascent of Pinnacle Peak and, later on that same trip, managed to reach Camp Muir. Climbing did not seem that much more difficult that it had 40 years earlier, though it did take me twice as long as before. My good friend Julius Boehm "romped" up Rainier last year on his eightieth birthday and looks forward to another ascent on his eighty fifth.

Pinnacle Peak
The Castle (to left)

However, at eighty I feel more like the seventy-year-old enthusiast who once, on Rainier, said to me, "I'll climb any mountain. I don't care how high it is or how steep it is, just as long as my horse can get me up there."

***

Have I mentioned, that when I completed my year at the New York State College of Forestry we purchased a well-used Model T Ford of about 1917 vintage with the intent of driving cross-country to the job I had just secured as a National Park Ranger on Mount Rainier? I found it in the used car lot of the Nash Agency and the price tag was only 160 dollars.

The Years of My Day

We had nothing approaching $160.00 at the moment, and that was one of the reasons we decided to drive home; we could not afford rail travel. When I mentioned my good friend C.B. Voorhees to the dealer he let me have the car for a very small down payment.

The extent of my driving experience at the moment was a few hours behind the wheel of a Dodge truck when in France, and the extremely hazardous round trip from our hostel at 90 Bd. St. Michel in the unit's Ford ambulance (more hazardous for the push carts and pedestrians of Paris than for me) in order to pick up some new arrivals and their baggage at the Care du Norde.

However, a classmate, Al Cline, gave me hours of introduction to the vagaries of the Model T on the day we picked up the vehicle, and I found two other classmates who had appointments on Yellowstone National Park, as sharing passengers and alternate drivers.

With Ruth, 18-month-old Kenneth, and myself, along with all our baggage and camping gear, the poor car was grossly overloaded.

In addition, the first day out of Syracuse was extremely hot, and our tires none too youthful and, for such a day, overinflated. We had nine flats the first day and made it only as far as Rochester.

In 1937, in a new Desoto Airflow I drove from Seattle to Philadelphia in only four days and did all the driving myself. On this 1922 journey we spent 18 days, averaging about 20 miles per hour. As far as Yellowstone our passengers did nearly all the driving, and most of the tire patching. From there on to Seattle, Ruth, Ken, and I were on our own.

Most of the highway across western New York, Ohio, and into Chicago was macadam and known as "turnpikes." Through the southern fringes of Chicago and for perhaps 50 miles west we had pavement, and all the rest was dirt, or a form of dirt called mud, or

Floyd Schmoe

in places across Wyoming, *no road at all* but two rough tracks through the sagebrush.

It amazes me as I look back upon that journey that we did not have more trouble than we did, though we had enough so that the boys who left us at Yellowstone were happy to have arrived in one piece. In central Nebraska on a narrow dirt road recently graded to a ridge down the middle and a track on either side barely wide enough for the car, and sloping toward deep drainage ditches, then full of water from a heavy thunderstorm, I skidded the car rear end first into the right hand ditch, where we lay on our side deep in mud and water.

A nearby farmer allowed us to pitch camp in his front yard and to telephone a garage about ten miles away in Grand Island. I also, much to my embarrassment, had to send a telegram to Ruth's sister Bertha in Wichita and ask to borrow $50.00 to pay the tow and repair bill. Fortunately no one was hurt and little damage was done to the car.

One day in Wyoming we drove and pushed for ten hours and covered less than ten miles. The "gumbo" mud was a foot deep and so stiff that it piled up under the fenders until the wheels would not turn. And that night we were drenched with more rain and threatened by flood in a campground along the Yellowstone River.

The only other near accident we encountered was on the last afternoon of our trip. We had opted for the newly constructed Blewett Pass cut-off between US2 and I-90, and on the steep narrow down grade discovered that we had no brake. The reverse band did not last long either so, in order not to take off into space on the next curve I took to the ditch and on up the hillside. We barely avoided another overturn but we did stop. For the remainder of the descent I employed an ancient device discovered by the early overland wagon trains. I found a heavy log and

The Years of My Day

attached it to the rear axle, dragging it behind the car to the foot of the hill.

About midnight that night, within a mile from our home, we found a barrier across Bothell Way where a new culvert was being constructed. It was miles out of our way to detour by way of Aurora Avenue, and we were very tired. I removed the barriers and the red lanterns, placed two long planks across the excavation and inched across.

Our little log cabin on the lake nearby, though it smelled strongly of the mice who had been the sole occupants for the last nine months, was a very welcome retreat that night.

Some years later while still living at Longmire Springs and working up a set of slides for my nature lectures planned for the coming season at Paradise Valley, I took my collection of animal and flower pictures to photographer I.D. Lindsley of Seattle to be made into colored glass lantern slides we used in the days before Kodachrome. L.D. and I worked almost all night in his laboratory and in the morning I drove the 100 miles back to the park – or almost back. On a straight stretch of road between Ashford and the park entrance I went to sleep at the wheel, drifted across the road, and went into a ditch at the only culvert on the road. I must have been driving 25 or 30 miles per hour for the car jumped the small stream and landed nose first on the bank beyond. Ruth and Kenneth were in the front seat with me and they were thrown down under the instrument board (we called it the "dash board" in those days when automobiles were still in the shadow of the horse and buggy) of the car. Neither were hurt.

Esther, still a baby, had been asleep in the back seat. When we had settled down into the creek and I recovered from the shock, I looked back and she was not there. Then we heard her cry. She was lying on the bank several feet ahead of the car, very much surprised but apparently unhurt. The sudden jolt had thrown her over my left shoulder, out the window – or the place where there

Floyd Schmoe

is a window on modern cars (the best we had then were called "side curtains") – and at least ten feet forward.

I was not hurt either although I noticed that the steering wheel had collapsed in a way that could only have happened by me leaning hard upon it. A day later my chest became sore and upon examination I found the print of the steering wheel upon "my radiator."

The car did not get off so lightly; the entire front assembly, including its radiator, was smashed in. Fortunately the first car that came by reported us to the garage in Ashford and soon a mechanic appeared in a tow truck.

We sold the $160 wreck and bought a brand new Model T, circa 1922 for around $600. That was our second, and first new, automobile and I can still smell the "newness smell" of paint and leather.*

June 1922. New York to Seattle in 18 days flat.

*Real leather. In those days the only plastic in a Ford was the
rim of the steering wheel, which we were told but did not believe it, Henry made out of soy beans.

The Years of My Day
Weddings

A wedding can be very expensive what with dress and flower, food and wine. If we had been financially able to provide such trimmings we would still have preferred the simple Quaker style, and fortunately our children agreed with us.

Ruth and I were both from poor families, though not so poor that we ever felt deprived. Both of us had paid our own way through college, and I had been entirely "on my own" from my second year in high school. We had learned almost as much no doubt from our struggle to obtain an education as from the schooling itself.

When it came time for our children to enter college they felt the same as we had. They wanted to work. Ken, in engineering at the University of Washington, had a native skill in mechanical and electrical work and easily found on-campus jobs during his spare time. Where I had earned twenty-five cents an hour bussing dishes at the Commons, he earned ninety cents in the experimental laboratory. Where I came out of school $1500.00 in debt, he had that much in the bank. Esther worked at baby-sitting and later as a part-time receptionist in a doctor's office. During her graduate work at the American University in Beirut she worked in the blood bank of the hospital.

Bill had the good fortune, and the good sense, to marry an experienced typist-secretary. Lil put him through college with minimal help on his own part.

***

I always weep at weddings – seldom at funerals – always at weddings. I guess women are different, they seem to love weddings.

We have had our share of weddings – about a dozen of them. Ken, the oldest, married first. It was January 4th, 1944. Agnes Harris lived in Victoria, British Columbia. She had come to Seattle

Floyd Schmoe

to attend high school, and to live with her aunt Bertha Smith. "Aunt Bertha" was a member of the Friends Meeting, so Agnes came to meeting and that is where they met. She was a beautiful girl, and we loved, so there were no regrets when they decided to marry. The wedding was a family affair. They stood before the large fireplace in our big new house overlooking Lake Washington and said their vows "after the manner of friends," as the Quakers say.

Esther and Gordon were next to marry. Gordon Hirabayashi was a student at the university of Washington at the time of the evacuation of all people of Japanese ancestry from the west coast during the war. Because he chose to violate the curfew order and resist the evacuation in order to test the legality of the action, he was drawn into the group of pacifists who assembled at Friends Center and in our home. When he was arrested and imprisoned, Esther, among others, became a regular jail visitor and gradually they came to be fond of each other.

Esther dropped out of school and volunteered her services as a nurses-aid in the hospital of Minidoka Relocation Center in Idaho. Gordon, between prison terms, went to live with his family who had relocated in eastern Oregon. Later he was asked by the American Friends Service Committee to head their services to relocated Japanese in Spokane.

On a visit home from the Idaho Center Esther picked up a truck for one of the internees and drove it to the camp for him. Passing through Spokane Gordon joined her to help drive, and to visit the camp. It was on this long drive that they became engaged.

They were married (also "after the manner of Friends") in Spokane on July 29th, 1944. Ruth and I drove to Spokane for the wedding.

Bill was the first to marry in a Friends Meeting. Registering as a C.O. (Conscientious Objector) he was assigned to "alternative service" and sent to Forestry C.P.S. (Civilian Public Service) at Glendora, near Pasadena, California.

The Years of My Day

Occasionally some of the Quaker boys in the camp attended Friends Meeting at the Villa Street Meeting in Pasadena, and often members of the meeting visited the Glendora Camp to provide social contacts and other services for the men. Active in the Villa Street Meeting was Charles Standing and his wife, and their four lovely daughters. It proved to be a perfect situation for matchmaking. All four of the Standing girls married Glendora CPS men within the year.

Bill and Lillian, and Bill's friend Lawrence Dunn, and Lillian's sister Irene, were married in a double wedding at Villa Street Meeting on August 26, 1947.

Ruth, Ruthanna and I had spent the year in Honolulu where I taught botany at the University of Hawaii. When school was out there was a shipping strike on and transportation was impossible to come by. Finally were heard that the troop ship General Meggs was in, crowded to the rails with Jewish refugees who had fled to China or eastern Russia before or during the war, but had been stuck there – some for ten years – in the ghettos of Shanghai, Mukden, and Harbin.

The General Meggs provided their first opportunity to escape. The news item also said that a few were disembarking in Honolulu. We hastily packed our bags and went to the pier to stand by incase we were permitted passage to San Francisco. Fortunately we were permitted to board. It was a pleasant passage, far different from the passage out the previous February when Ruthanna and Ruth had made the roughest trip sailors on the USS Matsonia had ever experienced. (During storms at seas sailors usually tell passengers: "This is the worst storm I ever saw," but this storm delayed the ship 24 hours and swept lifeboats from their davits 50 feet above the water line.)

The Meggs, however, was overcrowded and filthy. Ruth and Ruthanna found bunks in the for'castle where in the long swells of the mid Pacific the bow of the ship rose and fell a distance

Floyd Schmoe

of 50 feet or more, and where most of the women had been sick in their bunks since the first day out of Shanghai. I had a bunk with men at the opposite end of the 600 foot long ship where the incessant zoom upward, with the sickening fall back was almost annoying. Fortunately we are better sailors than most.

The weather was warm and we spent most of our days on deck. Meals were a problem however. We stood in line for hours and sometimes ate standing up. The Kosher food was good, but service was strictly "Army mess hall."

To most of these people America was heaven, the Garden of Eden, and the Promised Land all in one. We passed through the Golden Gate and under the high bridge at one o'clock in the morning. Like hundreds of others I stayed on deck for the occasion. It was quiet and all was dark until the bridge was passing overhead. Then I heard a sigh of relief and thanksgiving pass down the ship like a wave of salvation. I have experienced few more impressive moments.

Not all of the 1500 people on board were home yet, however. I had noticed one cluster of people who had camped the entire trip on deck, huddled together in the shelter of the forepeak. One day I approached them and found a man who spoke some English. He told me that they were four generations of the same Russian-Jewish family, that they had been in flight for more than ten years. First they had fled Russia for Romania, then for several years they were in U.N. camps in Greece. They had gotten to Holland, and finally across Europe and Siberia to Manchuria. From San Francisco they would go to Chicago, from there to New Orleans and then, "God willing," to Buenos Aires, where they hoped to settle. Most of the passengers had lost all their wealth and belongings but many of them had known better days and all of them had lived in hope.

The Years of My Day

Talking with one man I asked what he had done for a living. He said, "I made and peddled sausage to other refugees. Imagine a Jew...selling sausage," he exclaimed.

"But no," I said. "I meant, what did you do before the war in Austria?"

"Oh, I owned a factory that built locomotives," he replied. At the moment his entire wealth consisted of a suitcase filled with Chinese embroidery which he hoped to sell in San Francisco or New York in order to get back on his feet again.

Bill's wedding was next day. We had been worried, not knowing if we would be able to get home in time. But Pete was at the pier in San Francisco to meet us. He had a new car – not a 'new' car, but a car new to him – and he drove us down to Pasadena just in time. It was a lovely wedding, simple and touching.

I don't remember what I did the following winter, but in July of 1948 I took the goats to Japan.

Ruthanna was not married until November of 1957, more than ten years later.

She and Donn Higley had become acquainted while students at Western Washington University in Bellingham, but she had taken a couple of years out to fly as a stewardess for United Airlines. They were married at a Seattle church. Donn was the first "inlaw" who was not a Quaker, and anyway the Friends Meeting was not large enough to hold all the friends and relatives they wished to invite. Being a church wedding – though they said their vows in the Quaker manner – Ruth helped with the wedding gown, the cakes and punch, and perhaps with the flowers, I don't remember. Anyway it was a beautiful wedding.

Floyd Schmoe
Funerals

Ruth and I have felt the same way, or let us say, in a similar way, about funerals as we did about weddings. Simplicity and sincerity being much more to be desired than any form of show or ostentation.

The Society of Friends does not favor funerals as such. Cremation is usually preferred with a Memorial Service held some days or weeks later in the form of a meeting for worship. Our concern is more to celebrate and be thankful for the life that was lived rather than to mourn the loss.

Cremation followed Ruth's death and a Memorial Service was arranged for the following Sunday afternoon because Esther's and Bill's families had come so far to be with me and should not be expected to return in a few weeks. It was quiet, worshipful occasion during which numerous friends expressed their love and appreciation for the wonderful person Ruth had been.

Quakers do not suggest gifts or other such memorials, but since we have so many Japanese American friends who have a custom of giving money tokens on such occasion, money to the extent of some $900.00 was accepted by the University Meeting and placed in a fund to be used for the Meeting library.

I had requested that the cremation be total but was informed that such was either impossible or illegal, and was asked to accept the ashes. I was also informed that the laws of the state required that the ashes be deposited in a place of dedicated religious significance*, or wording to that effect – a law intended to benefit established cemeteries and mausoleums.

The Years of My Day

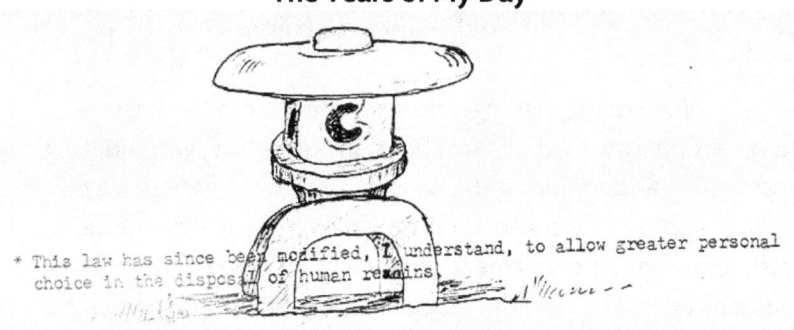

To me, however, any place I put Ruth's ashes would be a place of "religious significance," so I buried the small container beneath the stone lantern in our Japanese garden – a spot near home and family which I felt sure would please her far more than any other.
(*This law has since been modified, I understand, to allow greater personal choice in the disposal of human remains.)

Floyd Schmoe
Fun And Games 1900-1910

While riding, fishing, and swimming were the basic summertime sports of all farm boys, including me, with hunting and skating added during the winter, there were games we played on the school ground and at home which remain vivid memory. Basketball was a new game then but it swept the country. Ours was a dirt court behind the schoolhouse with hoops made by Uncle Bill, and backstops knocked together from wooden crates. In the spring basketball gave way to baseball, which was mostly just "playing catch," or batting out balls, though on Saturdays the older boys played match games in a corner of Bill Andrews' cow pasture. Bill was farmer-preacher and he would not allow his land to be used on Sundays.

Small boys and girls played "fox and goose" when there was snow on the ground or built snow forts and had snowball battles. A perennial favorite among us boys was "old sow." We used a battered tin can for a puck. Clubs or "sticks" were made of branches from the tough Osage orange hedge which bordered two sides of the school ground. The "field" was a 20-foot circle of small holes in the ground, with a larger "home" hole in the center. One player was always "it" and the object was to drive the can (puck) past all the other players who not only guarded their own holes, but the home hole. There was always one less hole in the circle than players, so if while defending the "home" hole a player neglected his own hole, the player who was "IT" might steal it, leaving the ousted player to be IT. When, and if, he who was IT succeeded in getting the can into the home hole every other player was to touch a "base" (usually the coal shed). Meanwhile, IT took a hole and the last one back was without a hole and became IT for the next round; a sort of field hockey with musical chairs variations.

The next most popular game played by the older boys, while the girls and the little boys played "ring around the rosy" and

The Years of My Day

"dare base," was our form of "cops and robbers." Those were the days and the range of Jesse James and the Dalton Boys, and they were the "bad men" of our game. Our crimes were usually train robberies or bank stickups. The "cops" were a sheriff's posse and the coal shed was our jailhouse. There were chases, ambushes, and shootouts involved.

There were more private games which we played at home. Our ice house with its piles of moldy sawdust provided a popular community playhouse, and later we had croquet on the lawn, and a tennis court.

Our most hilarious game was a clandestine affair played in the Meeting House on Saturday or Sunday afternoons when our mothers were shopping or busy at quilting parties and such. They usually followed a series of "Revival Meetings." The Meeting House had a small entryway, two rows of benches with a central aisle, and a raised rostrum, with pulpit, at the far end. (Kansas Quakers had departed from the simplicity of the traditional Friends Meeting House.) For our game the entryway was "Earth" and all its inhabitants were "sinners." The rostrum was "heaven." To get from earth to heaven the sinners had to escape "Hell." Hell was the big "Round Oak" stove which stood in the middle of the room and was presided over by the "Devil," and what "imps" he had been able to capture from the sinners. In our "upward flight" we went under benches and over them and few there were who reached the pearly gates.

We were only able to "use" the Meeting house when Uncle John White, the volunteer custodian and janitor, forgot to latch all the windows, and if, by chance, we got caught inside there was, literally, "Hell to pay."

The cruelest games we played were Halloween pranks of stealing neighbors' buggies, to be found the next day on top of the schoolhouse, or in the creek, putting burrs beneath the saddle of shoppers' horses at the store, or tin-canning stray dogs. One

Floyd Schmoe

Fourth of July, when tempted by the availability of firecrackers, I participated (much to my later shame) in the "canning" of a neighbor's mutt behind the grange store. We filled the can with firecrackers, tied it to the poor hound's tail, lighted the fuses and let it go. Except for the dog it was "great fun" until the terrified animal ducked into Uncle Bill's blacksmith shop and took refuge beneath the woodworking bench where the still exploding firecrackers set fire to dry wood shavings which had accumulated there.

The men were able to extinguish the fire and free the dog, but there were two or three boys who did not appear in public for a considerable time after that.

The Years of My Day
The Lecture Business

While a student at Syracuse I had been asked to speak to the local Audubon Society on the subject of "Western Birds," using a set of slides from the college library. During my first season on the National Park, I spoke each evening at the Guide House to people interested in the natural history of the mountain.

This gave me the idea that perhaps I could earn some extra money if I could arrange a lecture tour to eastern schools and clubs during the month vacation due me each year. Mid-winter was my slack season, and the time we would most enjoy getting away from the isolation of the Park, and it was also the normal lecture season. I could borrow and use the rather fine set of hand-colored slides L.D. Lindsley had created for use on the Park.

So I worked up a mailing list of high schools and colleges, outdoor and nature clubs, and such museums as the American in New York, the Philadelphia Academy of Science, and the Field Museum in Chicago. I had a modest brochure printed, and soon found myself in business.

The Director of the Milwaukee Museum of Natural History had been on the Park that summer with artists and photographers, preparing an exhibit of the timberline habitat for the museum. I had helped them in their study and collecting, and they had heard my lecture at the Inn. I was invited to speak twice on their winter lecture series, first on a Sunday afternoon, and again the same night. I would be paid a $50.00 honorarium.

It was February, I believe, and very cold. We went by train and Ruth, Ken, and Esther stopped off with her family in Wichita. Mr. Voorhees invited me to spend Saturday night at their palatial home in Kenosha, and to speak in the morning to his men's Bible study class at the First Presbyterian Church. It was the beginning of a very busy and profitable tour, but I thought for a time that night that it would also be the ending, not only of the tour but of me.

Floyd Schmoe

All the talks were well received but when, after a late lunch at the Milwaukee Athletic club where Dr. Bennett, Director of the Museum, took me, I finally got to bed. I was so exhausted from nervous tension that I could not sleep. Later I became very ill with stomach cramps and feared that I was suffering from "ptomaine poisoning," as perhaps I was. I did not know what to do about it and for an hour or so I was terribly sick. It has been my handicap all my life that it is almost impossible for me to vomit, and as a result I have suffered much more stomach pain than I should. I can remember only one time in life when I was able to do a really satisfactory job of "Throwing up." That was the night I gave my eighth grade graduation speech in De Soto. There have been many times when I have tried earnestly and failed.

Annual lecture trips became a regular feature of my year's work after that, and continued through the years I was at the University. Even with two trips to Hawaii to help with Japanese American relief at the close of the war, I paid our expenses by booking lectures at the University in Honolulu and a number of high schools about the islands.

Following my long series entitled, "The Mountain That Was God," I used my underwater work, and film made in the San Juan Islands while preparing my Masters, for a story I called, "I Live Under the Sea." This film and story, which had cost me perhaps $1500.00, took me not only to the University of Hawaii, but to the National University in Mexico, and the Cuban National University in Havana, as well as to a score or more of American and Canadian universities.

At first I wore the uniform of the National Park Service, but later I found a tuxedo the appropriate costume. At a lecture before the Cooper Institute in Boston, I was informed that "formal dress" was customary, so I went out and bought a second-hand suit of "tails." I felt very conspicuous that evening as I sat on a very high rostrum, then stood to be introduced to my first Boston audience.

The Years of My Day

After a few introductory remarks I asked for the house lights to be turned off so that I might present my pictures. The darkness was a relief but I was still tense. Standing at the edge of the platform with my back half-turned to the audience in order to see the screen, I was startled by what seemed to be a huge furry animal landing at my feet. It looked, in the dark, as big as bear, and I almost fell off the platform. It was the house cat, which had jumped up from the aisle to rub itself affectionately against my legs.

Looking at the brute and forgetting the audience, I said, "Cat, don't ever do that again." The people roared with laughter, and from then on I felt at ease. Boston people are no different from other folks.

Usually we drove east, and usually by way of California because of better weather. Also I could book several lectures in California.

There was another embarrassing moment in Wheeler Auditorium on the campus of Stanford University. I was waiting in the wings while the Chairman made my introduction and on a last minute impulse I hastily wet my hair in a nearby basin in order to comb it more neatly. I assumed I had a pocket comb, as I usually have, but when I heard my name called I could find neither towel nor comb, and had to step out into the spotlight dripping like a wet dog.

I do not know how many times I have driven cross-country, but we put more than 200,000 miles on the odometer of the 1935 De Soto Airflow, including a 1935 trip as far south as Mexico City.

I was to speak on Marine Biology at the Universidad d'Mexico. It was our first trip south and the entire family went along. Ruthanna was a baby and Bill was only seven. Wherever we stopped people gathered round trying to be helpful. Ruthanna was the center of attraction to the women and often they wanted to take her in their arms. Ruth permitted that but when she saw women with very dirty hands putting their fingers to the baby's

Floyd Schmoe

lips, or kissing her, she was frightened. "Montezuma's revenge" is a "maldad" too easily acquired even when the greatest care is exercised. For a small child dysentery can be serious. Although we happily escaped the "tourist trots" on this trip, Bill made a discovery no less unpleasant.

One of the hazards of motoring on country roads, or even freeways, south of the border, is the frequent encounter with people and domestic animals who are using the highway for purposes other than transportation. Pigs, goats, cows, and burros often sleep in the middle of the road, and people dry corn and beans, or winnow grain on the pavement. Burros, especially, feel a strong sense of territory as regards roadways, and are often reluctant to give right of way, or even share it.

One day when we were trying to coax a donkey, which had apparently congealed in the middle of the road, to give way, Bill expressed a wish to ride the animal. So, when we finally got the beats to its feet, I put Bill aboard and gave it a whack in a manner and in an area that I thought it might understand even if it did not comprehend *Los Ingles*. Surprisingly, perhaps even to itself, it took off into the bush with Bill hanging on for dear life.

He was soon scraped off in the shrubbery and scrambled back to the roadway. That evening at our hotel in Mexico City, Bill complained of itching about the waist. Ruth stripped him and found dozens of fat ticks with their heads so deeply anchored in his skin that they could not be removed intact. The heads that were left either continued to burrow or caused such infection that the boy was in misery for several days.

We had heard of course that the way to induce a firmly entrenched tick to back out is to touch its rear end with a lighted cigarette, but none of us smoked cigarettes. We had also heard that ticks carry Rocky Mountain Tick Fever, a deadly disease. Fortunately there were no such complications and Bill was cured of his itch to ride burros.

The Years of My Day

At the university I asked if an interpreter would be provided and was told that one would not be necessary. This was the case also when some years later I spoke to students at the National University in Havana. I am sure few if any American student groups could handle Spanish as well.

Floyd Schmoe
Oyster Farm

In 1948 I made a trip to Japan which remains vivid in memory; this time to an old man, Kokichi Mikimoto, king of pearl culturists. The Mikimoto Pearl Farms at Ago Bay, Ise Peninsula, were off limits to Americans at that time, but I went to the Army base at Toba and told the C.O. that I was a marine biologist from the University of Washington, and that a visit to the Mikimoto laboratories at Ago would be of special value to me and he wrote me a pass.

I was surprised to be met at Nakii, the end of the rail line, by the old man's private yacht, and even more surprised to find him waiting on the laboratory deck, very tall and dignified in a stiff black kimono and a brown derby hat. I bowed in my best Japanese manner but he put out a hand saying, "I bow to only two people, The Emperor and General MacArthur."

He then introduced me to a girl in white laboratory smock and we walked up the steep path to a large group of low buildings set amid mountains of oyster shell, which were the laboratories.

Inside the first building we found all the dozens of workers, mostly young girls, gathered at the windows. We joined them and I was told that the sister of the Emperor was expected momentarily.

Soon a very large yacht came around the point into the bay and approached the dock. I could see the old man standing stiffly at attention, and when the richly kimonoed lady stepped off with her escorts, Mikimoto-san took off his derby hat and bowed.

We waited at the entrance to the laboratory and all bowed stiffly as the party entered, the Princess escorted by the King of Pearls.

I had met a couple of Princes, one her nephew Akihito, but this was the closest I had come to a real Princess.

My guide and I followed the party on their tour and saw millions of dollars worth of what were undoubtedly the finest

The Years of My Day

culture pearls in the world, for the best and the rarest had been laid out for the Princess to see.

There were huge pearls, ropes made up of many strands of matched pearls, rare blue and pink and black pearls, and novelty pearls in the shapes of Buddha, fish, birds, etc.

A girl placed a huge rope of perhaps 50 strands around my neck and made a photograph of me.

At the end of my tour, while the royal party were having tea with Mikimoto-san, at his villa farther up the hill, my guide brought me a lacquered tray on which rested a large, live pearl oyster. "Souvenir," she said, bowing.

She then took the oyster to a table where a technician opened it deftly with a heavy knife, felt the white mantle of the oyster and removed two fine pearls.

She then gave me two smaller pearls joined together like Siamese twins. These, I was told, are purchased as wedding gifts to bring good fortune to newly married couples. Ruthanna has the two gift pearls but I do not know what happened to the twins.

The substance of pearls, known as "mother of pearl," or nacre, is produced by all shellfish of the order Molluscoidea, and pearls of gem quality are occasionally produced by the ordinary oysters and the freshwater mussels. The iridescent lining of the abalone shell is composed of nacre colored by traces of mineral elements.

From the standpoint of the clam this nacre, which is produced by the same or similar cells in the mantle of the animal as the calcarious shell, is purely utilitarian. It is to the shellfish what paint is to the house builder; it smooths and protects the surface of the structure. In one respect it is even of less value than paint, for paint provides beauty appreciated by the builder and his client, while the incidental beauty of a pearl is likely of no value to the oyster which produces it.

Floyd Schmoe

Pearls have been valued by their finders from the most ancient times. Until recent times they have been so rare, and the search for them so hazardous, that only princes and queens could afford to possess them.

With the discovery of methods of culture they have become common and within the reach of many people, though their value, due to a rare beauty, is still highly appreciated.

There is a story which recently found its way into the world press, that the culture pearl syndicate of Japan, of which the Mikimoto company is a part, in order to maintain a high standard of quality and maintain prices, releases only perfect specimens to the trade and holds back all that are blemished in color or roundness. Since probably less than half of all the pearls produced meet these standards there are large numbers of discards.

Among the pearl "farmers" of the Ise area, according to the story, some 800 pounds of these "culls" had accumulated, and in order to dispose of them safely they were taken off shore and dumped in the sea.

But that was not the end of the story. This is also a community of commercial fishermen, and soon quantities of pearls began to show up in the gullets of fish caught for the market. The fish were gulping down the pearls and soon the local market was flooded with bargain priced gems.

Pearls produced by "wild" oysters are "accidents of nature," a result of the animal's struggle to protect itself from parasites, or the intrusion of foreign objects such as a grain of sand or any other irritant. Since it cannot be expelled it is made harmless, or less objectionable, by being covered over with a smooth coating of nacre.

I have in my possession a large abalone shell from the California coast which, while still living, had been attacked by large numbers of small boring clams. Most of these parasites never managed to penetrate to the thick shell of the huge snail but a few

The Years of My Day

had, and these were covered from the inside by layer upon layer of nacre until mounds, as large as peas, were formed on the inner surface of the shell. Even these smooth bumps may have been uncomfortable to the abalone but they were less so than a boring clam would have been.

It is in the same manner that gem pearls are formed.

Pearl culture was undertaken by the Chinese as early as the 13th century and a method pf producing pearls in European freshwater mussels was invented by the great Swedish naturalist, Carl Von Linnaeus about 1750, but it was not until about 1912 that Kokichi Mikimoto, working with the Japanese pearl oyster (Pinctada), succeeded in producing gem pearls on a commercial scale, and started the culture pearl industry.

Cultured pearls are not "artificial" pearls. They are produced in the mantle of the host in exactly the same manner that "wild" pearls are produced. The difference is that pearl oysters are artificially propagated and the "seed," or basic irritant is introduced manually into the mantle of the living oyster, which is then returned to the water and carefully "cultivated" for a long enough time for it to build a pearl of commercial size. Culture pearls are created just as "test tube" babies are created.

As a boy in the Midwest I had seen "pearl" buttons being cut from Mississippi and Missouri River mussel shells; Davenport, Iowa being "the pearl button capitol of the world." I had seen the great piles of discarded mussel shells, sieve-like with the round holes from which buttons were cut, along the river bank. (A cousin, Terrance Schmoe, was a "pearl fisherman" for a time during the Depression along the White River in Arkansas – he showed me a handful of pearls he had found but they were of no great value – he later found moonshining more profitable.)

Most of these are ground into grit to be fed chickens, but some, I found, are shipped to Japan and from these the pearl "farmers" cut tiny beads to become the core of culture pearls.

Floyd Schmoe

In Mikimoto's laboratory that day I watched female technicians take live oysters from tanks of sea water, force the valves apart with a special clamp, cut a deep slit into the muscular mantle, and insert one of these tiny beads from Davenport, Iowa. Depending upon the size of the mother oyster, two or more seeds were implanted in each.

The clamp is then removed, the valves closed, and the oyster returned to the cages, which are suspended from rafts in the bay. These cages are lifted from time to time to be cleared of seaweed and other marine growth.

After sufficient time, usually six or seven years, the oysters are taken to the laboratory and the pearls removed. The flesh, which is edible, was even at that time of food scarcity, wasted, and the shells left in high, odoriferous piles. Surely a better use for both flesh and shell has since been found.

While waiting for the launch to return me to the rail head I wandered down to the bay and watched the girl divers at work. They were not diving for the oysters as the pearl divers of the Persian Gulf and Indian Ocean do, but for the spat, or larval oysters which hatch from eggs spawned into the sea, then become attached to strings of shell hung from rafts for that purpose. These ama, as they are called, work from a boat which is tended by a man. Each is equipped with a facemask for better vision, and a wooden tub for the spat and beside which they rest between dives. They wear nothing besides the facemask and a short cotton tunic held together by a cord. I did not time their dives but it seemed they sometimes stayed submerged for upwards of two minutes. It is a profession handed down from mother to daughter and some of the older women appeared to be fifty or more years old, though some of the girls were certainly teenagers. It is said that women make better divers than men.

Some years later when Ruth and I spent a few days at the hot springs resort town of Atami, we watched girls and women

The Years of My Day

diving for octopus and nori, or seaweed. They were diving in deeper and colder water. The octopus were small, not more than eighteen inches or two feet in total spread. When one was brought to the surface the diver bit it through the head to kill it. On the shore they had a fire to warm themselves and racks on which the octopus were hung to dry and be smoked.

Squid, which are more often seen on the market than octopus, are taken in nets at sea. Fleets of Japanese squid fishermen go as far as Australia for their catches.

At Atami Ruth had her first experience with that wonderful institution, the Japanese public bath. Every village has one, and almost every block in the cities. It is truly an institution because its value as a social center far outweighs its necessity as a sanitary device.

When we checked in at the Atami Inn we were puzzled by being told, "There is only one bath." We understood the maid to mean that only one bath is permitted, which would be absurd, as people go to the hot springs mainly for bathing.

When we were unable to understand her meaning she telephoned the proprietor of another hotel who spoke English, explained our problem, and had him tell me on the phone that what was meant was, "There are no separate baths for men and women, only one, which is used by both men and women."

I had no objection to that but Ruth was doubtful.

Our room was large, with a balcony overlooking the seas. On the balcony were two wicker chairs, but there were no other furnishings in the room. Soon our maid returned with a tray on which were freshly laundered ukata, the bathrobe worn even on the streets on warm summer evenings, and towels. She said the bath was ready.

It was a typical Japanese bath, the water so hot that it filled the room with steam. We entered a small mat-covered dressing room where we were to leave our towels and ukata in a wicker

Floyd Schmoe

basket. Men and women together were disrobing and washing themselves at fountains of running water which surrounded the tub (which was more like a shallow swimming pool than a conventional bathtub). It was all a bit too much for Ruth. We were both raised in provincial Kansas, but I had been abroad more than she had.

She said, "I'm going to take my bath in the morning," and returned to our room. After a delightful dinner served to us on a low table, brought to our room, the maid took the thick quilts, called futon (which serve as both mattress and cover) from their shelves, and spread our bed upon the soft tatami floor mats.

Guests sleep late in resort hotels, so Ruth found the bath empty at six the next morning, but workmen begin their day's labor early, and the bath at our inn had glass walls opening on a small garden. In the garden were men raking gravel paths and tending the shrubbery. She managed to enjoy a quick dip, but as she returned to the dressing room to towel, a man was disrobing. She snatched her towel and robe and ran to our room, to dry herself there.

The Japanese are a modest people though they may enjoy a communal bath. Bathers at public beaches often change from street clothes to swimsuits at the water's edge, and on a hot night they may sit naked fanning themselves on an open balcony. They have developed a sort of psychological privacy assuming that no one looks – which in fact they seldom do.

Under the influence of encroaching western mores co-ed baths are becoming less acceptable even to the Japanese and now are to be found only at small resort inns such as ours at Atami or more remote spas such as the great hot springs resort at Naboribitsu on Hokaido Island, and Beppo on Kyushu.

The Years of My Day
Ships

    I crossed the Atlantic first in May of 1918 on the Compagnie General Francais' S.S. Rochambeau. It was as rough a crossing with as strange a crew as anyone could imagine. May is a bad season the North Atlantic, and Old Ocean made no concessions for us. It was in the midst of the war, we carried troops, and an eager fleet of German U boats formed a reception committee stretching from the hump of Africa to the tip of Scotland. One passenger jumped overboard and another fell. We had a French opera troupe returning from a season at the Met, a couple of French aces who had been on a recruiting junket of America, and a dozen conscientious objectors assigned to "alternative service" with the American Friends Service Committee's unit in France. I was one of the latter.

    All the above were crowded into cabins, while the steerage and the baggage holds were filled with Czechoslovak volunteers from the Canadian prairies, rushing home to free their countries from the Austrians and Hungarians.

    The ship's officers were French, the kitchen and dining room staff Italian, the room stewards Indo-Chinese, and the "black gang" who passed coal in the inferno of the boiler room were tall Arabic-speaking Senegalese from East Africa.

    I ignored the signs that said, "Defense de entrée," one day, and went down to the stoke hold. From the grating above them I saw a score or more black men clothed only in dirty towels, wooden clogs, and sweat, passing baskets of coal from the bunkers to the boilers. In the glow from the open furnace doors, and dim lights, they looked like a bucket brigade of Satan's slaves in a hot and noisy hell of steel. The air was filled with coal dust and the temperature must have been around 130° F. The grating where I stood burned my feet through my shoes, and the floor plates of the boiler room must have been hotter still.

Floyd Schmoe

A Czech soldier went overboard in New York's lower harbor and was still swimming in the direction of Long Island when we passed beyond view.

On a calm day, as we neared the Garonne Estuary, a gray-haired 70-year-old French lady fell overboard. A day or two earlier the lifeboats had been cleared of their covers and swung overboard for quick launching in case of an enemy attack and this woman, strolling on the boat deck, had reached for the gunnel of a boat to steady herself as the ship rolled. But the boat, hanging loose from its davits, swung outboard and she fell overboard some fifty feet into the sea.

We were all amazed when word was passed to the bridge and a boat crew was beginning to lower a boat, to have an officer order them back. The ship did not hesitate and for the time perhaps I realized the meaning of the oft heard phrase, "C'est la guerre."

However it was not what we thought, for that evening, safe inside the estuary, we paused and a French gunboat came alongside and passed over our little old lady, dry and sailing in the white uniform of a sailor.

If the ship had stopped at the scene of the accident it would have been an easy target for an enemy torpedo. Instead the Captain had asked our naval convoy to make the rescue, and this had taken place so far behind us that we had not seen it occur.

Our little lady and her rescuers were given a big cheer by those who lined the decks.

From Bordeaux, where we docked about nine in the evening, we took a late train to Paris. I sat next to a friendly French girl in a crowded compartment, and before morning grew very sleepy. I nodded for a time, then dozed off in deep comfort. When I awoke I found the girl's arm around me and my head on her shoulder. I sat up then for a time, but when I awoke again in the same position knowing that I had not deliberately laid my head on

The Years of My Day

her warm shoulder, I left it there. C'est la guerre. Things were not so plush on my return voyage in July of the following year.

It was more than thirty years before I saw Europe again. The Cunard Line's S.S. Franconia was, fortunately, a "one class" ship, for nowhere, as onboard ship, does the English class-consciousness assert itself. We put in briefly at Le Havre to discharge Paris-bound passengers, then crossed to Southampton, where we birthed alongside the new Elizabeth II and our comfortable Franconia appeared immediately to have shrunk to half its size.

Opposite the docks at Le Havre I was surprised to see the huge concrete ski-jump-like paunch pads of the German "buz-bombs", used to blast London during the later weeks of the war, still standing.

My next crossing to Europe was by air, but in 1958 I took the Italian Line, M.S. Christopher Columbo out of New York for Naples, and returned that summer from Amsterdam on the sleek Hamburg-American M.S. Stattsdam. Of all the ships I have sailed on I have enjoyed Dutch and Norwegians most. Scandinavian and Dutch air service is also excellent.

While in Naples I took time off to spend a few days visiting Sorento, Capri, and the ruined cities of Pompeii and Herculaneum. I also made the ascent of Vesuvius, the volcano which in 79 A.D. covered these two pleasure resorts of the wealthy Romans with fifty feet of mud and hot ashes. Never since that terrible morning has the old devil mountain ceased to threaten the otherwise peaceful countryside. In 1958 the lava from a 1944 eruption had not yet entirely cooled.

I went on from Italy to Egypt on that trip, on one of the Adriatica Lines motorships out of Bari for Alexandria. It was the same ship I had taken in 1952 for Beirut.

On this crossing I had an interesting cabinmate.

Floyd Schmoe

My cabin was situated just across a narrow passageway from the ship's beauty parlor and barber shop. It was not air conditioned, so I left the door ajar for what fresh air was available. In the night I dreamed that someone was sitting on my chest and awoke to find a large black cat sleeping comfortably in that general area of my anatomy.

When the maid came in the morning to make up my berth I mentioned the cat and asked, "What is the cat's name?"

She finally understood what I meant – neither my Italian nor her English being quite adequate for such a profound discussion – but she was unable to answer my question so she called in the barber and a couple of girls from the beauty shop. It was no use. We did not communicate, so I said, "It does not matter," and went on deck.

Some hours later when I again descended to my room the little maid came running and brimming over with good news. The gatto," she said, "the gatto. His name is Loochea."

It was in that year that I did the trip down the Nile River.

Since at the age of five cousin Maurice Moon allowed me to look at his geography book in the one-room Prairie Center schoolhouse, I have had a great desire to see and know this amazing world which is our home, and in one way and another I have had opportunity to see much of it. Counting up I find that I have crossed the Pacific, or parts of it, 19 times, the Atlantic 11 times, The Mediterranean 6 times, and the Indian Ocean once. I have never been to South America or Australia. Those are oversights I must, if possible, correct.

The Years of My Day

Floyd Schmoe
Our Linda

Seattle sometimes refers to herself as "The Boating Capital of the World," and it is true that there are round and about Seattle more boats per capita than any other area of the nation, if not the world. And with hundreds of miles of scenic and safe, island studded waters, not only at our door, but all around us, it is not simply "too bad," but "cruel and unusual punishment" not to have some sort of watercraft in order to enjoy it fully. At least that is the way I felt after we had built our home on Lake Washington, and I had a glimpse of the waterways and islands of Puget Sound.

But with an income of less than $300.00 per month, and a growing family, there was no way we could afford more than a homemade rowboat, unless...unless we found some way to make it pay its own way.

On Mount Rainier, when we needed additional income, I had organized a sort of "boys camp on horseback," and from a basecamp outside the park's boundary, offered saddle and packhorse expeditions to the Wonderland Trail, which encircles the mountain. This did not endear me to the hotel company which had the concessions for all such activities within the park, but it was not illegal, and for two summers, with rented horses and hired leaders, I did a profitable business.

Now I thought – after returning to sea level – If I had a suitable boat I could take young people on organized cruises during the summer, and thus pay for a craft we could use the rest of the year. It was the same method employed by my friend Geroge Chidiac in order to own a car in Beirut.

So I began looking for a suitable craft.

There were plenty of good boats to be had in Seattle but none suited to my need, which was also suited to my bank account. I looked at hundreds of boats and at last found the Linda.

The Years of My Day

At the moment she was a rotting hulk, half submerged, at a Lake Union shipyard. She had been a beamy, ocean going, cutter-rigged, auxiliary yacht, 42 feet long, 16 tons registry. With considerable reconstruction she might be all that again.

I took Tony Jensen, who owned a small boat repair near the University, to examine my find and give an estimate on repairs.

Tony found the hull sound and that was about all that was. Still, that was the important part. I asked him if he could put it in "shipshape" for $1,000.00, which was about all I thought I could borrow on our little place on Lake Washington. He thought, "Perhaps."

I went to the coast Guard registry and discovered that the Linda had been built at Benecia, California, in 1889 as a pilot boat for service off the Golden Gate. She was older than I was, though I was still in better shape. Later she had gone to the south seas, but there was a story that, in between, she had belonged to Jack London and was used by him for his shenanigans on San Francisco Bay.

I had read London's book, "The Cruise of the Snark," and I was pretty sure this was not his "Snark." However, London had owned several boats at various times, and it made a good story.

I offered the agent $100, and he took it. Tony towed my craft to his yard, hauled her up on the ways, and started work. I told him that when the costs began to approach my one thousand dollar limit to let me know. He said that he would.

Within a week we had nothing but a hull with bare rib ends protruding like a rack of lamb. Soon, however, new decking appeared, and the framework of a spacious cabin.

Floyd Schmoe

Tony found a used engine and a suitable mast, and other gear. I began to worry about the bill. Once or twice I asked for an accounting, but Tony had never found time to total it up. In the meantime, I had signed on a dozen boys for a month's cruise to Alaska at $600.00 each. I hired Hubert Bauer, a former commander of the German navy, now doing research in oceanography at the University of Washington, as skipper; Sam Harby, a Physical Education instructor at the University, as mate; and Harry Holt, Principal of the high school of Bend, Oregon, as cook, and we were "Gung ho" to be off.

We let her in the water one hot July morning, trim and clean in new white paint, and properly christened with a bottle of ice water, manfully swung by five-year-old Bill in a new white sailor suit.

Then Tony presented the bill. It was something over $2,000.00.

I told him he could keep the boat – we would charter another. He didn't want the boat. We finally compromised on $1,600.00, which I was able to borrow. The boat leaked like a sieve, and we manned the bilge pump all the way to Sitka and back, though gradually the seams tightened and we were never in danger of swamping. On the whole it was a good voyage with a fine crew and fair sailing. We cleared a few hundred dollars.

The following summer, 1931, we went again with old Matt Peasley, of the popular "Cappy Rick" novels of Norman Reiley Reine, as Skipper. This time we had a new, more reliable engine, and a tighter ship. Instead of following sheltered inside passages this time we sailed the open seas from Sitka south. We had

The Years of My Day

planned to sail all the way to the Strait of Juan de Fuca, but after a couple of days of high seas, with several of the boys seasick, we turned "inside" again.

Inside we could anchor every night in sheltered coves but outside we had to work the ship day and night – four hours on and four off – in the ancient way. Captain Peasley, who had spent years "in sail," and at 19 had been the youngest captain of an ocean-going vessel off the Pacific coast, loved it that way, but Harry, whose galley stove and dining table stood all day at a 30° angle, was very unhappy. Peasley said, "When I was in sail the master never went to sleep until he was out of sight of land, but here, hell fire, we're never out of sight of land."

There were daily adventures. We saw more than fifty whales, and dolphins often swam beside our boat. On a dark night they left comet tails of light in the water, as bio-luminous plankton organisms were excited into action by their passing.

Most of the whales we saw were humpbacks, and a mating pair of these huge brutes put on a spectacular show of breaching and leaping early one fog-bound morning amidst ice bergs in Glacier Bay. On the way south from Sitka a big finback whale breached a number of times within fifty feet of our boat and we were able to secure a good picture of it. There was a fogbank offshore which showed up in the snapshot like distant land, and when L.D. Lindsley later made a colored slide form the negative he tinted the fog green.

When we examined the slide, L.D. asked, "What land is that in the distance?" and when I said, "The nearest land in that direction is Japan," he replied, "Then that's Japan."

We had tried trolling for salmon a number of times with no success, but when we were all to go ashore and climb Mount Edgecumbe, a volcanic cone which rises out of the sea a few miles off Sitka, Captain Peasley said he would do a bit of trolling instead.

Floyd Schmoe

Upon our return late that evening we were amazed to find several 20 to 30 pound king salmon hanging from the rigging.

We asked how he had done it. He told us he had cruised about with a couple of lines out for half a day and didn't get a strike, so he called a commercial fisherman who was getting fish and asked how he did it.

"How much lead you using?" the fisherman asked.

"'Bout three pounds, I guess."

"You need at least ten. These fish are down 60 to 70 feet."

So Peasley, not having more lead, tied a big Stilson wrench onto his line and immediately began to haul them in. He threw the small ones back but soon had a hundred pounds of fish. We had to feed most of it to the gulls.

We all learned much on those trips, not only about seamanship and marine life, but about ourselves and our ability to live and work together.

By the following summer the depression had settled down so heavily upon the country that even wealthy eastern families could not, or would not, send their sons on pleasure voyages, and we had to give up the venture.

The Years of My Day
Linda – Alaska

Three things happened on our cruise to Alaska that puzzled us, and for one of them we have never been able to find the explanation.

One morning, while pushing against the current in Wrangell Narrows, the boy on lookout called me forward to see what appeared to be a huge bird flying close to the water directly ahead of us. There was a heavy fog and visibility was a hundred yards or so.

I said "huge." This "bird" had wings ten feet long, and it was flying with a slow rhythmic beat almost as fast as we were moving.

As we moved closer we saw what it was; a fisherman standing in a dory rowing with long sweeps.

The second "mystery" was observed in Glacier Bay, also on a foggy morning. There were small icebergs floating in the bay and I was on the bowsprit keeping careful watch. We didn't want to ram one. Suddenly about a hundred yards in front of us a black shape that appeared to be as big as a submarine came straight up out of the water. I could see it only dimly in the foggy dawn and it frightened me. After rising perhaps 30 feet out of the water it fell sideways with a great splash. I saw then that it was a whale.

During the night I heard such sounds and thought they were made by ice falling from one of the surrounding glaciers. Now I knew the humpback whales were back.

There is a herd of fifty or more humpies which annually winter among the Hawaiian Islands, then migrate in the spring to feed and breed in Alaskan waters. Many of them return year after year to Glacier Bay. The great leaps are likely mating display.

The third mystery has not been solved. On the way north we were running late one very dark night to take advantage of the tide, but when the tide turned around midnight, we began looking for an anchorage.

Floyd Schmoe

One chart showed a narrow channel on the east shore a mile or two ahead, so we kept the land in sight and watched. Eventually we saw the opening which appeared more like a small river than a channel. Edging in slowly, and testing depth with a 16-foot pike pole, we found it to be deep. After half a mile there was still no bottom.

Finally we edged into the left shore and dropped anchor in about four fathoms. We lay almost against the rocky shore, but the water was still, so leaving one of the boys on watch we went below and slept. We were all tired. It had been a long day.

I awoke at dawn and went on deck. Dave was asleep. We still lay calmly beside the shore. I decided not to wake the others so Dave and I heaved the anchor, started the motor, and turned a round, heading back the way we had come in a few hours earlier. At least we thought we were heading out. I did not check the chart and it was still too dark to tell direction by the sun.

When after an hour we had not yet returned to the open channel, I became worried and began studying the chart. There was a network of narrow channels among the islands and I could not find any reference point which would indicate which one we had anchored in. Captain Bauer was equally confused.

We cruised for hours in narrow waterways and finally about noon we reached Stephens Passage with indications that we were nearing Juneau.

The only possible solution that we could arrive at was that sometime during the night while Dave was asleep, the tide had turned and we had dragged anchor until fast again, but on the opposite side of the narrow channel. If this was the case I had, by turning the boat around, continued on up the channel rather than returning out the way we had come in. Apparently we had spent the morning detouring around a large island, but I have never been quite sure.

One of my great adventures came the next day.

The Years of My Day

A few miles out of Juneau we passed an unusual barge equipped with cranes, from one of which hung an odd machine which looked like nothing I had ever seen before. It was a pear-shaped contraption about as large as a VW Bug, with several round ports, like eyes, and arms like claws at the ends, not unlike the legs of some giant beetle. We assumed it was a diving bell of some sort and we wondered what was going on.

We tied up that night at the city dock in Juneau, and next morning the small tug we had noticed at the diving barge came in and docked nearby. Talking with Captain Hall of the tug we learned that he and his crew were trying to raise the Islander, or at least salvage sone of the two million dollars worth of gold that was thought to be aboard the wreck.

About nine one night in 1901 the Canadian steamship S.S. Islander departed Skagway for Seattle loaded with miners returning from the Klondike and with an unknown amount of their gold. Steaming down Stephens Passage in the middle of a dark night at an estimated 18 knots, the slim, twin-screw Canadian plowed into an iceberg that had drifted down from the nearby Taku Glacier, tore a hole in her bow, and sank within 20 minutes. A few survivors managed to reach Admiralty Island two miles distant, but more than 70 were lost.

Grim tales were told of miners who refused to leave their hard-earned gold behind, and others who filled their pockets with nuggets, jumped overboard, and sank like a rock. It was said that the Captain was drunk when he came onboard at Skagway and asleep at the time of the crash. At any rate ice was to be expected off Taku Inlet and 18 knots was an excessive speed at night. Someone was at fault.

Diving stem-first in 365 feet of water the vessel plowed into the bottom then settled back, and after 31 years still sat upright on her twin keels. At Captain Hall's invitation we spent the next day on the salvage barge and watched the operation.

Floyd Schmoe

With powerful jets of water, directed from the diving bell, the men were boring channels beneath the hull through which cables would be passed to form a sling. These would later be made fast to two vessels, one placed either side of the sunken ship. The rising tide would lift the wreck.

In June and December tides run to 20 feet in Stephen Passage, and by the following June all would be ready. Two wooden hulls, which had been left over from the frantic shipbuilding of the first world war, were towed from Seattle's Lake Union and bridged together by 90-foot spars. This floating platform was anchored above the Islander, the cable ends attached to hand winches on either side and, at low tide, all cables were cranked taut. Five or six hours later, at high tide, the sunken hull had been lifted clear of the bottom.

The entire flotilla was then towed toward Admiralty Island until the wrecked vessel again grounded. This simple process was repeated twice each day and within a few weeks time the barnacle-encrusted hulk sat high and dry, at low tide, on the beach. It was a clever operation.

Because relatives of lost miners still lived, the entire operation was kept secret, and I never was able to learn how profitable it proved to be. But the rumor was that everyone involved had new automobiles and new houses that autumn.

When we were aboard the previous July we were shown and given our pick of a store of booty which had already been taken from the ship. There were supplies from the galley, personal affects from cabins, instruments from the bridge, decorations from the public rooms, even skulls and other human remains.

I was interested in the effect of time and salt water upon various objects. Steel cable woven around a hemp core could be crumbled between fingers, though the hemp remained sound. A pair of ladies' shoes still showed the wax polish. A brace of pistols was welded together in a mass of rust.

The Years of My Day

One day the grapple brought up a case of champagne, the foil seal on the bottles unbroken. The find was greeted with shouts of joy by the crew, but these turned to moans when the bottles were opened. Salt water had replaced the wine through or around the corks.

At 365 feet the pressure on the surface of an object is approximately 180 pounds to the square inch, and sea water, being heavier than wine, gradually seeped into the corked bottles.

I was given the coffer compass box from the bridge. Pressure had broken the glass cover. The needle had crumbled, but the painted markings of the dial were still bright and easily readable. It is now a part of the display at Northwest Seaport in Kirkland.

When we returned to Seattle I found several human bones which some of the boys had taken and hidden under a bunk of the Linda, but then had thought better of the idea and left them there. They are buried in our garden near the Lake Washington house.

After lunch that day Captain Hull asked me if I would like to go down to the wreck. I was waiting for the chance.

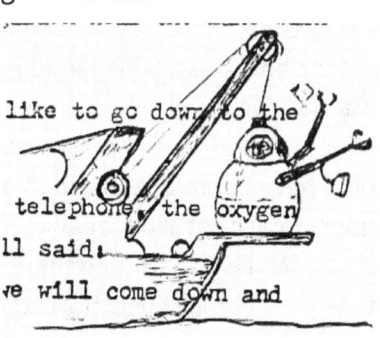

Seated in the bell, I was instructed in the use of the telephone, the oxygen control, and the exterior lights and tongs. Captain Hull said, "You have oxygen for eight hours. If anything happens we will come down and get you before it runs out.

I didn't ask, but as the heavy dome was lowered over my head and being bolted down, I wondered just how that might be done.

We tested the telephone, then I was hoisted up, swung over the side, and lowered into the cold green water. I was

Floyd Schmoe

stopped there and asked to inspect the seal of the hatch to see if there were any leaks. I replied that water was dripping on my right shoulder, but Hull said. "That's alright," and down I went.

For the first hundred feet the color of the water changed from light green to dark blue, to almost black, and from there on down I saw only the sparkle of the luminous organisms that were disturbed by my passing. When we touched bottom I turned on the outside lights but could see only a cloud of muddy water that had been raised by contact with the bottom. I was told to watch and I would be moved closer to the hull. Soon a wall appeared out of the gloom, a wall of barnacles, marine worms, sponges, anemone, seaweeds, and other marine organisms all tangled together into the amazing community of plants and animals which thrive at such depths.

There were starfish and real fish...some large sculpins and larger rockfish, and a big red snapper looking in the port light at me. Reaching out with the tongs, which operated from inside by a series of levers such as those on a backhoe or bulldozer, I took a basketball-sized bite of this living assembly, which we later examined on deck. The most notable thing which I remember was that the barnacles, which made up the bulk of the material, were six to ten inches in length, a giant species (Balanus nubilis, I believe), found only in deep water. I never saw anything which could have been recognized as a sunken ship, though it lay there almost intact not ten feet away.

While I was sitting there the voice from above said, with a tone of excitement which worried me, "Hold on, we're going hunting."

Then I heard the motor of the tug start and pull away from the barge.

It may have been only ten minutes, but it seemed a lot longer before I heard it return.

The Years of My Day

Then a voice said, "Hello, you still there? We got a couple of deer. We're bringing you up. Venison for supper." I couldn't imagine what was going on.

On deck a few minutes later I was amazed to see two deer, their feet tied, lying on the deck of the tug.

While I was below they had seen three deer swimming across the three-mile-wide channel. We thought later that they must have been chased by wolves or bear. Otherwise they would not have attempted so long a swim, thought deer do commonly swim from island to island along the coast.

Thinking of fresh meat, the entire crew had deserted me and took off after the deer. All three were near exhaustion and one sank and drowned before it could be picked from the water. On deck they were too exhausted to stand, but the men had tied their feet to prevent their struggles.

Actually we had no venison for supper. No one had the heart to kill one of the deer, and we all agreed to take them ashore on Admiralty Island and set them free.

It is of interest to me, as now I remember the incident, that none of the six or seven men, all of them except myself, were enthusiastic deer hunters who could, and no doubt had, shot number of deer, would not look a captive animal in the eye and cut its throat. It may just be that it is the latent spark of compassion for a fellow creature, which resides deep in most of us, which can someday be fanned into a flame of salvation. I hope so.

Floyd Schmoe
Along the Way

After the World Conference of Friends, at Oxford University in the summer of 1952, I filtered down across Europe on my way to our "Houses for Hiroshima" work camp in Japan. This was my first, and perhaps only, round the world circuit, and I was enjoying it.

From Innsbruck, Austria, where I slept in the $50.00 per day bridal suite of an old but grand hotel for $10.00 because it was eleven at night when I arrived and this was the only remaining room in the hotel, I took a morning train south over the higher Brenner Pass into Italy. I was to spend the day and night in Venice, Jewel of the Adriatic. On the train I became acquainted with a young American G.I. stationed in Germany. He and his German bride were on their honeymoon and they were also going to Venice.

We reached the Venice terminal about ten at night and the clerk at the hotel bureau in the station informed us that there was a music festival on, a half dozen symphony orchestras were competing that moment in the Plaza San Marco, and there was not an empty hotel room in the city.

While the three of us sat on the stone steps facing the Grand Canal, a ragged Italian boy, much wiser than his 14 years, came and asked, "You want a room?"

That we did, two rooms if possible.

"Come with me," he said. We followed, along the canal, across several bridges, along smaller canals, more bridges, through an inky black tunnel beneath buildings, into a tiny square beside a canal, where a dozen men and women sat gossiping.

A woman (the urchin's mother or aunt, no doubt) flew at him like a riled setting hen, berating him for bringing strangers into their midst. While he fended her off with a stream of shrill Italian, he kept assuring us a soothing, "Okay, okay."

The Years of My Day

Once the "Squall" passed over, we were led into a nearby house. An old grandmother was routed from her bed to a mattress in another room, and I was made welcome.

The honeymooners were taken to another house facing the square and we never met again.

The room was musty and hot. When I opened the shutters for a possible breath of air, Granny closed them again. There were robbers about.

I told my hostess I'd be back and went for a walk. In the Plaza San Marco two orchestras battled from opposite sides of the square and the sidewalk cafes were filled.

I found a table on a side street, ordered dinner, and listened. At Midnight the square emptied, the musicians packed their instruments, and I found my way back to the little square beside the canal. All was quiet but the door was unlocked. I opened the shutters, took a feather mattress off the bed to sleep on a firmer, cooler mattress beneath, and turned off the light.

The "robbers" came in but they came on buzzing wings. There must have been thousands of them and they all wanted a piece of the action, which was me. I wondered what the Venetian mosquitoes ate when I was not there, and I resolved to be there only until the first train left in the morning.

The 7am Rome Express was loaded to the gills. Latecomers clung to the outside steps. It was already moving when I reached the last coach. Someone took my bag. Someone else hauled me aboard. I climbed over bodies and bags for ten coaches and back again. There was not a seat on the train, not even in the aisles.

I had slept very little where I had sheltered under my sheet in the oven-hot, mosquito-filled room, and I was tired. I wanted to sit down.

At last I found a compartment where an Italian farmer and his family occupied one side. An Italian soldier and some other man sat opposite them. The Italian farmer had three small children and

Floyd Schmoe

each had a seat. I asked if I might hold a child on my lap and have his seat.

The farmer ignored me. I stood for an hour, looking as tired as I felt.

Finally the soldier asked the farmer to take up the child and give the American a seat. Again the farmer refused.

Snatching the child almost violently, the soldier plopped it down in its father's lap and said to me, "Sit down." I sat.

The farmer cursed the soldier and glowered at me. For several miles the air was tense.

I have learned to arm myself against such dangers. A polaroid camera with instant pictures is one of the best weapons, but it is too expensive. The ammunition costs too much. I have found a cheaper defense. A few candy bars, even a pack of gum, will usually suffice. That day I had a handful of toy rubber balloons in my pocket. I blew up one for each of the children. Soon we were all batting them back and forth about the compartment, and long before we reached my destination the farmer and his wife were sharing their cheese and wine with me.

I stopped off at Perugia to walk the few miles up to the walled city of Assisi, there to spend a day and night communing with the spirit of my favorite saint, the gentle Francis of Assisi.

I have told of that visit in another place.

From Assisi I went on to Rome where, among the ruins of the Coliseum, the Forum, and the Catacombs, and amidst the grandeur of the St. Peters and the Vatican, I had a small number of human adventures not easily forgotten.

I took a bus out along the old Appian Way to the underground burial place of the Christian Martyrs, and an hour or two later was walking back toward the center of the city, when I passed a young man, obviously American, whom I had noticed on my way out. He was standing at a corner making the thumbs up

The Years of My Day

gesture toward passing motorists, which in America will often secure free transportation.

He was still there on my return, still gesturing towards Rome. In passing I said, "No luck yet?" He answered with the same pleading thumb, and said, "They no spika da Inglish."

Later, returning from Vatican Square along the Tiber, an American soldier, recognizing me as a fellow stranger, stopped and asked if I spoke Italian.

When I said no he asked, "How do you get by?"

I told him that I was not doing very well myself, but with a bit of French, less of Spanish, and a lot of body English, I was managing to cope.

He asked me if I knew the location of a certain dealer in watches and jewelry, and when I told him I did not he asked me if I would make inquiry for him.

We hailed the next friendly looking person and I said, "Pardon me, but do you speak English?" He shrugged.

"Parlez Vous Francais?" Again he shrugged.

"Sprechen Sie Deutch?"

He answered with a gesture to himself, "Grecko."

Whereupon my friend (of Greek ancestry) embraced the stranger and I left them screaming hilariously at each other in Greek.

Since a gold Swiss watch had been displayed I surmised that the jewelry firm being sought was a buyer of fine watches smuggled into Italy from Switzerland, a profitable sideline of some American travelers.

My last similar adventure came just before I was due to depart from Rome on a train to Bari, on the east coast, where I was to board the steamer (that of the tan cat whose name was Luchia) in the morning.

I was in the middle of the city, near the fine new central railway station, and I did not have much time to spare, but I could

Floyd Schmoe

not find the station. I inquired of a nearby "Poliziotto," but he knew even less English than I knew Italian, so we called another policeman, and still another, none of whom could decide, even after lengthy consultation, just what the poor "Americano" wished to know. I tried everything I knew except "Station"...la gare, der bahnhof, no one knew. At the last moment a Pan American airline stewardess chanced to pass by and I stopped her. "Please, can you tell me where the railway station is?" I asked. She smiled and pointed. There, a block ahead, in large electric letters, were the words, Stazione Grande Mussolini.

My granddaughter Judy, driving into Italy one time, had a similar embarrassment. At her first stop she inquired where she might purchase "petrol." Then "das benzine." No response. "L'essence?" she asked. Finally the light dawned, "Ah, si si, la gasoline, no?" the man replied.

One day in Paris when I was studying sculpture at the Academie Julian, a lady stopped me on the street and asked, in very bad French, if I could direct her to the Odeon Theater. I told her in equally bad French, that I was walking in that direction and I would show her the way.

For a block or two we walked and struggled with our French. Finally she said, "Vous a na pas Francaise, nest ce pas?"

"No, I replied," I am an American."

"Well, I am too," she exclaimed. "so why are we talking like this?"

The Years of My Day
Small Affairs

    A few years ago Bill, who then lived in Houston, was driving Ruth and I through the southern parishes of Louisiana where we admired the huge live oaks draped in long streamers of Spanish Moss, and the fleets of brightly painted shrimp boats anchored in the sleepy bayous.

    Seeing the name Evangeline on a shrimper we remarked on the pathetic history of those refugees from Acadia.

    Bill said, "Yes, all these people are of French-Canadian descent. Notice the names on the mailboxes: Prideau, La Cross, Dumont, etc."

    He continued, "Even the dogs here have French names. I was talking with a native one day, and he had a hound dog with him, so I asked, 'what's the dog's name?' He said, 'Fido.' That's not French, I said. 'It is if you spell it Phydeaux,' the man replied."

    Many of the men in the area have deserted the shrimp fleet now for higher paying employment on the oil rigs offshore, but many others, more acutely allergic to sustained effort still spend the winters trapping muskrats and the summers relaxing behind a fishing pole. Muskrats from the Louisiana swamps, and skunks trapped by Missouri and Indiana farm boys, are just about all that remains of the great American fur trade which made the Astors wealthy and opened up the west to settlement.

    The idiom of the south and its droll humor provides perhaps the most unique store of our native wit. I remember one summer day many years ago, when walking the 13 miles from the railway to Calico Rock, Arkansas, to the inland hamlet of Wild Cherry, I paused midway to make inquiry at a small country store. When I asked, "Sir, how far is it to Wild Cherry?" he paused for a long minute, stroked his white beard as in deep reflection, and answered, "Wal, I'd jedge it's bout five miles. That is if you're ridin'. If you're walking, hits ten."

Floyd Schmoe

On another occasion, while canoeing with a friend on a branch of the Arkansas River, we came upon an ancient black man who, while fishing from the bank, had apparently snagged his hook on some underwater obstruction. We pulled over and, taking the line in my hand, I slid my paddle down it and freed the hook. As we moved away the old man stood up and, bowing low, stated in mellifluous tones, "Gentlemen, your kindness and consideration shall not be neglected."

Crossing to Japan one summer on a freighter, we ate with the ships officers who were served by two stewards, one a black southerner and the other Cockney Englishman. Both were droll. For the entire fourteen-day crossing they engaged in a running battle of words. In addition the southerner talked to himself.

One day the two met at the pantry door behind my chair. As usual the black man was holding conversation with himself. When the Englishman asked a question he turned upon him angrily and said, "Can't you see I'm talkin' to myself? Never interrupt a man when he's talkin' to his self."

Travel by freighter is often pleasant. The quarters are good, the food ample, and the atmosphere relaxed. American law requires that if a vessel carries more than twelve passengers it must also carry a ship's doctor. Because of this, most freighters provide accommodations for only twelve passengers. Since company is limited and contacts intimate much of the pleasure, or lack of it, is dependent upon mutual compatibility.

On this trip our fellow passengers were a family of evangelical missionaries who constantly squabbled amongst themselves, and whose children were intolerable brats.

Our purser had, by grave misjudgment, seated the family at the captain's table. We noted that after a few days at sea the captain was not appearing at meals. I assumed that he was being served in his quarters and in conversation with him on occasion mentioned his absence.

The Years of My Day

"It's those damn missionaries," he exploded. "I'll be damned if they didn't try to convert me at the very first meal."

Floyd Schmoe
Hobbies

The dictionary says, in effect, that a hobby is something that you do when you are not doing anything else. Presumably it is a pleasurable avocation.

I have had lots of hobbies because I have never worked at a job that took all my time or energy, and I have always found things I enjoyed doing in my spare time. In fact, you might say that "trying everything once" has been my lifelong hobby.

Fortunately this is not literally true. I have never tried crime in any serious way, or engaged in any of the more popular vices. Check over the Ten Commandments just now, as codified in the Bible, I believe I might score a B, if not a B+.

Never have I placed "any other god" before that creative spirit of love which we Quakers call "the light within," and for which – having no better name – we use the word God. Nor have I, since the childish days of innocently repeating the profanity I heard around Uncle Bill's blacksmith shop, often, if ever, "taken the name of the Lord in vain." (Actually, however, I have found the vulgarity of speech heard around army camps, or among certain sailors, far more distasteful to my ears than the sincere "God damn" profanity of otherwise decent folks.)

As to remembering the "Sabbath, to keep it holy," I'll admit that there have been times when I considered hard work, whatever the day of the week, more "holy" than hymn singing. And even Mother – who once objected to us kids playing ball on a Sunday afternoon - got out and drove a team to a hay wagon, when storms (which have no respect for the Sabbath) threatened the year's crop.

As to honoring "thy father and thy mother, that thy days may be long upon the land," there were times when the "honoring," broadly interpreted by my parents, and enforced with a hickory

The Years of My Day

stick, came hard, but gradually it grew in sincerity until few if any exceptions remained.

Most people take the fourth commandment to refer only to the killing of a man, and fortunately I have never been placed in a position where I would want to destroy another, need to in self-defense, or be in danger of doing so by accident, even though in sixty years of driving a car I have had some narrow escapes.

However, feeling as I do now that all life is sacred, I bear heavy guilt for killing wild and domestic animals not only by myself but by others.

All farm boys of my day (and most today) liked to hunt and fish. Some still find trapping fur-bearing animals a pleasant as well as a profitable occupation.

Mom, bless her, objected to guns and traps, but she found little support in her family. She was especially opposed to the "wolf hunts," and "turkey shoots," which every year were organized by the local "sportsmen." Dad loved them and encouraged us boys in shooting rabbits, squirrels, and even hawks, which occasionally raided the chicken pens.

I had my first "attack of conscience" I think when, one autumn day as Geary and I were husking corn, and a jack rabbit ran across the field, and I killed it with an ear of corn. Actually it was on impulse and entirely by chance. I just happened to have the ear in my hand and I just happened to hit the running jack. I couldn't do it again in a hundred tries. It was like a "hole in one."

But as I ran to pick up the beautiful animal, still struggling in its death throes, I remember feeling sorry that I had caused it pain.

At about the same time, when I was ten or twelve, I began trapping skunks, muskrats, and opossums along the creek which crossed our farm. That winter I earned $12.00 from furs, the most I had ever earned, and with it, at Christmas time, I bought a ticket to Wichita to visit relatives in "the big city."

Floyd Schmoe

I think I had no severe pangs of conscience until one morning I found a neighbor's cat caught in one of my traps. The skunks and opossums I killed quickly with a shot from my rifle, and the muskrats usually drowned themselves, but the cat I could not shoot. I turned it loose, but the sight of its mangled and bleeding paw haunted me for days. I hope that it recovered.

My most traumatic experiences were the killing of animals for meat, or the destruction of a horse with a broken leg. Years later, when I was a ranger on Mount Rainier, I found it necessary to shoot two horses; one badly injured in a fall, and the other so old I felt it could not survive the winter on the range. Rather than allow old Adam to starve or be killed by a cougar, I shot him. Both actions pained me greatly and at that moment I found myself, as the Indians are said to have felt, mentally asking forgiveness from the Great Spirit who was father of us both.

Fortunately I soon gave up trapping and hunting and in time came to deplore all killing, whether in war or as "sport," or even for food or clothing. I can excuse the Eskimo who needs the flesh of the seal and the whale, and the fur of the polar bear and arctic fox. But I cannot excuse the commercial killing of whales, seal, and wildfowl, not even the "game management" destruction of coyotes, wolves, lions, and elephants.

I am aware of course that situations develop where such "management" seems the lesser of two evils, but I sure better methods can, with study, be learned.

As to why "nature," which is to say "God," allowed, or caused, predation to become the way of life for more than half of all creatures on Earth, I have no answer. Being ignorant of causes and reasons, I call it "God's mistake."

But we started out to talk about hobbies.

From my earliest memory I have been a collector. My first, more or less, organized collection was of the leaves of native trees.

The Years of My Day

I remember that when I was no more than six or seven years old I had a book full of pressed leaves. There are more than 100 species of trees and shrubs indigenous to eastern Kansas, and I found most of them, though I did not learn the names of all of them.

Next I went for birds' eggs and butterflies. Mom discouraged the taking of birds' eggs, except those of the crow who destroyed a lot of corn in the field and even invaded her garden and chicken pens. Raiding crows' nests was exciting and dangerous. They nested in colonies high in the cottonwood trees in our lower pasture. The nests were high and the crows ganged up on nest robbers. They are bold in defense of their eggs and young, and do not hesitate to fly into the face of the enemy.

Then I discovered fossils and arrowheads. Eastern Kansas was once part of a great inland sea where fish, shellfish, sponges, crinoids, and many other forms of marine life abounded in such abundance that the limy shells of such animals, in settling to the floor of the sea, formed thick layers of limestone which, centuries later, became elevated above the level of the ocean, and were exposed in ledges and cliffs along the streams.

This stone – which we used for buildings, bridges, and stone walls – was simply a mass of clam, snail, and mussel shells, many of them preserved intact in the sedimentary rock. These fossils, few of which I could identify, I broke out of the rock and hoarded.

Fortunately the museum of the University of Kansas at Lawrence was free to the public and Mom took me there on several occasions. Lawrence, 16 miles to the west of Prairie Center, was our nearest "city," and about once a year we went there to shop or to see the circus. At the museum I learned about fossils from diatoms to dinosaurs, and I saw hundreds of Indian artifacts.

A cousin of my cousin Earl White lived near Lawrence and once I went with Earl to spend a couple of days. Lee was older than

Floyd Schmoe

I, and a student at the University. He knew about Indians and had a collection of artifacts. He took me arrowhead hunting in their corn fields, which lay on high ground overlooking the Kaw River.

I found my first piece of chipped flint, part of a broken arrow point, or scraper, and I was hooked on archeology. I had never heard the word, but that was what I wanted to be...an archeologist.

When we moved to Miami, Oklahoma in 1912 and I entered high school, I had my first contact with scientific books, and I also came to know and love a classmate, Albert Jones.

"Spider," which was the only name I knew him by, was a kindred spirit. He knew Indians, and fossils, and birds, and he knew where arrowheads could be found.

During the three years I lived in Miami, Spider and I spent most of our free time hunting Indian artifacts, and Spider even learned to make arrow points by flaking flint in the Indian way. We both acquired a sizable collection of flints, several hundred specimens, in fact.

Spider, if he is still living, must have thousands, but I gave all mine away, most of them to the museum of Friends University in Wichita, but a few are framed and hang on the wall of Ruthanna's living room on Finn Hill.

I suppose my second great hobby would have to be labeled "girls." I went skating with Eva Hales, and looked longingly at shy, mysterious (to me) Thea Baer, and I fell madly in love with Judith Garrett during a single afternoon, but I did no serious dating until my last year in high school.

The first two years at Miami High provided a number of group affairs with the two Indian girls, cousins Musa Gobin and Mary La Fallier, and assorted others at ball games, picnics, hay rides, and church socials, but no one girl stood out above the others.

The Years of My Day

My junior and senior years at Wichita High School were different. I went out first with my lovely cousin Clara Moon and she introduced me to others of her group. First there was Margaret Townsend – fragile, brilliant, and pretty – but the competition was too great. Then I saw Ruth and for half a century there was no other.

Girls led to another love – if not truly a hobby – canoeing.

My roommate, Fred Fellow, was dating Helen Israel, and since Helen and Ruth were as much attached to each other as were Fred and I, our twosomes were often foursomes. To facilitate togetherness Fred and I bought a canoe, and dreaming of future bliss, we named it The Honeymoon. Many happy hours were spent exploring and drifting, and picnicking on the waters and shores of the Little Arkansas River in and around Wichita that summer.

Ruth, our home, and our children were both hobby and vocation "until death did us part." More recently I have taken up a number of other avocations.

I had dabbled a bit in both clay and oils in college, studied sculpture seriously for a few months in Paris, and done pencil sketches for my columns and my books, but though I had thought of it many times since watching Mom with her paint and canvas when a small child, I did not take to the brush until I was past seventy. I still paint something occasionally, mountains, trees, and portraits of Tomiko's cats, but only when the mood strikes me.

At the annual Arts and Crafts Show in Bellevue a few years ago I saw a mobile of stylized fish which swam lazily in the air currents. Then I came home and did a similar one for myself. I had seen Calder's ponderous steel creation in eastern museums, and his more sensitive wire sculptures in Paris, but though they moved, they did not move me. These fish, however, floated and drifted as light as falling leaves, and they fascinated me.

Even so, I doubt I would have pursued the hobby of mobile making very long, except that I found them in demand. All my

Floyd Schmoe

friends seemed to want one. And, to my surprise, they were willing to pay for them. I suppose I have made a couple hundred, each different, and now they float in breezes from Sweden to Japan and Australia. I never seem to catch up with the demand.

While lecturing at Pendle Hill in 1956 I killed time by doing some pottery work in the studio. I was not interested in pots, though I found "potting" fun, but I was interested in original figurines. Schools of leaping dolphins, flights of gulls, and scale models of whales. Funny little owls and pelicans, cub bears, and pussy cats.

Some years ago Ruth had taken up weaving and owned two Niadou looms. Some of our friends and children still wear beautiful skirts and scarves she wove. For me she wove four yards of heavy wool tweed which, after she died, I took to Hong Kong, on our way to meet Ruthie in Thailand, and on the return trip picked up a beautiful jacket which I love and wear often. It will last me as long as I live.

I sold Ruth's looms when she no longer had need of them, and bought a small kiln for my pottery, and a furnace for my foundry. I have not yet learned to use the foundry with skill, but from it have come my most impressive works of art.

If I could do it well I could sell all the bronze dolphins and masks I could make.

The Years of My Day

In 1944 I made Who's Who. I know, it's a commercial rip-off. So is the Miss America Contest. Both have a similar ethic. No amount of money can buy the space.

In 1979 an international publication called, Men of Achievement, based in England, listed me. Regardless of my qualifications, I do keep good company.

Among other ego boosters I have a certificate signed by President Woodrow Wilson, for the American Red Cross, in appreciation of service in Europe during the first World War. I have a personal letter from the Emperor of Japan thanking us for our work in Hiroshima and Nagasaki, and I have numerous decorative scrolls in Japanese and Korean script from government officials and private agencies, in appreciation of work done in their countries. For some years the Crown Prince of Japan sent us Christmas cards.

But Gerry and Mitzi Yuen, my Canadian grandchildren, top that. In August of 1978 they hosted Queen Elizabeth and Prince Phillip at the Commonwealth Games in Edmonton.

Floyd Schmoe

*In celebration of the Birthday of
His Majesty the Emperor
The Consul General of Japan, Mr. Kenichi Yanagi
requests the honor of your company
at a Reception
on Saturday, April 29th, 5:30 to 7:00 p.m.*

R.S.V.P.
622-8520

*421 West Highland Drive
Queen Anne Hill*

In 1956, as Ruth and I were on our way to Korea, we happened to pass through Tokyo on April 29th, the Emperor's birthday, and were invited by our friends, Mr. and Mrs. Tojo, to attend the public celebration on the lawn of the Imperial Palace. Both the Emperor and the Empress appeared and the Emperor spoke to his guests. Ruth was exhausted from travel and the day was very hot, so she did not attend.

Each year Tomiko and I are invited to the home of the Consul General of Japan, in Seattle, to toast the Emperor and celebrate his birthday.

The Years of My Day

In Honor of His Excellency
Mr. Takeo Fukuda, the Prime Minister of Japan

The Consul General of Japan and Mrs. Sono Uchida
request the honor of the company of
<u>Mr. & Mrs. Floyd Schmoe</u>
at a Reception
on Saturday, March 19, 1977, 5:30 to 6:30 p.m.
at the Washington Plaza Hotel, Vashon Room

~~R.S.V.P ---~~
Reminder

Floyd Schmoe

St. Francis in the garden

-Sculpture, Floyd Schmoe, 1970s

The Years of My Day

Mount Rainier oil painting
My first attempt at painting in oil, 1970

(Editor's note: To keep the print-on-demand price of this book reasonable, we elected to keep the interior black and white. For full color version of this painting see the Floyd Schmoe page on our website azzurripublishing.com)

www.ingramcontent.com/pod-product-compliance
Lightning Source LLC
Chambersburg PA
CBHW070421010526
44118CB00014B/1847